U.S. FOREIGN POLICY and the THIRD WORLD:

AGENDA 1985-86

John W. Sewell, Richard E. Feinberg,
and Valeriana Kallab, Editors

Paul R. Krugman
Steve Lande
Craig VanGrasstek
Christine E. Contee
Anthony Lake
Stuart K. Tucker

Transaction Books
New Brunswick (USA) and Oxford (UK)

Copyright © 1985 by Overseas Development Council, Washington, D.C.

Library of Congress Catalog Number: 85-987
ISBN: 0-87855-990-6 (paper)
ISBN: 0-88738-042-5 (cloth)
Printed in the United States of America

Library of Congress Cataloging in Publication Data
Main entry under title:

U.S. foreign policy and the Third World

1. Developing countries—Foreign economic relations—United States— Addresses, essays, lectures. 2. United States—Foreign economic relations— Developing countries—Addresses, essays, lectures.   I. Sewell, John Williamson. II. Title: U.S. foreign policy and the Third World—agenda 1985-86.   III. Series.
HF1413.U535   1985   337.730172'4   85-987
ISBN 0-88738-042-5
ISBN 0-87855-990-6 (pbk.)

The views expressed in this volume are those of the authors and do not necessarily represent those of the Overseas Development Council as an organization or of its individual officers or Board, Council, Program Advisory Committee, and staff members.

U.S. Foreign Policy and the Third World: Agenda 1985-86

Acknowledgments

Agenda Project Directors and Editors:
Richard E. Feinberg, John W. Sewell, and
Valeriana Kallab

Editorial Associates:
Carol J. Cramer and Linda Starke

The editors wish to express sincere thanks to members of the ODC Board, Council, and Program Advisory Committee, and to the many others both within and outside the ODC who so generously provided advice and critical comments on various drafts of the chapters comprising *Agenda 1985-86*.

Special thanks are due to Lisa M. Cannon for editorial assistance, to Nellie Rimkus for administrative planning, to John Kaljee for the cover and grid design and the visual presentation of the statistical annexes, and to Robin E. Ward for expediting the manuscript.

The Overseas Development Council gratefully acknowledges the help of the Ford, William and Flora Hewlett, and Rockefeller Foundations, whose financial support contributes to the preparation of the ODC's U.S.-Third World Policy Perspectives series, of which *Agenda 1985-86* is part.

Contents

Foreword

Agenda 1985-86 is the tenth Overseas Development Council assessment of U.S. policies and performance in U.S. relations with the developing countries. Initiated by the Council in 1973, the *Agenda* is designed to provide policy decision makers and the public with a comprehensive, nonpartisan overview of current U.S.-Third World policies and options for U.S. actions in the period ahead. Over the first decade of its issuance, the ODC *Agenda* has come to be widely relied upon for its periodic critique of this sector of U.S. foreign policy from a point of view that acknowledges and seeks to reinforce the positive, constructive importance of the U.S.-Third World interrelationship for both the United States and the greatly differentiated countries of the developing world.

To analyze a greater range of important themes in U.S. relations with developing countries more frequently and in depth, the ODC in 1984 launched its new U.S.-Third World Policy Perspectives series, incorporating the *Agenda* into this series on an alternate-year rather than annual basis. The two-year interval is a more realistic retrospective as well as forward horizon for the critical analysis of the U.S. policy-making process.

In contrast to the *Agenda,* which continues to assess U.S. policies across the broad spectrum of U.S.-Third World issues, other volumes in the new Policy Perspectives series each offer several perspectives and recommendations on different aspects of a *single* policy theme. Volumes issued in 1984 are *Adjustment Crisis in the Third World* and *Uncertain Future: Commercial Banks and the Third World;* forthcoming 1985 volumes are *U.S. Trade Policy and Developing Countries* and *Development Strategies: A New Synthesis* (descriptions are provided at the end of this volume). We invite readers' comments, criticisms, and suggestions on the views expressed and the themes selected for this new series, which is an important component of ODC's policy analysis program.

For those concerned about U.S. relations with the developing countries, 1985 is a particularly crucial year. In recent years, the United States has often misperceived the nature of U.S. security interests, downplaying their close relationship to American economic, social, developmental, and humanitarian interests in the Third World. This *Agenda* analyzes the effect of this trend on four issue areas of great importance to the United States as well as the developing world—trade and industrial policy, international finance, development cooperation, and foreign policy—and finds that current policies, while sometimes successful in the short run, have sown the seeds of long-run difficulties and costs to U.S. interests. Thus future choices, whether by the Executive Branch or Congress, by the public or private sector, are particularly important if fundamental U.S. interests in the development of the Third World are to be realized.

John W. Sewell, *President*
Overseas Development Council

U.S. Foreign Policy and the Third World: Agenda 1985-86

U.S. Foreign Policy and the Third World:
Agenda 1985-86

Overview and Summaries of Recommendations

Testing U.S. Reassertionism: The Reagan Approach to the Third World

Those who argued that the permanent bureaucracy, U.S. Congress, or immutable national interests would prevent any administration from altering the course of U.S. policy toward the Third World were proven wrong during the first Reagan Administration. The White House asserted control over the Executive Branch by placing carefully chosen appointees in positions with authority over North-South issues. And these officials did not hesitate to redefine and assert their own views of American priorities. Congress, for the most part, lacked the interest, will, or means to deflect Administration initiatives or to propose its own.

Since taking office, the Reagan Administration has pursued significantly different policies from those followed during the 1970s in the key areas of macro-economic policies, international finance and debt, North-South trade, development assistance, and diplomacy toward radical, nationalist regimes. Not all policies followed during the Nixon, Ford, and Carter years were discarded, but the Administration overturned many inherited traditions. It did so in order to rid the global economy of the inflation and other imbalances that had characterized the 1970s and to reassert U.S. economic and strategic power after a period of what many perceived to have been unnecessarily sharp decline. The Administration moved boldly and forcefully to give primacy to U.S. macro-economic policy over macro-economic coordination with allies; to sidestep slow-moving international bureaucracies in favor of more manageable regional or bilateral accords; to transform U.S. for-

3

eign assistance by emphasizing security rather than long-term development; and to draw sharp distinctions between friendly and hostile regimes.

After four years, it is now possible to assess the reassertionist experiment. Not only did the Administration succeed in remolding U.S. policies, but—when judged by its own criteria—it also scored more successes than setbacks. Yet when alternative criteria and a longer-term horizon are applied, the victories appear more fragile and the future more worrisome.

In the area of macro-economic policy, the Administration largely rejected the efforts begun in the mid-1970s to improve the coordination of policies among the major industrial countries. Previous administrations had acted on the belief that since the relative weight of the U.S. economy had decreased, the United States had to work with Western Europe and Japan to orchestrate global prosperity. The Reagan Administration chose instead to concentrate on righting domestic macro-economic policies, believing that instabilities in the international economy were less the result of the diffusion of economic power than of mistaken *domestic* policies in key countries.[1] In their view, attempts at international coordination were bound to fail unless faulty domestic policies were corrected and, conversely, would be unnecessary if such corrections were made. If nations pursued inflationary fiscal and monetary policies, exchange rates and other international economic variables were bound to be volatile, but if key governments followed prudent policies, international stability would follow automatically.

Many Reagan officials believed that the 'interdependence' school had exaggerated the relative decline in American power.[2] While conceding that Europe, Japan, and some developing countries had increased their share of global power, Reagan policy makers argued that the U.S. was still, by far, the single largest economy in the world.[3] Moreover, in some areas—such as finance—the U.S. role had become relatively more important and could set the framework and tempo for others. And although U.S. 'openness' to international trade and financial flows had expanded, the U.S. economy was still relatively self-sufficient and therefore autonomous.

The Administration's perception of national strength also imbued its policies toward the Soviet Union. All administrations in the postwar period have, quite appropriately, sought to limit Soviet influence in the Third World. However, the Reagan Administration was more willing than previous administrations to employ economic, diplomatic, and paramilitary instruments of coercion against regimes considered too close to the Soviet Union, and at the same time was less interested in exploring avenues for the peaceful resolution of regional conflicts.[4] Believing that the world was rife with hostility and struggle, senior

Administration officials argued—at times even publicly—that the United States ought not be constrained by some international legal and moral norms that worked to the disadvantage of U.S. policy.[5] Covert paramilitary action assumed a prominence that it had not enjoyed since the Vietnam war.

Administration foreign assistance policy also reflected an eagerness to reassert U.S. power. Reversing the decade-long trend toward multilateralism in aid, the Administration sharply cut back on new budgetary commitments to the World Bank and other multilateral development agencies, reserving new resources for bilateral aid programs. Within U.S. A.I.D., it redirected funds toward friendly states perceived to be in jeopardy from internal (El Salvador, Sudan) or external (Honduras, Pakistan) threats while cutting aid to governments considered unfriendly (Nicaragua, Tanzania). The bilateral aid program deemphasized the direct provision of services and skills to the poor that had typified A.I.D. in the 1970s. Instead, A.I.D. sought to emphasize reforms of national economic policies in favor of market mechanisms and private entrepreneurs. In trade, the Administration pursued policies more in line with past administrations. Under the influence of U.S. Trade Representative William Brock, the Administration advocated trade liberalization within multilateral mechanisms. But frustration with the General Agreement on Tariffs and Trade (GATT) drove the Administration to circumvent multilateral institutions and to negotiate bilateral or regional deals. Strategic concerns also motivated the Administration to pursue preferential trade arrangements—in the Caribbean Basin and with Israel—that violated the most-favored-nation principle that has been the cornerstone of U.S. (and international) trade policy since World War II. The Caribbean Basin Initiative (CBI) generously provided the small Central American and Caribbean nations with freer access to the U.S. market without extending these concessions to other trading partners.[6]

Finally, the debt crisis drove the Administration to violate its own free-market rhetoric and many conventional practices in finance. To stabilize shaky credit markets, official institutions abandoned their traditional 'arms length' posture for one of close collaboration with commercial banks, orchestrating a quiet revolution in international finance.[7] The U.S. Treasury, the Federal Reserve System, and the International Monetary Fund (IMF) mobilized their own resources and coordinated the actions of the private credit markets to manage a global financial crisis. The irony is that the result of the Administration's actions has been a much stronger role for the public and not the private sectors in international finance.

These discontinuities in U.S. policy have their roots in strategic conceptions, ideas, and circumstances. The Administration believed that the East-West clash was by far the greatest challenge to U.S. foreign policy.[8] It sought to marshal the nation's resources by injecting this paramount interest into a wide range of programs. If the Administration was not always as clear-headed and united on tactics, it tended to harbor a straightforward vision that argued for directing resources to fortify friendly forces and depriving perceived adversaries in order to weaken or destroy them.

While the Administration naturally preferred to work with cooperative allies, it was also prepared to act unilaterally when others found its strategic vision to be too unidimensional or simplistic or its tactics too blunt and aggressive. Some in the Administration possessed an underlying distrust of many in Europe and the Third World who seemed to lack the clarity or will to take tough decisions. Consequently, many U.S. policies took on a decidedly anti-multilateral tenor.

Officials believed that the United States possessed sufficient power to pursue this course. Where previous administrations knew that the United States had the capacity to veto the initiatives of others, the Reagan Administration acted as though it could go further and impose its own solutions on recalcitrant nations, whether allies or not. It believed that the international correlation of forces still favored the United States if its leaders employed its power with more decision and firmness than its predecessors.

The philosophy of the Administration combined belief in the free market as the most efficient and ethical mechanism for the allocation of resources with a vision of Marxism as a hostile, aggressive ideology whose adherents in the Third World were inherently and irretrievably anti-American and typically pro-Soviet. This integrated world view was to some degree a reversion to earlier, cold war attitudes. However, the magnified emphasis on the free market—clearly the most efficient allocator of resources in many circumstances—was more hostile toward government interventions that arguably were necessary to correct for market failures or to enhance the general welfare. The Administration also tended to ignore the deep rifts that had arisen among Third World radicals, and between them and the Soviet Union. These views permeated the Administration's approach to all aspects of relations with the developing countries, including foreign assistance. Strategic and ideological perspectives combined to make the Administration skeptical of multilateral development agencies—notably the World Bank—that were at least partly under the influence of Western Europe and the Third World and whose programs were seen as overly statist and redistributive. Taking a cue from their domestic agency counterparts, some Reagan appointees declared that many of the poverty-oriented programs of the 1970s "frankly, haven't worked."[9] Rather, they tried to convince official lending agencies that the economic preferences of the Administration were the correct policy model for the developing countries.

However, circumstances often intervened to force the Administration to abandon its preferred philosophy. When private financial markets patently failed, as in the debt crisis, the Treasury Department pragmatically turned to government activism to stabilize the international financial system. When domestic firms demanded trade protection, the Administration sometimes abandoned its anti-statism at the water's edge. And when the country in question was one of strategic interest, for example Egypt or the Philippines, the ability to use aid to promote market mechanisms was muted. Strategic interests sometimes convinced the Administration to blunt its hostility toward radical regimes; thus it adopted a relatively low-key posture toward Iran to avoid driving Khomeini toward the Soviets.

Of course, the Reagan Administration did continue some of the North-South policies of previous administrations. Trade policy, for example, continued to combine an acceptance of preferential treatment for developing nations with efforts to coax newly industrializing nations to gradually open their markets. After an initial wariness, the Administration came to appreciate the value of the IMF. Moreover, some of the Administration's "new directions" actually represented a return to earlier notions. Old Washington hands were fully familiar with U.S. government programs that subsidized overseas investment, with IMF 'shock treatments' that sought a rapid reduction in budget or current-account deficits, with World Bank advocacy of price mechanisms, and with A.I.D. balance-of-payments loans that were accompanied by broad policy advice. Nevertheless, these antecedents should not obscure the important departures that the Reagan Administration brought to its Third World policies.

The Scorecard: Successes

The Administration often succeeded both in compelling the bureaucracy to accept its agenda and in producing the hoped-for policy outcomes. This was not so in all cases; sometimes, as discussed later, the Administration was unable to push through its programs or to move events in the desired direction. But if judged on the basis of its own criteria, the Administration can properly boast of real accomplishments.

During the Reagan Administration's first two years, the United States imposed deflation and austerity on the rest of the world. The combination of Administration-recommended fiscal deficits and tight monetary policy contributed to high international interest rates and the global recession. In response to U.S. monetary and fiscal policies (and in some cases to domestic preferences), European governments adopted restrictive policies of their own, while many developing nations had no choice but to adjust their economies downward. The second half of the first Reagan Administration saw the domestic fruits of this strategy, as the U.S. economy combined rapid growth with low inflation. Massive foreign savings flowed into the United States and helped to fund the twin fiscal and trade deficits. The soaring dollar symbolized the world's faith in the U.S. economy and the apparent triumph of the Reagan strategy. Moreover, the relatively strong performance of the U.S. economy, compared with that of Europe and many developing countries, halted and marginally reversed the postwar trend toward the diffusion of economic power away from the United States.[10]

In terms of its own objectives, the Administration's strategy toward the debt crisis also was a success. The international financial system and the major U.S. banks were stabilized as large-scale defaults were avoided. With U.S. backing, the International Monetary Fund compelled banks to lend enough to keep the major debtors liquid, while advising the developing countries to adopt austerity programs. The direct financial costs to the U.S. government of the various rescue packages were small; those official resources that were pressed into service were mostly short- or medium-term and were non-concessional. The debtor nations bore the brunt of the adjustment process by slashing their imports and borrowing needs with striking speed. If many nations rescheduled outstanding principal, they nevertheless dutifully met an interest bill inflated by the sharp rise in the real cost of money on international markets.

The Administration also succeeded in imposing some of its priorities on the multilateral development banks. Standing alone, the United States forced the International Development Association (IDA) to reduce sharply its future lending levels in real terms. The Europeans have so far proved unwilling to fund a supplemental IDA program without U.S. participation. In addition, the Administration has blocked any major increase in the World Bank's capital and has voted against more individual loans in the banks than any previous administration. Closer to home, the Administration systematically targeted its bilateral aid program toward political and security objectives by increasing security assistance relative to development assistance.[11]

President Reagan has claimed not to have lost "one inch of soil" to communism. No radical revolutions occurred in major Third World states, no Cuban brigades appeared in new locations in Africa, and Soviet troops remained within existing parameters. It might be argued that Soviet influence did increase in several countries, either directly (Nicaragua), or via 'proxies' (as through the Syrians in Lebanon), and that U.S. influence declined elsewhere (Argentina, Morocco, Saudi Arabia). But as its handling of the withdrawal of U.S. Marines from Beirut illustrated, the Administration was very adept at 'rolling with the punches' and minimizing the impact of setbacks.

An assessment of the Reagan Administration's trade policies hinges on the criteria employed. If living up to its rhetoric and keeping U.S. markets open to developing-country products is the yardstick, then the Administration's record is defensible. If opening up developing-country markets to U.S. exports is the criterion, the Administration was frustrated by stalemates in the GATT and the contraction of developing-country markets due to the global recession; in its major Third World trade innovation—the Caribbean Basin Initiative (CBI)—the Administration beneficently granted one-way concessions. However, if the overall trade balance is the measure, then the Administration failed massively—although the widening gap was more the result of uneven global growth rates, recession in the Third World, and the high dollar than of trade policy per se.

In sum, the Administration achieved many of its objectives in macro-economic policy, international finance and debt, and development assistance. If keeping U.S. markets open to developing-country products is the criterion, it did credibly well in trade. And in its dealings with Third World radical regimes, it suffered no grievous losses.

Administration successes can be attributed to its own strengths, the weakness of potential opponents, its pragmatism under pressure, and to plain good fortune. If the Administration did not possess a detailed, fully coherent strategy toward the Third World, it did harbor a set of principles and attitudes that were generally shared by its hardliners and moderates alike. In contrast, the rest of the world was severely divided. Europe was split between conservatives, who tended to share many of the Administration's sentiments, and social democrats, who themselves were fractured along ideological and national cleavages. The Third World was wracked by fratricidal regional conflicts, a widening gap between the more dynamic newly industrializing states and the stagnant less developed countries, and a global recession and debt crisis that had forced many developing nations to turn inward and to adopt more cautious foreign policies. The heady days of OPEC and 'The New International Economic Order' seemed distant as nations scrambled to regain their creditworthiness on international capital markets, to meet IMF-designed stabilization targets, and to boost their manufacturing exports to industrial-country markets. The Soviet Union itself often seemed passive in parts of the Third World, whether due to preoccupation with its own economic difficulties, its political succession problem, the lack of suitable opportunities, or, possibly, to the fear of an American response. The Soviets did relatively little to exploit such crises as the Falklands/Malvinas war, the Iran-Iraq clash, the domestic vulnerabilities in Pakistan, or the instabilities in Southern Africa, and pursued generally cautious policies in the Caribbean Basin.

Finally, fortune seemed to smile on Ronald Reagan. The drop in the price of oil and the remarkable political stability maintained in many countries, despite severe economic downturns, were among the favorable trends that made life easier for officials in Washington. Advantageous economic developments at home, recession abroad, and the absence of coherent domestic or foreign opposition provided propitious conditions for the reassertionist experiment.

The Scorecard: Setbacks

If the Administration performed better than many of its critics anticipated, it nevertheless suffered significant setbacks. Some frustrations occurred when ideas conflicted with reality or when objectives proved to be incompatible. Other failures resulted from ill-conceived strategies or from the neglect of important issues, while still others emerged, ironically, out of the Administration's own successes.

If the global adjustment process proceeded substantially as the Administration desired, the 1980-82 recession at the same time brought serious costs. Most immediately, the contractions in developing countries—which account for about 40 per cent of U.S. overseas sales—cost the United States more than $18 billion in export earnings, about one million jobs in U.S. export industries, and some $10 billion in direct investment income to U.S.-owned firms.[12] Seemingly good loans turned bad as the creditworthiness of many debtor nations suddenly deteriorated. The prices of their stocks fell and banks were obliged to 'beef up' their reserves against potential losses. New loans and investments slowed to many developing countries, especially in austerity-ridden Latin America and Africa.

Administration incentive to private firms—in the form of tax breaks for corporations, reduced government regulations, and low inflation—were unable to overcome the effects on the U.S. trade account of uneven global growth rates and the high dollar. The U.S. trade balance with all developing countries benefited from the tumbling price of oil, but the trade balance with Latin America and the Caribbean swung from a positive $1.3 billion in 1981 to a negative $17.9 billion in 1983.

The uneven global growth rates—with the U.S. outpacing Western Europe and many developing countries—combined with the high dollar to produce a flood of imports and sluggish U.S. exports. In this sense the United States paid the costs for the lack of international coordination of macro-economic policies and exchange rates. Greater coordination might have stimulated some European countries to adopt a more growth-oriented fiscal policy. Even taking into account the strength of market forces, more interventionist exchange-rate policies by central banks might have yielded a somewhat steadier and lower dollar. In any event, the Administration's philosophy prevented it from taking the initiatives required to test these hypotheses.

Similarly, U.S. trade policy was hampered by the absence of positive measures to assist workers and firms adapt to international competition. Existing programs clearly needed improving, but the Administration chose to cut funds for rather than reform the Trade Adjustment Assistance Act. And honoring its free-market principles at home if not offshore, the Administration chose not to require firms receiving trade protection to prepare for eventual competition in open markets. These actions risked heightening protectionist pressures: Workers who feel vulnerable and unprotected and firms that cannot compete will press for trade barriers. At the same time, since the Administration did not have plans to help phase down or restructure declining industries, it was less prepared to make concessions in bargaining with developing countries. The Administration's refusal to place potentially attractive concessions on the table was one reason why many developing countries were unenthusiastic about a major new round of trade negotiations under the GATT. Paradoxically, if the United States is to continue to foster a liberal international trading regime, it may have to adopt more interventionist policies at home.

In international finance, the Administration's very success in passing the burden of adjustment onto the debtor nations exacerbated an already chronic debt crisis. As new lending dried up and developing countries complied with their debt service obligations, many debtor nations were paying more to their creditors than they were receiving in new loans and investment. This perverse transfer of funds from poor to rich countries threatens to lower consumption and investment levels in developing nations, and to place additional political pressures on debtor governments to question the prevailing debt and adjustment strategies.[13]

Contradictions also marked the Administration's aid programs. On the one hand, confounding expectations, the Administration has wisely increased aid budgets, and further growth is projected. On the other hand, however, A.I.D. increasingly directed its resources toward nations that the Departments of State or Defense considered important to U.S. security. Recipients of large amounts of U.S. aid sometimes rejected A.I.D.'s conditions in full confidence that their bureaucratic and congressional allies in Washington would block a cutoff of funds.

As a result, in many countries A.I.D.'s "policy dialogue" took a back seat to strategic ties. In other countries, A.I.D.'s programs inherently lacked leverage because of their small size.

More difficult to judge is the Administration's impact on the *content* of A.I.D.'s programs. The Administration did not formally reject the basic human needs emphasis of the aid legislation of the 1970s, although these programs often did not easily meld with A.I.D.'s current interest in expanding the private sector and in policy dialogue. If carefully designed, these new approaches could still rebound to the benefit of the poor through enhanced job creation and productivity. But the Administration entered office with few concrete ideas on how to actually promote the private sector abroad and was hazy as to whether the target was indigenous firms or U.S. companies or both. A final assessment of the impact of these programs is not yet possible, largely because most of the projects are in the early stages of implementation and results will not be available for several years.

The Administration's diplomacy in the Third World focused on containing, and if possible reversing, the radical revolutions of the 1970s. Although the Administration suffered no grievous defeats in dealing with radical Third World states, it did not overturn earlier 'losses' (except for tiny Grenada). The Ayatollah Khomeini, Muammar el-Qaddafi, Fidel Castro, the Sandinistas, and the MPLA (Angola) were all still in power at the end of the first Reagan term, and the Soviets remained in Kabul and the Vietnamese in Phnom Penh. The Administration might counter that the direct costs to the U.S. budget of its harassment of these regimes were rather small. However, there were the intangible costs in the struggle for international opinion of a policy that shunned international legal norms, most notably in refusing to accept jurisdiction of the World Court regarding Nicaragua's complaint against the United States.

Also hard to measure are the lasting effects of the global recession and the handling of the debt crisis on developing-country perceptions and attitudes. Certainly some Third World leaders were made more wary of participating too vigorously in a highly unstable international economy as well as less trusting that the North would seek to resolve future crises in an equitable manner. As a result, they were also less receptive to donor prescriptions for their economic ills. To some, the United States seemed more agitated by the existence of radical governments than by the development needs of the Third World. For U.S. officials more interested in being feared than being respected, this outcome was not necessarily bad. But the lingering resentments seemed likely to generate future tensions in North-South relations.

In sum, the Administration's significant successes were clouded by the persistence of some old problems and the emergence of new dangers, raising doubts about its lasting contribution to prosperity and peace in the Third World. The apparent progress in macro-economic policy and international debt was brittle; some simmering problems had been ignored and new ones loomed ahead. Trade policies were incomplete and in important areas frustrated, while some aid strategies lacked coherence. Several unfriendly radical rulers checked Administration parries and seemed likely to outlast even a second Reagan Administration.

Raising the Sights

The setbacks noted above were measured against the Administration's own yardsticks. Yet these criteria themselves were rather narrow and defensive. The emphasis on bilateralism or sub-regionalism was born more of frustration than of promise. The programmatic emphases on deflation, financial market stability, and the avoidance of new trade protectionism amounted largely, although not exclusively, to crisis containment rather than to progressive innovation.

Resort to more ambitious criteria raises more serious questions about the results of the Administration's first four years. If the criteria include emphasis on the values of world order and community, a reduction in international tensions, an increased U.S. capacity to accommodate to a politically pluralistic globe, resumption of strong economic growth, and improved well-being for poor people in developing countries, a harsher appraisal emerges.

The Administration has shied away from many traditional forms of supranational cooperation. "If federal government is bad, international government is ten times worse," remarked one White House official.[14] Yet this distrust of international authority ignored the need for collective action in international relations to harmonize national economic policies, to prevent one nation from undertaking actions harmful to others, to correct for structural and cyclical market failures, and generally to contain international tensions. Policy makers traditionally have felt that the United States, as the major power, has an important stake in a series of global political, economic, and environmental institutions and systems. Yet, the Administration ignored these imperatives in adopting hostile attitudes toward the arduously negotiated Law of the Sea Treaty, the infant-formula code, the International Planned Parenthood Federation (because of its abortion-related activities), the International Fund for Agricultural Development (IFAD), the World Court, several U.N. agencies, and, not least important, the international financial institutions.

The Administration consciously sought to increase international tensions in regions populated by regimes considered to be antithetical to U.S. interests. Economic sanctions and covert actions were used to 'bleed' Afghanistan, Cuba, Nicaragua, and Vietnam, and the United States seemed to acquiesce in South Africa's destructive warfare against Angola and Mozambique. Such conflicts potentially hurt U.S. economic interests, embroil regional friends, risk escalation to a direct U.S.-Soviet confrontation, and cause human suffering. Moreover, such policies deepen the suspicion of many in the Third World that the United States is intolerant of Third World nationalism and political experimentation. In reaction, Third World radicals are more likely to anticipate U.S. hostility and seek the security umbrella of the Soviet Union. Thus, the policy risks generating the very results it seeks to prevent.

Whereas the Administration understood the usefulness of economic ties to bolster friendly states, preconceptions—its assumption that radicals are incorrigible—blinded it to the strategic value of economic links to radical regimes. The disinclination to use economic instruments as 'carrots' to alter the behavior of difficult governments left the Administration more dependent on a narrower range of coercive measures. Moreover, deep hostility toward radical states sometimes clouded Administration policy and prevented it from carefully distinguishing between policies designed to unseat governments and those aimed more precisely at moderating a given regime's behavior. Yet the former seemed to interfere with the latter in Nicaragua. The Administration's ambivalent policies toward Nicaragua also made it suspicious of peace plans forwarded by major Latin American states, including Mexico, that were seen as too tolerant of the Sandinistas.[15]

The Reagan Administration can hardly bear sole responsibility for the global recession of the early 1980s. Nevertheless, it did adopt a mix of fiscal and monetary policies that had grave consequences for many developing countries. Most Latin American countries will not regain pre-1980 levels of per capita income until well into the next decade. Sub-Saharan Africa is even further disadvantaged. Moreover, the Administration has shown relatively little interest in assisting most developing countries to meet their long-term financial needs. As a result, U.S. commercial and political interests in economic development also have suffered.

The overall impact of Reaganomics and the global recession was to produce a less integrated international economy. The boom in North-South capital markets ended, international trade contracted, and many developing countries adopted restrictive trade and exchange-rate policies. (Developing countries also looked more toward each other for markets, and the relative importance of South-South trade grew markedly [see table C-12 in the appendix].) This partial de-linking of North and South ran counter to traditional U.S. foreign policy objectives that have sought to integrate the developing countries into the global economy.

The Fragility of the Current Situation and Future Challenges

The preceding analysis suggests that the Administration may well have sowed the seeds of future difficulties when it carried its reassertionism and 'domesticism'[16] too far, when it defined security too narrowly and sought to impose its philosophy too dogmatically, when it impatiently shunned international cooperation and refused to listen to the views of others, and when it allowed ends to justify means. Sometimes its focus on quickly regaining American prestige caused it to lose sight of basic American values and longer-term interests.

Ultimate judgments of the North-South policies of the Reagan Administration will depend upon its ability during the second term to sustain its successes and to correct its mistakes. Especially crucial will be policy in the key areas of macro-economics, debt, trade, foreign assistance, and diplomacy in conflictive regions.

Macro-Economic Policy

Much of the perception—and the reality—of renewed American strength is a result of the strong U.S. economic performance during 1983-84. Nevertheless, the twin deficits in the fiscal and external accounts seem unsustainable. The United States may now find itself in the same position as the many developing countries which during the 1970s enjoyed an artificial, deficit-funded expansion—only to confront international constraints that forced a downward adjustment. The trick will be to manage a gradual closing of the twin deficits so as to avoid a recession that would burst the bubble of renewed U.S. vigor, and which could send the global economy into another tailspin. Greater coordination with the major industrial economies would reduce the dangers of miscalculation and actions that are collectively self-defeating.

The prospects for the developing countries in the period ahead will depend substantially on how the United States manages macro-economic policy. The best set of U.S. policies for the developing countries would be fiscal reform that cuts the budget deficit, allowing the Federal Reserve to cut interest rates. This in turn would permit an expansion in other industrial countries and hopefully lead to a widespread, durable global recovery. But if that sustained recovery does not come, or if fears of renewed inflation force monetary authorities to drive up interest rates (and perhaps the dollar), the results for the Third World could be disastrous. Everything could go wrong—export demand could fall, interest payments rise, and the burden of dollar-dominated debt could increase.[17]

Developing-Country Debt

The current strategy toward Third World debt depends upon a sustained recovery in the industrial countries, declining interest rates, and improving commodity prices for developing-country exporters. Even if these optimistic assumptions hold, the political problem of negative net financial flows from debtors to banks—and the consequent slower recovery of living standards—will persist. A corrective strategy is required to attack both ends of the equation.[18] Official lenders can increase their own flows while encouraging private lenders to do the same, whether through co-financing and guarantee mechanisms or through helping developing countries to improve their creditworthiness by adhering to adjustment programs. Official agencies can continue to urge banks to lower their interest rates and other financial charges while more prudent U.S. fiscal policies work gradually to reduce the demand for credit and thereby to yield a more marked decline in interest rates. It may be necessary to reschedule or "cap" interest payments if interest rates rise again.

Trade

The Administration may be hard pressed to maintain its fairly good record of resisting protectionism at home if it cannot correct its two failures in trade policy: its inability to reduce protectionist barriers abroad and the huge U.S. trade deficit. A reduction of the trade deficit substantially hinges on bringing U.S. growth rates more into line with those in other industrial countries and our major developing-country trading partners, as well as realigning the U.S. dollar.

Trade liberalization provides the Administration a major opportunity to put its preferred economics into practice. Encouraging developing countries to join a meaningful North-South trade round in the GATT will require the United States to be more willing to make reciprocal concessions. The Administration's own bargaining hand may be strengthened by adopting a more activist policy in assisting declining domestic industries to adjust to new market forces.

Foreign Assistance

Foreign aid always has been used to achieve a broad range of goals. But the current emphasis on short-run political and security goals at the expense of economic development and meeting the needs of poor people is detrimental to longer-term U.S. goals and to the address of poverty. The question is less one of scarce resources—foreign aid is projected to increase substantially—than one of the allocation of resources among competing programs. Reordering priorities is essential if the aid program is to be made congruent with long-term U.S. interests in the Third World.

The United States needs to direct far more development assistance to the world's poorest countries. In this respect Africa presents the second Reagan Administration with the greatest development challenge of this decade. Million of Africans are now threatened by one of the most serious famines of recent history. The United States has responded generously and, led by A.I.D., is providing a large portion of the food and other emergency supplies being channeled to the hardest hit areas. But the real policy challenge is how to address Sub-Saharan Africa's chronic underdevelopment and to strengthen fragile African economies so that they can withstand natural and external economic shocks in the future. The region's long-term economic potential is good, but additional resources are necessary to develop it. Currently Sub-Saharan Africa receives just under 30 per cent of total OECD aid. This share needs to increase, and donors need to coordinate existing programs much more effectively.[19]

In 1982, in the midst of the debt crisis, the Treasury Department dropped its initial skepticism toward the IMF. In 1985, the Administration urgently needs similarly to reconsider its hostility toward the World Bank. As stabilization programs are completed and as the IMF gradually withdraws from many developing countries, the stage may be set for the World Bank to play a much greater role. The Bank may be the most effective single institution to assist developing countries making the transition from austerity and stabilization to structural adjustment and renewed growth, and to help provide a framework that would give greater confidence to lenders and investors. However, if the Bank is to play this role, the resources available both to the Bank itself as well as to the International Development Association will have to be increased.

Diplomacy

The State Department should be given greater scope to bring its good offices to bear on resolving regional disputes. Even where U.S. influence is limited, an activist diplomacy that engages all parties to the conflict—regardless of the regimes' professed ideologies—can often produce results. This was most recently demonstrated by the Administration's successful efforts to improve relations between Mozambique and South Africa. Sometimes the lead should be granted to regional powers with good entreés to the parties at conflict. In Central America, the United States should assume a more positive attitude toward the peace proposals put forth by leading Latin American powers—which address the key U.S. security concerns in the region—even if that implies accepting a *modus vivendi* with the Nicaraguan government. Among other reasons, only if peace is secured in Central America will U.S. financial aid and the opportunities offered by the Caribbean Basin Initiative be able to stimulate economic recovery and long-term development.

A review of recent U.S. policies toward radical states provides evidence that economic 'carrots' and 'sticks' can work—provided that they are employed as part of a coherent strategy with realistic, limited objectives. In the short term, economic inducements can help to moderate a regime's foreign policy, if not necessarily its internal politics. In the longer run, policies of diplomatic engagement can also encourage trends toward economic decentralization and political pluralism within revolutionary states.

All of these proposals imply a broadening of goals and a lengthening of the Administration's time horizon. While seeking to conserve the gains made during the first Reagan term, they introduce important mid-course corrections to address neglected issues and to avoid predictable dangers that lie ahead. Herein lie the challenges for the second term.

Notes

[1] For the most coherent explanation so far of the Administration's 'domesticist' approach by a participant, see Henry Nau, "Where Reaganomics Works," *Foreign Policy*, No. 57, Winter 1984-85, pp. 14-37.

[2] As described in Kenneth Oye, "International Systems Structure and American Foreign Policy," in Kenneth Oye, Robert Lieber, and Donald Rothchild, *Eagle Defiant* (Boston: Little, Brown, 1983), pp. 3-32.

[3] See Chapter 1 in this volume by Paul Krugman, a former member of the Administration's Council of Economic Advisors.

[4] This issue is analyzed in Chapter 5 by W. Anthony Lake.

[5] For example, see Jeane J. Kirkpatrick, Address Before the American Society of International Law, Washington, D.C., April 12, 1984.

[6] The trade policies of the last four years are assessed in Chapter 3 by Steve Lande and Craig VanGrasstek.

[7] The growing role of the public sector in international finance is discussed in Chapter 2 by Richard E. Feinberg.

[8] See *Realism, Strength, Negotiation: Key Foreign Policy Statements of the Reagan Administration* (Washington, D.C.: U.S. Department of State, May 1984).

[9] As quoted in Christopher Madison, "Exporting Reaganomics—The President Wants To Do Things Differently in AID," *National Journal*, May 29, 1982, p. 962.

[10] See Krugman chapter,pp.32-34.

[11] The trends in the U.S. aid program are scrutinized in Chapter 4 by John W. Sewell and Christine Contee.

[12] *U.S. "Costs" of Third World Recession: They Lose, We Lose*, Overseas Development Council *Policy Focus* No. 2 (1984).

[13] For a fuller discussion, see Richard E. Feinberg, "Overview: Restoring Confidence in International Credit Markets," in Richard E. Feinberg and Valeriana Kallab, eds., *Uncertain Future: Commercial Banks and the Third World* (New Brunswick, N.J.: Transaction Books, for the Overseas Development Council, 1984), pp. 9-14.

[14] Interview cited in Oye, op. cit., p. 25.

[15] See Guy Erb and Cathryn Thorup, *U.S.-Mexican Relations: The Issues Ahead*, Development Paper 35, Overseas Development Council, 1984.

[16] For an explanation of the Administration's 'domesticist' strategy, see p. 4 of this chapter and footnote 1 above.

[17] See Krugman chapter, p. 47.

[18] Op. cit., footnote 13.

[19] The Overseas Development Council and the Council on Foreign Relations are jointly sponsoring the Committee on African Development Strategies which will issue a series of recommendations for U.S. development policy toward Africa in mid-1985.

Summaries of Recommendations

1. U.S. Macro-Economic Policy and the Developing Countries
(Paul R. Krugman)

Although the traditional concern of North-South economic discussion has been with issues of aid and trade, in recent years the macro-economic policies of industrial countries have moved to center stage. In particular, U.S. macro-economic policy, through both its direct and indirect effects on the macro-economic situation worldwide, is crucial to the medium-term prospects of poorer countries.

The key to understanding the role of U.S. macro-economic policy lies in recognizing that its international effects are not limited to the simple multiplier effects of U.S. economic expansion on export demand and employment in other countries. Far more important are the induced responses of other governments. This is especially important for the case of fiscal policy, where the direct impact of the U.S. budget deficit is probably to increase demand in the rest of the world, but where the induced policy changes in other countries offset and perhaps even reverse this effect.

Less-developed countries are particularly exposed to the consequences of U.S. macro-economic policy. Those countries, with their large dollar-denominated external debt, are highly vulnerable to the combination of tight monetary and loose fiscal policy, which worsens their debt burden by raising both interest rates and the value of the dollar. Indeed, external shocks due largely to U.S. policies have made the recessions in these countries far deeper than that in the United States itself.

The outlook for developing countries therefore depends importantly on U.S. macro-economic policies. An alternative to the recent pattern—a fiscal-led boom, with monetary policy progressively tightened in an effort to restrain inflation—would be a U.S. fiscal reform that allows a sustained reduction in both interest rates and the international value of the dollar, and more durable global growth. This scenario would be far better for developing countries.

2. International Finance and Investment: A Surging Public Sector (Richard E. Feinberg)

Rhetoric and reality sometimes can be far apart. Over the last four years, the U.S. government has combined passionate faith in the free market with international financial policies that relied heavily on official action. When the deterioration in the creditworthiness of many Third World nations generated a near panic among the commercial international banks, the task fell to official agencies to contain the crisis. Less willing than before to act alone, the alarmed private sector increasingly sought the clasp of the visible hand of government before risking capital in uncertain Third World markets. To renew the flow of funds to developing countries, the Reagan Administration participated in emergency bail-out packages, agreed to increase the resources and authority of the International Monetary Fund, and supported other official efforts to reinvigorate private flows. Prodded by Congress, the Administration also introduced tougher government regulation of international banking. In addition, government agencies worked with the banks to alter traditional procedures for the restructuring of existing debts.

Although U.S. firms with overseas subsidiaries did not face the same sort of acute crisis, U.S. direct investment in developing countries shared the same basic experience as the credit markets: The private sector retrenched and the public sector stepped up its activities. However, despite its positive attitudes toward direct investment, the Administration did not introduce any major policy changes. It concentrated instead on expanding existing institutions—particularly the bilateral Overseas Private Investment Corporation (OPIC) and, to a lesser degree, the multilateral International Finance Corporation (IFC) of the World Bank. The Administration did, however, advance two minor initiatives targeted at increasing investment in the politically important Caribbean Basin. These various efforts to stimulate U.S. direct investment failed to offset the disincentives caused by the global recession.

The same forces that drove the Reagan Administration to intervene in financial markets forced governments of diverse ideological stripes to intervene more heavily in the allocation of foreign exchange and domestic credit. The dismal economic environment hit the private sector particularly hard in many Third World countries, and the public sector frequently acted to steady markets and protect living standards, bringing about an impressive shift of relative power and resources to the public sector. However, as the global recession ends, some emergency public-sector activities are receding and the long-term trend toward increased state ownership of productive firms seems to have peaked in some countries.

Although considerable progress has been made, it would be a grave mistake to imagine that the debt problem has been definitively solved. The key to the continuing successful management of global financial problems can be found in the lessons of the recent past: Changing international circumstances demand a pragmatic adjustment in the relations between the public and private sectors.

3. Trade with the Developing Countries: The Reagan Record and Prospects (Steve Lande and Craig VanGrasstek)

The United States and the developing countries share common goals in maintaining relatively open access to the U.S. market. The developing countries need an export market in order to earn foreign exchange, foster more sophisticated industries, and create employment. Liberal trade policies also serve American interests by stimulating foreign demand for U.S. exports of services and capital goods, by generating income to repay debts to U.S. banks, and by creating employment in U.S. export industries.

Access to the U.S. market is threatened by growing protectionist pressure in the United States. This pressure is largely directed at the labor-intensive industries in which the developing countries have a comparative advantage.

The developing nations and their economic allies in the United States are not helpless bystanders in U.S. trade policy; they can and should work with one another in order to form a counterweight to the protectionist lobbies.

• **Textiles.** Textile and apparel exports will continue to be restricted by the quotas negotiated under the Multi-Fibre Arrangement (MFA), and the politically powerful U.S. lobby of textile producers will advocate stricter import controls. But international and domestic threats to developing-country market access can be challenged effectively. Textile-exporting nations can act as a more cohesive bloc in the MFA negotiations and can use the threat of retaliation (i.e., cutting off U.S. access to their own markets) to negotiate from a position of strength. And within the United States, the recently strengthened coalition of agricultural and retail groups can counter the power of the U.S. textile lobby; it can point to serious concerns raised by developing-country retaliatory threats to argue that further textile restrictions are not in the U.S. national interest. Such moves can also be complemented by the efforts of those within the U.S. textile industry who profit from open market access—for example, by mills that sell their fabric to Mexican and Caribbean producers.

• **Application of Import Relief Laws.** Due to growing protectionist pressure in the United States and to changes recently made in U.S. trade legislation, the number of import-relief cases brought against developing-country exports may increase in the coming years. Exporters in developing countries must be prepared to defend themselves in such cases.

Because the anti-dumping and anti-subsidy laws are administered on a technical rather than a political track, there is little opportunity to influence their outcome through concerted pressure. In contrast, the 'escape clause' and 'presidential retaliation' statutes are subject to much greater political influence. The President should continue to both resist pressures to apply these laws and oppose their protectionist revision in Congress. With respect to export subsidies and other interventionist practices common in the developing world, the United States should favor the view expressed in the Subsidies Code of the GATT, which sees most Third World subsidies as legitimate means for overcoming structural disadvantages.

• **Changes in the U.S. Generalized System of Preferences (GSP).** In its 1984 renewal of the U.S. GSP, which will stay in place through mid-1993, Congress added a new element of negotiability to the program: The President is now empowered to make GSP-eligible products subject to either greater or less security of eligibility under the program. This change may work to the benefit of the least developed and mid-level beneficiary countries; but for the newly industrializing countries, it is virtually certain that tough negotiations lie ahead. These countries should be prepared to bargain with the United States on the tariff and non-tariff barriers they erect to products of interest to the United States, as well as on other matters, such as 'intellectual property rights' (e.g., counterfeiting).

This change in the GSP program is a departure from the principle that trade preferences for developing countries should be non-reciprocal. The United States should use its power to remove products from the GSP sparingly, if at all.

• **Trade Negotiations in the Second Reagan Term.** The Reagan Administration is gearing up for trade negotiations during its second term, and the newly industrializing countries are near the top of the agenda. The United States is eager to discuss 'new issues' such as (a) trade in services, (b) trade-related investment, (c) high-technology products, and (d) intellectual property rights.

The more advanced developing countries have good reason to resist discussions on these topics, but the United States is prepared to use unilateral retaliation to force them to negotiate. Given that negotiations are practically inevitable, the developing countries would do well to fashion a coherent and united position. They may want to engage the United States in 'plurilateral' discussions as a middle road—instead of multilateral or bilateral talks. If they do negotiate at the bilateral level, they should attempt to extract concessions in return for those they make themselves.

For its own part, the United States should take the interests of the developing countries into account when proposing any international standards in the 'new issues.' Equal standards should not be imposed on countries of manifestly unequal economic status. Any new rules should make allowances for the differing levels of economic development and industrial sophistication.

4. U.S. Foreign Aid in the 1980s: Reordering Priorities (John W. Sewell and Christine E. Contee)

The U.S. foreign aid program is in danger of losing sight of its primary objective: to alleviate poverty among the world's poorest people. Under the Reagan Administration, the program has become increasingly oriented toward political and security concerns. Bilateral aid is preferred over less politicized multilateral programs, and within the bilateral program, short-term political and security objectives have received far more attention than long-term development. The new "four pillars" approach of the Agency for International Development contains two relatively non-controversial and potentially useful elements, the emphasis on institution building and technology transfer. The other two program instruments, policy dialogue and the private sector initiative, are more controversial. The private sector emphasis is undoubtedly useful in certain circumstances, but it remains disturbingly unclear *who* is benefiting, or even if the approach has been clearly defined. In a similar vein, the emphasis on policy dialogue is potentially promising, but A.I.D.'s staff and resource limitations, coupled with the Administration's reluctance to increase funding for the multilateral banks—the logical leaders in policy dialogue—call into question the ultimate effectiveness of A.I.D.'s efforts in this area.

In relation to gross national product, the U.S. aid program remains very small compared to those of other industrial-country donors. Yet it is clear that resource scarcity is not the primary problem—the U.S. foreign aid budget increased by nearly $5.4 billion during the first Reagan term.

Getting the aid program back on track requires reversing existing priorities. The legislative mandate of the 1973 Foreign Assistance Act must be reaffirmed. This means restoring the balance between development-oriented and security-oriented aid. In the last four years, military and security aid rose 67 per cent while development assistance, multilateral contributions, Food for Peace (P.L. 480), and other bilateral economic programs grew by less than one-third. Reaffirming the mandate also means targeting far more aid to the low-income countries of the Third World, which currently average only 50 cents per person of U.S. aid; the upper middle-income developing countries, in contrast, receive over three times that amount. The useful elements of the "four pillars" should certainly be retained as tools to achieve the primary objective of equitable growth and poverty alleviation. Finally, the low priority currently assigned to U.S. support of the multilateral organizations also must be reversed. Increased support for these institutions—particularly for the International Development Association—contributes toward the U.S. objective of alleviating poverty. Equally important, the multilaterals are vital sources of capital and policy advice for the middle-income countries and support the U.S. objectives of fostering policy reform in developing countries and reinforcing a healthy, open international economy.

5. Wrestling with Third World Radical Regimes: Theory and Practice (Anthony Lake)

The two major schools of thought on how American policies might best deal with 'radical regimes' in the Third World—the *globalist* view, emphasizing East-West aspects of the problem, and the *regionalist* perspective, focusing more on local questions—suggest different tactical goals and methods. The former emphasizes the removal or punishment of such regimes through the use of economic and political sanctions and even by force. The latter seeks their containment and moderation through policies of diplomatic and economic engagement.

The record of the past eight years offers the opportunity to test these theories as applied in practice by both the Carter and the Reagan Administrations, although neither pursued either globalist or regionalist policies in their pure form.

After reviewing contrasting approaches to radical regimes in Nicaragua, Afghanistan, Indochina, Southern Africa, Libya, and Iran, the author offers some general conclusions:

In no case was there any success in removing a radical regime, or even significantly affecting its internal behavior. The limits to American leverage are narrower than either liberals or conservatives like to believe. It may well be that there are opportunities to encourage trends toward pluralism within revolutionary states once they have had full experience with the difficulties of trying to manage their economies through central (and generally inefficient) bureaucracies. But in their first years in power, revolutionary regimes may be the least receptive to external efforts to influence their internal policies, perhaps because of the very fragility of the infant institutions they seek to protect and build.

There were, however, some partial successes, either potential or real, affecting the *foreign* policies of these regimes. Yet when the goal of rollback was pursued at the same time as efforts to induce foreign moderation, the former seemed to interfere with the latter.

It is not difficult to stand by and allow, or even to encourage, the 'bleeding' of a radical regime in some local conflict, as a warning to revolutionaries elsewhere. But in the long run such policies serve neither American interests nor American ideals.

The 'carrots' preferred by regionalists and the 'sticks' of the globalists have each had some limited effects. Not surprisingly, Washington has exercised the greatest influence when it has combined the two. Policies of diplomatic engagement paid off for both the Carter and Reagan Administrations. Efforts to isolate radical regimes do not seem to have succeeded. In any case, barrages of hostile rhetoric have proved self-defeating in both foreign and domestic political terms.

Thus it would seem clear that no single theoretical approach always, or even almost always, works. Effective policies can best be shaped by examining each situation rather than by pretending to know the theoretical answers even before the questions are posed. Pragmatic policies in Washington depend, however, not only on the wisdom of policy makers; they must also be understood and sup- ported by the American public. The first requirement is for an understanding that a policy of pragmatism depends on leadership in Washington that consistently elucidates and educates, thus giving itself the political room it needs for maneuver abroad.

U.S. Foreign Policy and the Third World: Agenda 1985-86

Chapter 1

U.S. Macro-Economic Policy and the Developing Countries

Paul R. Krugman

For most of the postwar period, discussion of North-South economic relations and of the role of the United States in world development has focused on the micro-economic issues of trade and aid. In the mid-1980s, however, it seems clear that for at least the next few years the most important concern of developing countries will have to be the world *macro-economic* environment: unemployment, interest rates, and exchange rates in the industrial countries. For heavily indebted countries in particular, the prospects for successfully extricating themselves from their current difficulties depend critically on the course of growth and interest rates in the advanced nations.

The key to the future world macro-economic environment in turn lies to an important though not exclusive extent in the monetary and fiscal policies of the United States. In addition to their direct influence on the world's largest economy, U.S. macro-economic policies have a special, strategic role in influencing monetary and fiscal policies elsewhere in the world. Through its direct and indirect effects, U.S. policy is arguably the most important factor shaping the economic environment of developing countries. Yet the channels of U.S. influence, and the implications of alternative U.S. policies, are not well understood by many who are interested in the problems of poorer nations.

This chapter offers a framework for understanding how U.S. macro-economic policy influences the world economy as a whole, and developing countries in particular. It then applies this framework to recent events and to the analysis of future prospects. Although the focus here—given the time of writing—is on the problems of those middle-income countries with substantial private bank debt, the analytical framework should also be useful to those interested in the prospects of poorer nations.

The Rediscovery of U.S. Economic Predominance

Someone once remarked that in the textbook accounts of history, the middle class always seems to be rising. Most magazine articles and books on trends in the international economy prompt a similar observation: in these accounts, the degree of U.S. dependence on the economies of other countries always seems on the rise. When it was first argued by Richard Cooper and others, the idea of the "economics of interdependence" was a challenge to conventional ways of thinking.[1] By now, however, it has become conventional wisdom and, as such, it is probably accepted too readily.

There is no question that the U.S. economy of the 1980s is far more dependent on international transactions than that of the early 1950s. Nor is there any question that the U.S. government has a much larger stake in the economic policies of other governments than it did a generation ago. But despite this gradual, long-term trend toward increased interdependence with the rest of the world, the United States still possesses both a great deal of economic autonomy and a powerful ability to affect the economies of other countries. The past five years have demonstrated that the time has not yet arrived when the United States will have lost its ability to strike out on an economic course of its own and to shape the economic environment of others.

To put recent events in perspective, imagine an international economist— one interested in policy—who went to sleep at the end of 1979 and awakened in late 1984. Such a professorial Rip Van Winkle probably would have formed a set of judgments about the role of the United States in the world economy based on the experiences of the 1970s— emphasizing the diminished role of the United States in the world and the decreased autonomy of U.S. macro-economic policy. On awakening, he would find these expectations largely overturned by events.

What we thought we had learned by the end of the 1970s was that the United States was no longer the predominant economic power. Once upon a time the United States had been the unmoved mover of the international economy. U.S. macro-economic policies were of vital interest to other countries, but the U.S. government felt free to make those policies with little regard for international considerations. During the 1970s, however, both the nation's leadership role and its autonomy seemed clearly weakened. The rapid U.S. recovery from the 1975 recession failed to spark a matching recovery in other industrial countries; indeed, unemployment rates in Europe continued to rise.[2] Partly as a result of its more rapid recovery, the United States developed what at the time was regarded as a huge trade deficit, and the dollar began falling sharply on world exchanges.

Faced with the failure of its unilateral expansion to bring about world recovery, the United States began to seek coordinated action. The second half of the 1970s was the era of "locomotive" and "convoy" theories arguing a need for simultaneous expansion by several countries.[3] At the same time, the United States was forced into an acceptance of the limits of its own autonomy. Its shift toward tighter monetary policy in 1979 was at least in part motivated by the desire to stop the slide of the dollar. By the end of 1979, then, the age of interdependence seemed to have arrived.

On awakening in late 1984, our napping Rip Van Winkle surely would be driven to self-doubt. To begin with, the Federal Reserve's long attempt—from 1979 to 1982—to fight inflation with recession not only produced the nation's worst economic slump since the 1930s but also was associated with a worldwide recession. Rightly or wrongly, many people believed that the United States had exported its recession to the rest of the world. After 1982, the country experienced a rapid recovery. Like the earlier U.S. emergence from the 1975 trough, this one did little for recovery in other industrial countries, with unemployment again continuing to rise in Europe.[4] Again, moreover, U.S. recovery contributed to a growing U.S. trade deficit—this time one that dwarfed the earlier bulge.[5] Yet the trade deficit of the 1980s somehow failed to lead to a slide in the dollar; on the contrary, the dollar rose to ever greater heights.

In trying to understand the dollar's strength, our reawakened economist would find many people attributing it to a U.S. budget deficit that has driven up interest rates and attracted foreign capital. And he would find widespread acceptance of the view that U.S. fiscal deficits are shaping not only domestic but also worldwide economic events—that by bidding up interest rates and the value of the dollar, the U.S. budget deficit has a contractionary influence on other industrial countries and also intensifies the problems of debtor nations.

Thus instead of continuing an inexorable trend toward growing interdependence, the 1980s so far seem to have been a time of "counter-revolution" in the role of the United States. Once again the United States appears to be able to go its own way in macro-economic policies. And once again many countries *believe* that U.S. macro-economic policies are a critical factor in their own environments, though the channels of influence have changed.

Even if announcements of the end of U.S. economic predominance were premature, however, we still need to understand why the last five years have looked so different from the previous five. To do this, we need to back away briefly from current events to consider some general aspects of international economic interdependence.

The Economics of Interdependence

The study of international macro-economic linkages is by no means a new field. The Great Depression of the 1930s was international in scope and demanded an analysis that explained why macro-economic policies in one country influence the economies of other countries. With the development of Keynesian economics in the 1930s and 1940s, a mechanism was quickly found that appeared to explain the phenomenon of coordinated, worldwide booms and slumps. This was the so-called foreign-trade multiplier.

As analyzed more than a generation ago, the foreign-trade multiplier was presumed to operate as follows: Suppose that the United States shifts its monetary or fiscal policy in a contractionary direction, raising interest rates or increasing taxes. This contraction will reduce the demand for U.S. products, leading to a fall in income and employment. With this drop in income, Americans will cut back their spending, producing a further round of contraction, and so on—the familiar multiplier analysis of introductory textbooks. However, as people in the United States spend less, part of the reduction in demand will be a reduction in demand for *foreign* products, leading to a decline in imports. This will set in motion a parallel process of contraction abroad. Furthermore, these multiplier processes will interact: As foreign economies contract, their demand for U.S. exports will fall, reinforcing the U.S. contraction; as the U.S. economy contracts, the demand for imports will fall, reinforcing the foreign slump.[6]

Stated this way, the concept of the foreign-trade multiplier seems to give a convincing account of international interdependence. To this day, much of the discussion of international interdependence remains couched in these terms,[7] and the common sense of non-professional discussion is, as usual, largely based on the professional conventional wisdom of a few decades ago. Yet, for two reasons, the foreign-trade multiplier seems an increasingly inadequate model of international interdependence. First, attempts to quantify the importance of interdependence have led to disappointing results. Since the late 1960s, a number of efforts have been made to produce world econometric models linking the national econometric models that have become standard tools of economic forecasting. These attempts—of which Nobel prizewinner Lawrence Klein's Project LINK is the best known—require an immense amount of data collection and statistical analysis. What they seem to imply in the end, however, is that interdependence is not all that important. A representative estimate would be that an expansionary monetary or fiscal policy that raises U.S. gross national product (GNP) by 1 per cent will raise the output of other industrial countries by only something like two-tenths of 1 per cent. While the predicted effects are not negligible, they fall far short of providing a strong case for the crucial importance of interdependence. This suggests that, however appealing the foreign-trade multiplier concept may seem in words or algebra, it is not very important in practice.

Second, the change in the international rules of the game since 1970 makes the conventional account of interdependence even less convincing. In the 1970s, the fixed-exchange-rate system broke down, and exchange-rate flexibility seems to offer countries an opportunity to insulate themselves from the effects of other countries' macro-economic policies. If the U.S. government wants to engineer a boom during an election year, and if West Germany is concerned about inflation, the Germans can simply hold to a path of monetary and fiscal discipline and let the deutsche mark appreciate against the U.S. dollar. Economists can offer technical arguments about why floating exchange rates may fail to fully insulate economies from macro-economic disturbances abroad, but the basic point remains that the conventional explanation of interdependence, which upon quantification looks weak even in a world of fixed exchange rates, looks even weaker in a world of flexible exchange rates.

Taken at face value, this result invites the dismissal of international macro-economic interdependence as a major issue. But it must be remembered that the period since 1970 has been marked by two worldwide, coordinated slumps. Furthermore, governments have continued to demand changes in each others' macro-economic policies and to blame other governments for their problems. These need not be decisive pieces of evidence, since common external causes, especially jumps in the price of oil, surely had something to do with the coordinated slumps, and since the propensity of governments to blame others for their own problems largely reflects a human tendency to pass the buck (or franc, in this case). Nonetheless, the continuing, widespread acceptance of mutual interdependence as reality is enough to warrant a reexamination of the issue. Perhaps Project LINK and its like failed to find much interdependence not because it is not there, but because they failed to approach it in the right way. In the past few years a 'new view' of international interdependence has emerged that makes precisely this argument.[8]

The new view starts with the observation that the conventional approach to the issue treats governments as being rather passive. Except for the government that initiates action, governments are assumed simply to sit still while the multiplier process works itself out.

But in fact governments of course do react to the changed environment. The new view argues that the crucial channel of interdependence is not the direct impact of one country's policies on the economies of other countries, but the indirect impact of induced changes in the *policies* of other countries.

The following (not at all abstract) example illustrates the point. Suppose that the United States, concerned about inflation, resorts to a tighter monetary policy. Initially, this would bring higher U.S. interest rates, a recession, and appreciation of the dollar against other currencies. Conventional analysis suggests that the recession would not be shared with the rest of the world. The U.S. recession would indeed reduce U.S. demand for exports from the rest of the world, but the rise of the dollar would simultaneously make foreign goods more competitive vis-à-vis American goods, providing an offsetting stimulus. On balance the effect on the rest of the world is likely to be small—or perhaps even stimulative.

But the new view envisions a different result. For a variety of reasons, other countries are unlikely to accept the rise in the dollar without trying to do something to sustain their currencies. Canada, for example, is closely linked to the U.S. economy and will fear an inflationary impact if the Canadian dollar declines too much. Italy, while less closely linked to the United States, is heavily dependent on imported oil, which is priced in dollars. Japan fears that a further slide in the yen will provoke a protectionist reaction in the United States. France views the value of the franc as an important political symbol. And so on.

How will these governments attempt to sustain their currencies? They may first try to limit the dollar's rise by intervening in foreign-exchange markets. Experience has shown, however, that exchange-market intervention, unless backed by a change in underlying monetary policies, is largely ineffective: It is quickly swamped by offsetting private capital flows. Consequently, as countries attempt to keep their currencies from falling, they will be forced to alter their domestic policies. In particular, they will react by tightening their monetary policies in order to raise interest rates. And it is this *induced* response, rather than the *direct* effects of a U.S. recession, that explains why tight money in the United States can produce a global recession.

Now it is immediately apparent that induced policy responses by foreign governments can give U.S. macro-economic policy much more leverage over the world economy than it would have otherwise. What the attempts to quantify the foreign-trade multiplier showed was that, despite its size, the U.S. market is not important enough for a U.S. recession to generate directly a matching recession in the rest of the world. If other countries care enough about the value of their currencies in terms of the dollar, however, their induced policy changes in response to a U.S. monetary contraction can indeed set in motion a worldwide slump.

The other major implication of the new view of interdependence is that the extent to which U.S. policies are transmitted abroad depends a great deal on the mix of policies that the United States selects. Our example has focused on the effects of U.S. *monetary* policy. Consider, however, another not-so-abstract example: Suppose that the United States adopts an expansionary *fiscal* policy while retaining a tight monetary policy. In this case, although domestic demand would increase, interest rates would also rise—and the effect might well be a rise rather than a fall in the dollar. If foreign governments reacted by tightening their monetary policies to sustain their currencies, the effect could easily be to reduce production outside the United States. That is, while an expansionary U.S. *monetary* policy would tend to lead to a worldwide recovery, an expansionary U.S. *fiscal* policy would be much less likely to do so—and might even lead to a deeper recession abroad.

It is not at all farfetched to suggest that this last point is an important element in the current, uneven world recovery. The U.S. recovery has been achieved despite unprecedentedly high interest rates, due to an equally unprecedented fiscal stimulus resulting from the huge budget deficit. The high level of U.S. interest rates, and the resulting strength of the dollar, has inhibited the willingness of other countries to loosen their own monetary policies. They could, of course, use fiscal stimulus instead—but that is another story—one that will be considered in this chapter.

Two conclusions have emerged thus far: First, despite the disappointing results of econometric exercises, there is a good case to be made for the proposition that a high degree of interdependence exists between the macro-economic policies of the industrial countries. This interdependence arises not from the mechanical operation of some multiplier process, but through the effects of one country's policy choices on the policies of other countries. Second, it matters a good deal whether monetary or fiscal policy is used to affect demand. An expansionary monetary policy in the United States encourages expansion everywhere, but an expansionary fiscal policy may not, and may even have a contractionary effect abroad.

Interdependence and the Less-Developed Countries

Much of the above discussion of interdependence among industrial countries applies equally to developing nations. However, the interdependence between these countries and the industrial world, in particular the United States, has some additional features that in the last several years have made less-developed countries particularly dependent on U.S. monetary and fiscal policy. Three features in particular stand out: the existence of large outstanding foreign debt; vulnerability to loss of creditor confidence; and the role of the International Monetary Fund.

Substantial foreign indebtedness is not a new thing for less-developed countries. Despite heavy borrowing during the 1970s, the ratio of debt to GNP for these nations as a group rose only modestly from the early 1970s to the early 1980s, and the ratio of debt to export earnings did not rise at all.[9] But the stability of these ratios masks an important change in the *nature* of developing-country debt. Much of the new lending of the 1970s took the form of private lending by banks rather than the public lending that had been dominant previously. This was particularly true for the most heavily indebted countries, especially the major Latin American debtors.

The important difference between public and private lending from the point of view of international interdependence is that private lenders are more acutely conscious of the need to protect themselves against risk. In the 1970s, the major risk appeared to be that of rising interest rates resulting from increased inflation. To protect themselves, lenders resorted to two strategies. First, much of the debt incurred during the 1970s was "floating-rate" debt, with the interest rate tied to recent Eurocurrency rates. Second, lenders shortened the maturities of their loans. Both strategies had the effect of protecting banks from locking themselves into long-term loans at low interest rates and then finding that short-term rates had risen.

The unintended consequence of this change in the character of lending, however, was to introduce a new and direct dependence of debtor nations on conditions in international financial markets. As already noted, a rise in interest rates abroad can put pressure on a country's exchange rate by inducing a capital outflow. In the case of heavily indebted developing countries, however, a rise in Euromarket interest rates also has a direct, adverse effect on their current accounts—an effect that has no counterpart in the interdependence among large developed countries.

The second main way in which developing countries differ in their dependence on the economic policies of others is closely related to the first, but not exactly the same. It is the vulnerability of these nations to crises of confidence. All market economies are, of course, vulnerable to the possibility of capital flight. Even in a wealthy industrial country such as France, a lack of investor confidence can lead to a weak currency and be a major factor in inducing a government to adopt austerity measures. The external debt of such countries as Brazil and

Mexico, however, poses a much more direct and acute problem of confidence. Because of the high ratio of debt to exports, and because of the relatively short maturity of the debt, by the early 1980s the foreign exchange needed to pay interest and principal on long-term debt (and to repay short-term loans) exceeded 100 per cent of foreign-exchange earnings.[10] In other words, countries had to borrow to service their existing debt. In good times this poses no problem—such a state of affairs is normal in business. But when conditions turn adverse enough for creditors to become unwilling to make new loans or to roll over old ones, a balance-of-payments problem can quickly turn into a serious crisis.

Dealing with such a crisis requires reassuring one's bankers. For developing countries, this means reaching agreement with the IMF. The Fund has some resources of its own to offer, but, more important, private lenders usually will not deal with a country whose policies have not met with IMF approval. As noted, the key channel of interdependence among industrial countries is not the mechanical operation of multiplier effects but the induced responses of governments. In the case of developing countries, this channel is made formal and explicit when the IMF requires credit restrictions and budget cuts as part of its conditionality. In a direct sense, the current deep recession in Latin America results mostly from the effects of tightened monetary and fiscal policies within the Latin American nations themselves rather than from the multiplier effects of reduced exports, but few would deny that these domestic policy changes are in large part responses to the worsened external environment created by developments in the industrial countries.

Having described the channels through which U.S. macro-economic policy affects the developing countries, let us return to the example used earlier—a U.S. shift toward tighter monetary policy—to show how these channels operate. As pointed out above, the initial impact of U.S. tight money will be higher U.S. interest rates, a recession in the United States, and a stronger dollar. As other industrial countries attempt to limit the dollar's rise, they will tighten their own monetary policies, so that both the rise in interest rates and the recession will in effect be exported by the United States to the rest of the industrial world. What happens next is that the combination of recession in the industrial countries and higher interest rates puts pressure on the balances of payments of developing countries, especially those carrying heavy loads of short-term or floating-rate debt. These countries may lose the confidence of their bankers, and if they do, they are forced to accept tough austerity measures prescribed by the IMF. It is through these austerity measures that the recession is in turn exported to the developing world.

This is a hypothetical case. But it is a not at all bad portrait of what happened to the world economy from 1979 to 1982. The important point is that because of the way that governments respond to external pressures, an initial shift toward monetary restraint in the United States can have worldwide consequences. Indeed, U.S. tight money may actually produce a deeper recession in developing countries than it does in the United States itself.

This account of interdependence may, however, still seem to leave very recent events unexplained. Why has the rapid recovery in the United States not generated a strong worldwide recovery? And why do the developing countries remain in such serious trouble? The answer lies in the fact that the U.S. recovery has not been a mirror image of the U.S. recession. The 1979-82 recession was clearly generated by tight monetary policy, bringing with it a sharp rise in real interest rates and in the value of the dollar on foreign-exchange markets. But the recovery, in contrast, has not been led by a loosening of monetary policy. Except during a critical few months during 1982, monetary policy in the United States has remained tight. The driving force behind the U.S. expansion has been fiscal policy—the Reagan Administration's deficit. As indicated earlier, a recovery led by fiscal policy has very different international implications from one led by monetary expansion.

The crucial difference is that because of the opposing pulls of fiscal stimulus and tight money, real interest rates in the United States have remained high and even have risen as the economy has expanded. Faster recovery in the United States than in the rest of the world has contributed to a widening trade deficit—just as it did in the later 1970s. Because of high U.S. real interest rates, however, this widening trade gap has been willingly financed by foreign capital inflows, so that the dollar not only has not depreciated but has become even stronger. Faced with a rising dollar, other industrial countries have not felt free to loosen their own monetary policies and generate an increase in domestic demand. As a result, the U.S. recovery has been exported to the rest of the industrial world only through the direct channel of the foreign-trade multiplier—and this channel is, as mentioned, a relatively weak one. The result—outside the United States, and Canada, closely linked to its neighbor—is a recovery that is by and large too slow to bring about any major reduction in unemployment or slack capacity.

Finally, the developing countries find that the increase in demand for their exports, though welcome, is limited by the failure of industrial countries other than the United States to experience a vigorous recovery. And with interest rates remaining high, they have received no relief at all on the financial front. As a result, their fundamental balance-of-payments position has been improved only at high domestic cost. What is most needed, particularly for countries caught up in the debt crisis, is an improvement in the external environment dramatic enough to restore lender confidence and allow a resumption of normal financial flows. The peculiar world recovery that has been in progress since 1982 has failed to deliver this kind of uplift.

In sum, then, a view of interdependence that stresses the induced policy reactions of governments indicates that U.S. macro-economic policy continues to play a crucial role in the economic outlook for developing countries. This role is much larger than the far-from-negligible, direct role of the United States as a market for developing-country exports: In addition, U.S. policy influences the policies of other industrial countries, and plays a crucial role in determining world interest rates. In this way U.S. policy is critical in defining the external constraints that in turn are the key determinants of the domestic macro-economic policies of developing countries.

The Special Role of the United States

The discussion so far has taken for granted that the United States initiates changes in the world economic situation and that the rest of the world responds. This point of view has not, however, really been justified. Don't shocks originate in policy changes in other countries— for example Japan or West Germany? And doesn't U.S. policy depend on other countries' actions as much as they do on ours?

A partial answer is to acknowledge both that shocks can originate from the actions of other governments, too, and that the U.S. government can find itself constrained in its own policies by the policy choices of others. As argued in this section, the sharp change in U.S. fiscal policy under the Reagan Administration has in fact been paralleled by equally sharp changes—in the opposite direction—in other industrial countries. Also, as noted earlier, the failure of other countries to keep pace with the U.S. recovery in the late 1970s, and the resulting decline in the dollar, did help pressure the United States into a shift to tighter money in 1979. Thus the asymmetry between the United States and other economies is not total.

The symmetries should not, however, be exaggerated. Despite the gradual decline in U.S. predominance since its postwar peak, the nature of interdependence between the United States and the rest of the world is still qualitatively different from that experienced by other countries. The United States continues to have far more freedom of maneuver, and far more effect on the world economy, than any other nation.

In part this is simply a matter of size. The United States still accounts for roughly a quarter of world output, roughly a third of the output of the market economies, and roughly 40 per cent of the output of the industrial countries. The U.S. economy is perhaps two-and-a-half times as large as that of Japan, its nearest competitor. Thus size alone would make U.S. policy more important to other countries than their policies are to the United States. In addition, the analysis of interdependence presented earlier indicates that the size of the United States gives it more freedom of action than other industrial countries possess, and that the political fragmentation of the rest of the industrial world enhances U.S. leverage over other countries.

To illustrate, consider again what happens when an industrial country tightens its monetary policy. If the country were West Germany or France, it would have to worry about whether the move would be matched by other European governments. An independent monetary tightening by a European country would lead to an exchange-rate appreciation and loss of competitiveness in relation to both the United States and other European nations, posing serious economic and political risks. In contrast, when the United States changes its monetary policy, it in effect ensures that the policy is coordinated across an economic region as large as Europe; the stresses caused by the resulting exchange-rate movement are far less significant than they would have been for a smaller country.

Conversely, consider the European response to a tighter U.S. monetary policy. If the European Community were able to act as a unified whole, it might choose to maintain its policies unchanged in the face of a U.S. policy shift, accepting the exchange-rate depreciation that results. Given that policies are not coordinated, however, the reaction is different. Suppose that the United Kingdom and West Germany decide to tighten their monetary policies to sustain their currencies against the dollar. France would then have to do the same to defend the franc, not only vis-à-vis the dollar, but versus the pound and the mark. Tighter French monetary policy would reinforce the incentive for West Germany and the United Kingdom to raise interest rates—and so on. In the end, the extent to which European governments independently allowed their decisions to be driven by U.S. policies might be much greater than if they had been able to act in concert.

Closely connected to the advantage of size is the fact that the United States is still relatively closed to trade. Although the share of trade in U.S. gross national product more than doubled during the 1960s and 1970s, trade is still much less important to the United States than to other industrial countries. What this means is that international considerations, especially the exchange rate, are much less important to U.S. policy than to the policies of other countries.

Assume, for example, that the United States follows a policy that leads to a fall in the dollar. This decline will lead to a rise in prices of imports and of import-competing goods and will thus contribute to inflation. For two reasons, however, the effect will be less than for other countries. First, imports are a smaller share of spending in the United States than elsewhere, and a rise in import prices therefore does not have as great an impact on U.S. inflation. Second, in many cases foreign firms will not immediately react to a dollar depreciation by raising their U.S. selling prices. Because imports are not that large a share of the U.S. market, many foreign firms will treat U.S. domestic firms as price leaders, and they will avoid changing their own dollar prices until they are sure that an exchange-rate change is both large and permanent. The result is that when the dollar declines, U.S. import prices do not rise in the same proportion. Indeed, some estimates suggest that a 20-per cent dollar depreciation may raise U.S. import prices by as little as 10 per cent.

But suppose, instead, that U.S. policy changes in a way that leads to a *rise* in the dollar. Then the major inhibiting factor for most governments becomes concern about the effects on the international competitiveness of national industry. Although this is by no means a negligible issue in the United States, it is not as crucial as elsewhere. As became very obvious in 1984, the U.S. manufacturing sector—unlike that of any other industrial country—can indeed prosper through sales to the domestic market even while doing badly in international competition.

Thus the relative self-sufficiency of the U.S. market strengthens the factor of sheer economic size in giving U.S. macro-economic policy unusual freedom of action. Moreover, the role conferred by the economy's size is reinforced by another factor: the special international role of the U.S. dollar.

The extent to which dollars are used in international transactions and international prices are quoted in U.S. dollars is in part simply a reflection of the direct importance of the United States in the international economy. But the role of the dollar stretches well beyond this. The dollar is used as the standard in many transactions into which the United States does not enter at all. For international interdependence, the role of the dollar is particularly crucial in two areas: in setting the price of oil and in denominating international lending. The importance of these international roles of the dollar for the impact of U.S. policies on developing countries can be illustrated by considering the case of Brazil. For Brazil, direct economic links with the United States are not all that central; the U.S. market accounts for only about one-sixth of the country's exports. However, 60 per cent of Brazil's import-spending is for oil, the price of which is set in dollars. And the bulk of Brazil's huge foreign debt is denominated in dollars. When the U.S. exchange rate rises, what matters for Brazil is not the effect on U.S.-Brazil trade, but the fact that the burden of paying for oil imports and debt service is directly increased.

All of the factors discussed so far are based on objective economic data. For completeness, however, the analysis should also allow for a political factor that has contributed to the recent apparent resurgence of U.S. macro-economic predominance. It has been argued that the ability of the United States to recover faster than other nations without a depreciating dollar rests on the mix of policies used—on the combination of loose fiscal policy and tight monetary policy. The natural question this prompts is: Why wasn't this option used in the 1970s? Why did the exchange-rate consequences of expansion constrain U.S. policy in 1979 but not in 1984?

The answer is a rather strange one. In 1979, there was a consensus in the United States that budget deficits are a bad thing. A strategy of supporting the exchange rate with a mix of tight money policy and loose fiscal policy—though advocated by some academics—simply was not on the map of the politically feasible. When the loose-fiscal, tight-money mix actually arrived, it was not as a result of deliberate strategy. A fiscal stimulus to demand arose—not as a piece of deliberate Keynesianism, but as an inadvertent by-product of supply-side tax cuts. Tight money was imposed not as part of a unified strategy but against the administration's wishes by an autonomous and inflation-conscious Federal Reserve. In effect, the United States stumbled into the policy mix that has demonstrated how much autonomy its economy still possesses. Supply-side policies have thus played a key role in reasserting U.S. macro-economic predominance—not because they work as such (for there is no evidence that they do), but because they have removed the inhibition against budget deficits.

The purpose of this article has been to argue the case that the United States remains in a class by itself both in its ability to set its own macro-economic course and in its ability to shape the world economic situation. Like the popular emphasis on internationalization, however, this argument can be carried too far. It is a good idea, then, to offer some reasons for caution.

The first caution is that U.S. policy is not the only thing happening in the world. The worldwide monetary tightening after 1979 was not wholly imposed on the world by the United States. It also reflected independent, and in some cases earlier, moves toward tight money by other countries, including the United Kingdom and West Germany. The loosening of U.S. fiscal policy since 1980 has been matched by a sharp move toward *tighter* fiscal policy in these two nations and Japan.[11]

The second caution is that other industrial countries probably have a good deal more economic autonomy than they have been willing to exercise. For example, if European countries really want an economic expansion, they are surely capable of getting one by combining a modest willingness to use fiscal stimulus with a moderate degree of coordinated action.[12] U.S. monetary and fiscal policy may be dictating European policies, but allowing this to happen is itself something of a policy choice on the part of European governments.

Caveats aside, it remains clear that the United States continues to have a special position. When one tries to picture the future economic environment of the developing countries, it is hard to avoid thinking of U.S. policy as the key.

U.S. Responsibilities and Interests

If U.S. macro-economic policies exert substantial leverage over the economies of other nations in general, and over developing countries in particular, should this be a concern of U.S. policy? Should the effect of U.S. monetary and fiscal policies on poorer nations be taken into account when these policies are formulated?

There are two kinds of response to this question. One is admirable but not very useful. This is the altruistic answer: The United States should care about the welfare of others and thus has a responsibility to conduct its macro-economic policies in such a way as to respect other countries' interests as well as its own. The problem with this answer is that it does not address political reality. International altruism, while not entirely gone from the U.S. scene, is not in the mid-1980s an argument sufficiently forceful to make much difference to U.S. policy.

Even if one cares about the developing countries for their own sake, then, one had better be able to argue that what is good for them is also good for the United States—that it is in the enlightened self-interest of the United States to shape its policies with their international repercussions in mind. If we would like to be able to make this argument, we must, however, ascertain that it is true. What is the U.S. stake in the effects of its policies on poorer nations?

The most familiar case made for a U.S. interest in the economic health of developing countries highlights the importance of these countries as markets for U.S. exports. This argument points to the sharp declines in U.S. exports to Latin America resulting from the debt crisis and suggests that these lost exports translate into large U.S. employment losses. It should be immediately recognized, however, that this kind of calculation is in fact a version of the foreign-trade multiplier analysis rejected earlier. It assumes, in effect, that U.S. policy can be taken as a given, so that the employment effects of reduced exports follow directly from reduced demand.

This is not a good description of the situation. Unemployment in the United States does not fundamentally represent a difficulty in generating demand. There is nothing easier than creating demand through expansionary monetary and fiscal policies—even generating an expansion of demand large enough to offset a worsening foreign-trade position, as the experience of the last two years has reconfirmed. The constraint on U.S. employment growth is not the lack of ways to expand demand, but the Federal Reserve's fear that too rapid an expansion of demand will lead to a resurgence of inflation. Since export-led growth in demand is just as likely to be inflationary as domestic-demand growth, the Federal Reserve would have moved toward a tighter policy domestically if, for example, exports to Latin America had been higher. The distribution of employment growth would have been different, but there is no reason to believe that, in the end, employment growth would have been any higher. Appealing though it may be, the argument that the United States should be worried about the developing world because U.S. jobs are on the line is not well grounded.

A better argument rests on the U.S. financial stake. Some developing countries owe U.S. banks a great deal of money, and it is a reasonable concern of the United States that it not follow policies that make it impossible for that debt to be serviced. The concern reaches beyond the interests of banks and their stockholders: A serious debt crisis could threaten the solvency of major banks, which in turn would pose problems for the smooth operation of the financial system. (This threat should not, however, be exaggerated. Even a debt repudiation by several countries need not produce a 1931-style banking crisis if the Federal Reserve acts intelligently, and all indications are that reasonable contingency plans are in fact in place.)

The problem with the financial argument is that it seems to suggest that at least as far as U.S. macro-economic policies are concerned, the only developing countries whose interests we need to be concerned about are those that owe us money. This is a disturbingly cold-blooded conclusion. Surely there must be a solid economic reason to take a wider view? Unfortunately, it is quite hard to come up with such an argument. If the United States has an interest in taking into account the effects of its policies on the developing world as a whole, that interest arises out of political and strategic concerns rather than strictly economic costs and benefits.

Looking Ahead

The world economy is in better shape now than it was in the depths of the crisis in the fall of 1982. Economic recovery has brightened the picture, even if the recovery is mostly in the United States. Debtor nations have improved their trade balances dramatically, even though some of the gain has been swallowed up by higher interest rates and though the domestic costs have been high. One need not be a congenital pessimist, however, to argue that the current situation is not stable. A crunch of some kind is coming, and the key to getting through it—for the world economy in general, and for the developing countries in particular—lies in U.S. monetary and fiscal policy.

The reason for the impending crunch is that the world recovery, in its present form, cannot go on much longer. The moderate overall pace of growth in the industrial countries has been based on a rapid reduction in unemployment and excess capacity in the United States, while economic slack continues to worsen elsewhere. The problem is that the United States will soon start to run out of spare capacity. What will happen as the U.S. economy begins to approach the point of inflationary overheating? Instead of offering a single forecast, let us consider four scenarios. None of these would surprise the author if, like the Rip Van Winkle envisioned earlier, he were to take a five-year nap and be presented on awakening with a summary of intervening developments. No doubt reality will surprise us again. Nonetheless, here are four possible scenarios for the period ahead:

• **Renewed inflation.** The U.S. boom continues unabated, and inflation begins to accelerate. The Federal Reserve, either politically intimidated or hamstrung by international concerns, accommodates the inflation, which surges to double-digit levels. The dollar drops, and other industrial countries take advantage of this to loosen their own monetary policies.

For the developing world, in direct, economic terms, this scenario would be good news. Primary producers and debtors have a stake in inflation, whatever their judgments about its ultimate desirability. From a U.S. perspective, however, the political consequences of a resumption of inflation are disturbing to contemplate.

• **Monetary squeeze.** The boom continues unabated. As inflation begins to rise, the Federal Reserve steps hard on the brakes. Interest rates and the dollar rise even higher. Other industrial countries are driven to tighter monetary policies, and OECD growth slows down sharply.

This possibility is a disastrous one for the developing countries. Everything goes wrong: Export demand falls, interest payments rise, and the burden of dollar-denominated debt rises. This is the scenario in which debtors' cartels and repudiations can be expected.

• **Soft landing.** The U.S. boom comes to an end without any need for a tightening of monetary policy. Interest rates and the dollar level off or drift down. As U.S. growth slows, however, recovery in the industrial countries peters out.

For developing countries, this case is not as bad as the previous one. It is possible that the improvement in their financial prospects can continue even without continuing strong growth in the industrial countries, through a combination of import substitution and export promotion. This is a case in which industrial-country trade policies could prove crucial: How much increased exporting by developing countries will the industrial countries accept?

• **U.S. fiscal reform.** A fiscal reform package sharply cuts the U.S. budget deficit. The resulting cooling-off of demand allows the Federal Reserve to lower interest rates. The dollar falls, encouraging other countries to loosen their monetary policies. OECD growth continues at something like its recent pace, with slower U.S. growth offset by faster growth elsewhere.

This is of course a much better scenario for the developing world—perhaps not as good as an all-out resumption of inflation, but with a promise of more durable success. The important point is that this 'happy ending' depends on whether or not sound reforms in U.S. fiscal policy are in the cards.

Notes

[1] See in particular Richard N. Cooper's *The Economics of Interdependence*, Council on Foreign Relations (New York: Columbia Unversity Press, 1968).

[2] The overall unemployment rate for the EEC was 2.8 per cent in 1973; it rose to 4.2 per cent in the 1973-75 recession, yet it continued to rise to 5.7 per cent in 1979, after several years of 'recovery.'

[3] For an account of the various initiatives toward international macro-economic coordination, see George de Menil and Anthony M. Solomon, *Economic Summitry*, Council on Foreign Relations (New York: 1983).

[4] From 1979 to 1982, the unemployment rate in the EEC countries rose from 5.6 to 9.1 per cent. In the fourth quarter of 1983, the rate stood at 10.2 per cent.

[5] The 1984 U.S. trade deficit is projected at $130 billion, compared with $42 billion in 1978.

[6] For the classical analysis of the foreign-trade multiplier, see Lloyd Metzler, "A Multiple-Region Theory of Income and Trade," *Econometrica* 18 (1950), pp. 329-354.

[7] For a recent example, see *OECD Economic Studies*, Autumn 1983 (Paris: OECD).

[8] Much of the 'new view' of policy interdependence described here derives from a recent conference on the subject at the Center for Economic Policy Research in London. Also see Gilles Ordiz and Jeff Sachs, "Macroeconomic Policy Coordination among the Industrial Economies," *Brookings Papers on Economic Activity*, 1 (Washington, D.C.: The Brookings Institution, 1984).

[9] See William R. Cline, *International Debt and the Stability of the World Economy* (Washington, D.C.: Institute for International Economics, 1984).

[10] For estimates, see Morgan Guaranty Trust Company, *World Financial Markets*, October 1982.

[11] For a fuller discussion of this issue, see Olivier J. Blanchard and Lawrence H. Summers, "Perspectives on High World Real Interest Rates," *Brookings Papers on Economic Activity*, 2 (Washington, D.C. The Brookings Institution, 1984).

[12] A coordinated European fiscal expansion is advocated in R. Dornbusch et al., *Macroeconomic Prospects for the European Community* (Louvain-la-Neuve, Belgium: Center for European Policy Studies, 1983).

Chapter 2

International Finance and Investment: A Surging Public Sector

Richard E. Feinberg

In times of crisis, the public sector often intervenes to stabilize shaky private markets and to protect the national interest. Even conservative politicians then set aside their philosophical preference for market mechanisms in favor of government action. Responding to the global recession and the Third World debt crisis, public-sector institutions—including governments in industrial and developing countries and multilateral agencies—have become increasingly active in international credit and investment markets, even when those in power have been ideologically disinclined to do so.

When the deterioration in the creditworthiness of many Third World nations generated a near panic among international banks, the task fell to official agencies to contain the crisis. Reluctantly but ineluctably, the Reagan Administration:

• Contained its hostility toward multilateral financial institutions and approved the doubling of the resources available to the International Monetary Fund;

• Supported the initiatives of two men of impeccably conservative credentials—Federal Reserve Board Chairman Paul Volcker and IMF Managing Director Jacques de Larosière—as they impinged upon the management prerogatives of the commercial banks by indicating how much they should lend to which developing countries; and,

• Contrary to its general policy of 'getting government off the backs of the people,' worked with Congress to increase the authority of those regulatory agencies that oversee international banking.

With fewer inhibitions, the Reagan Administration also entered into the other main area of non-concessional capital flows: direct investment. The inclination to provide official incentives to firms to increase their overseas investments arose less from the need to manage a crisis than from the strongly held belief that private investment was the best engine for growth, whether at home or abroad. Here, too, the Administration sought to energize both bilateral and multilateral agencies to alter the allocation of resources that the private market, if left to itself, would have generated.

Similarly, Third World governments of diverse ideological stripes intervened more heavily in the allocation of foreign exchange and domestic credit in the 1980s. Pursuing counter-cyclical fiscal policies, many governments ran budget deficits that absorbed a rising share of available domestic credit in order to cover recession-driven revenue shortfalls. Under pressure from the debt crisis to husband scarce financial resources, governments also stepped in to determine the distribution of foreign exchange. For its part, the indigenous private sector in many developing countries contracted relative to the public sector, as a result of scarce, expensive credit and generally adverse business conditions that led to widespread bankruptcies.

These trends toward official intervention in credit and investment markets have been obscured by a dominant orthodoxy that trumpets its free-market rhetoric and that frequently cites anecdotal cases to prove that markets are, indeed, being unfettered. Certainly, the Reagan Administration could not be expected to highlight a pattern of statist reforms in its own policies. The liberal opposition to the Administration inadvertently contributed to the obfuscation. The critics were busily accusing the Administration of passivity, and so missed the scope of the reforms. In looking for a single, grand solution to the debt crisis, many in their ranks failed to grasp that the Administration's incremental, *ad hoc* responses, while perhaps not dramatic in isolation, added up to a quiet revolution in international finance.

The story told here is not intended to suggest that the public sector has or should take control of international finance and investment. Rather, the purpose is to demonstrate that in these spheres, as elsewhere in the global economy, public and private actors can have vital, *complementary* roles to play and that, particularly during crisis periods, an assertive public sector can serve the general welfare and save the private sector from its own structural weaknesses.[1]

Rise and Decline of Finance Capitalism

The 1970s was the decade of international banking. In the early postwar years, the banks had been unassuming, secondary players responding to the demands of their traditional corporate clients for trade finance. Suddenly, an immense inflow of deposits from oil-exporting nations and other sources supercharged the banks with excess liquidity. The banks found eager clients in Third World countries that sought credit to offset the higher costs of energy and other imports while attempting to maintain strong growth rates. Bank loans to non-oil developing countries rose from $10 billion in 1973 to $49 billion in 1980. Whereas the private financial markets accounted for less than one-third of developing-country accumulated debts in 1970, they held 55 per cent in 1980.[2]

The boom in commercial bank lending was also the result of the passivity of industrial-country governments. Instead of accepting responsibility for managing the financial imbalances of the 1970s, officials were pleased to watch the private markets handle the recycling of petro-dollars to Third World borrowers. In particular, the institution created to help countries correct maladjustments in their balance of payments—the International Monetary Fund—had failed to keep pace with a growing global economy. IMF quotas (which in part determine the amount of resources available to the Fund) declined from 16 per cent of world trade when the Fund was created in 1944 to 4 per cent at the start of the 1980s. Despite some reforms during the 1970s, IMF resources and lending shrank even more as a percentage of world financial flows. The loans being authorized by the private banks soon far surpassed those of the IMF and World Bank combined. The ready availability of private finance enabled developing countries to avoid submission to the rigorous conditions that typically accompany IMF credits.

The explosive growth of international private lending in the 1970s largely took place outside of any regulatory framework. The national regulatory authorities in Washington were then primarily concerned with managing domestic savings and credit flows, monetary growth, and the protection of domestic depositors, borrowers, and investors. As characteristically occurs, government agencies lagged behind the pace of change in private markets, and the regulators were slow to recognize the growing importance of the banks' international activities. Moreover, some U.S. government officials resisted proposals to tighten supervision of international lending. They argued that increased official scrutiny would simply drive banks to take their business abroad. Some questioned whether government bureaucrats were better equipped to judge the quality of loans than were 'hands on' bankers. Some even argued against increased reporting requirements, on the grounds that the information was proprietary and that bankers ought not be burdened with further non-productive paperwork.

But governments were not entirely quiescent. As early as 1975, industrial-country governments reached some agreements on their individual and collective responsibilities for supervising international banking. In 1977, U.S. federal regulatory agencies instituted the Country Exposure Report, requiring banks to submit semi-annual reports on country exposure levels. But these were side shows during a heady decade of international finance riding high on expanding private markets.

The Public-Sector Response to Panic in Private Markets

Voluntary private lending to many developing countries came to a screeching halt in mid-1982. The credit markets suddenly found themselves mired in a deteriorated global economy. The length and depth of the global recession, the steep descent in commodity prices, and the new and persistent reality of high interest rates transformed seemingly creditworthy countries into dubious risks. In some cases, when bankers stopped to add up their clients' debts to all external creditors, they discovered surprisingly large sums; the higher debt-service ratios meant that outstanding loans were of diminished quality. Frightened, many banks closed their windows to new loans, and tried to shorten or reduce existing exposure. But while such a strategy might make sense from the vantage point of an individual bank, it cannot work if all banks attempt it, for the debtor nation soon runs out of foreign exchange and becomes illiquid. Thus banks can become prisoners of their own logic and precipitate the very crisis they hoped to avoid.

To forestall a collapse of private markets, governments had to take action. To renew the flow of funds to developing countries, the Reagan Administration participated in emergency bail-out packages, agreed to increase the resources and authority of the IMF, and supported other official efforts to reinvigorate private flows. Prodded by Congress, the Administration also introduced tougher government regulation of international banking. In addition, government agencies worked with the banks to alter traditional procedures for the restructuring of existing debts.

Rescue Packages

To finance a rapid growth rate, high consumption levels, and massive capital flight, Mexico began borrowing heavily in 1979. Banking on Mexico's oil reserves and stimulated by competition for market shares, private creditors were willing to continue to pump in money even when oil prices began to slip. As late as June 1982, Mexico raised $2.5 billion in the Eurocurrency market. But during that summer, a gaping current-account deficit and a falling peso altered the nation's creditworthiness. Suddenly cut off from new lending—on which it had come to rely for servicing old loans—the Mexican government was forced to suspend debt payments.

Under pressure to avoid default by Mexico, a major debtor, the U.S. government demonstrated that it could act quickly and decisively. In a few intense days, the Administration pasted together an emergency package of over $8 billion—more than the entire annual budget of the Agency for International Development. The official sources were multiple: short-term 'swap' lines of credit from the Federal Reserve System and the Exchange Stabilization Fund of the Treasury Department (often through the Bank for International Settlements), the Commodity Credit Corporation, and the U.S. Strategic Petroleum Reserve (for advance payments on oil purchases). In addition to the immediate relief, the IMF soon agreed to put up nearly $4 billion over a three-year period.

The U.S. government and the IMF also acted to block the banks' flight from Mexico. They supported Mexico's request for rolling over debts due in the near term. More dramatically, at a meeting conspicuously hosted at the New York Federal Reserve and welcomed by its President, Anthony Solomon, Jacques de Larosière warned the many assembled bankers that the IMF could only proceed in Mexico if the banks provided $5 billion in new loans. That evening, Federal Reserve Board Chairman Paul Volcker reinforced de Larosière in a remarkable speech in Boston, announcing that these "new credits should not be subject to supervisory criticism," so long as they "enable a country to strengthen its economy and service its international debt."

These meetings and speeches amounted to a sharp departure from the traditional 'arm's length' relationship between the regulators and the international banks. Thus began a pattern—repeated for Argentina, Brazil, Chile, Yugoslavia, and other countries—in which official agencies, generally led by the IMF, would seek to overcome the anarchical, self-destructive tendencies of panicky credit markets by bringing all the banks together to persuade them to act in their collective self-interest. Official agencies would indicate how much credit they could provide and the gap the private sector would have to fill for the debtor country to meet its external obligations, including debt service. Having provided the analysis of the debtor country's earning and financing needs, and sometimes actually assembling hundreds of concerned bankers, officials left it to the banks to divide the burden among themselves.

To keep banks involved in lending to key debtors, officials employed a combination of positive and negative inducements. The 'carrots' consisted of official credits, an IMF-monitored economic stabilization program, and favorable treatment of new loans by the regulators. The 'sticks' included the withholding of IMF and other official loans until the banks agreed to lend new money and, reportedly, exhortations by the regulators—especially toward the more reluctant, smaller, regional banks—to play ball. This mix of measures persuaded the banks that their self-interest lay in more orderly retrenchment rather than disorganized retreat. Banks would just have to live with most of their existing exposure and even extend some new loans, albeit in amounts considerably below the levels of the 'go-go' years.

The International Monetary Fund

Initially, the Reagan Administration was unenthusiastic about increasing IMF resources. Some political appointees in the Treasury Department feared that a large quota increase might result in less rigorous conditionality and strengthen those tendencies that they believed were transforming the IMF's proper role as short-term lender-of-last-resort into one of a development agency. The Administration also expressed concern that an excessive quota increase might produce an inflationary expansion of global liquidity.

The near-collapse of the private capital markets reversed the Administration's position and drove it to support an accelerated and substantial increase in quotas. As a result, IMF resources were increased by 47.5 per cent, to Special Drawing Rights (SDR) 90 billion. Furthermore, the Fund's General Arrangements to Borrow (GAB) were boosted from approximately SDR 6.4 billion to SDR 17 billion. In sum, resources potentially available to the IMF were approximately doubled.

The IMF did not hesitate to make use of these enlarged resources to fill some of the gap being left by reluctant private lenders. Net IMF credit to non-oil developing countries rose sharply in absolute terms: from $200 million in 1979 to $10.2 billion in 1983. IMF lending jumped from an amount equal to less than 1 per cent of commercial bank lending in 1979 to over 50 per cent in 1983 (Table 1).

Increased resources enhanced the IMF's ability to perform its traditional role of providing policy advice to member governments. But in response to the crisis in the private financial markets, the IMF took on additional roles. The Fund assisted the industrial-country governments and banks in formulating and coordinating their policies toward the Third World. De Larosière enunciated policies that governments and private lenders should follow to manage debt and adjustment problems. He frequently gave speeches laying out the most recent IMF forecasts for global growth rates and balance-of-payments developments, analyzing progress made in coping with the crisis, and describing recommendations for future measures. These pronouncements—themselves the product of continual discussions among industrial-

Table 1. Shifting Sources of Finance for the Non-Oil Exporting Developing Countries, Net Flows ($ billions)

	1977	1978	1979	1980	1981	1982	1983
Commercial Banks	15	25	22	25	51	25	17
IMF	−.2	−.3	.2	1.5	6.1	7.1	10.2
Ratio	∞	∞	*110:1*	*17:1*	*8:1*	*4:1*	*2:1*

Sources: IMF, *International Capital Markets: Developments and Prospects, 1984*, p. 104, and *World Economic Outlook, 1984*, p. 197.

country governments, banks, and the IMF—served as common guideposts for policy makers.

As already noted, the Fund's coordination of policies extended to persuading and coercing the banks to continue modest lending. The Fund helped to impose discipline on markets whose boom—and now bust—mentality had threatened to destabilize the international financial system and their clients' economies. Finally, the Fund worked to coordinate the activities of other lenders—public and private—to increase their collective leverage over borrowers. Commercial banks, government agencies, and often the World Bank waited to approve new credits until the IMF gave the signal that the debtor government had agreed to appropriate stabilization measures. The U.S. government did occasionally give priority to perceived diplomatic interests and provide new loans in the absence of an IMF agreement (as in Honduras, El Salvador, and Israel). But more often the Administration joined commercial banks to starve recalcitrant debtors of desperately needed credits until they bowed to IMF prescriptions. Conversely, the IMF reinforced the bargaining strength of the banks by leaving the impression that it would withhold credits should debtors default on commercial obligations.

Taking on the multiple roles of economic forecaster, policy planner, market disciplinarian, gatekeeper of access to new credits, and police officer for financial norms and obligations, the International Monetary Fund boldly reorganized international credit markets during their worst moments since the Great Depression.

Co-Financing

The IMF was not alone in seeking to stimulate new bank lending to developing countries. With the support of the Reagan Administration, the World Bank and the U.S. Export-Import Bank (Eximbank) also attempted, with partial success, to catalyze private finance through various "co-financing" and guarantee schemes.

Instead of financing entire projects by itself, the World Bank has since the mid-1970s sometimes delegated a portion to private lenders. Co-financing allows the Bank to gain greater mileage from its own limited resources and to stimulate private lending. The World Bank ties some, but not all, co-financed private loans with formal memoranda of agreement and "optional" cross-default clauses. To make such arrangements even more attractive, the Bank in 1983 announced several new "B-loan" mechanisms for increasing its linkage to the commercial portion of the financial package. The World Bank may guarantee the private credit, take a portion of the commercial loan for its own portfolio, or agree to refinance the final commercial maturity under certain conditions.

During fiscal years 1980-84, World Bank co-financing operations involved an annual average of $1.4 billion in private credits. The Bank noted with disappointment that its co-financing program was being retarded by the shortage of World Bank-style investment projects in recession-ridden developing countries.[3] Nevertheless, the Bank expressed satisfaction that the nine "B-loans" completed or substantially completed during FY1984—totaling $1.1 billion—covered a substantial portion of the estimated $5 billion in new commercial bank loans extended during the first nine months of its 1984 fiscal year (July 1, 1983-March 30, 1984).

The Reagan Administration also looked to the U.S. Eximbank to stimulate new credits by covering some of the political and commercial risks incurred by banks and suppliers that provide trade finance. The Administration supported increases in Eximbank guarantees and insurance, which reached $8.5 billion in FY1983 (while showing less enthusiasm for Eximbank's own direct credit program). In addition, the Administration prompted the Eximbank to open special guarantee and insurance lines of $1.5 billion for Brazil and $500 million for Mexico.

The Foreign Credit Insurance Association (FCIA)—an amalgam of private insurance companies—was created in 1961 as an affiliate of the Eximbank to issue commercial and political-risk insurance. FCIA premiums were intended to generate a profit for its members, although the Eximbank set broad policy guidelines and covered political risk and large commercial losses. However, losses incurred as a result of the global recession caused the FCIA to nearly collapse and forced the Eximbank to agree to underwrite all of the risk covered by FCIA insurance policies, making the Association merely an agent of the Eximbank. In effect, the retreat of the private-sector insurers compelled the public sector to step in and absorb the entire risk in insuring private trade finance.

The co-financing schemes of the Eximbank and the World Bank might have been more effective were it not for institutional constraints. Facing record losses in the Third World, the Eximbank became more cautious in some markets. The World Bank refused to grant banks a mandatory cross-default clause that would force its own loan into default if a member government defaulted against the co-financed commercial loan. The overall budgetary ceilings that the Reagan Administration was imposing on the World Bank were less binding than the reticence of the commercial banks and the recession-induced shortage of new projects, but such caps could slow the growth of co-financing in the future.

Despite these limitations, a rising proportion of new loans being made to developing countries were associated with World Bank co-financing and export credit agency co-financing and insurance—or were part of IMF-coordinated loan packages. Less willing than before to act alone, the alarmed private sector increasingly sought the clasp of the visible hand of government before risking capital in uncertain Third World markets.

Commercial Debt Rescheduling

For the banks, the biggest challenge has been to protect their existing exposure, endangered by the deteriorated international environment. Since most developing countries could clearly not meet the schedule for repayment of principal, debts had to be restructured. Whereas official creditors had their "Paris Club," no formal creditor-debtor framework existed for conducting commercial bank debt negotiations when the crisis broke in 1982. Bank debt restructurings had been sporadic and involved an annual average of only about $1.5 billion during the period 1978-1981. Yet in 1983-84, over $100 billion would require rescheduling. In helping to design and manage the process whereby commercial bank debts could be restructured, official agencies played a major role in at least six ways.

First, the IMF calculated the debtor nations' financing needs. These projections informed official and private creditors about the amount of debt that could be served and how much needed a new repayment timetable, as well as how much new lending would be needed. In an important departure from previous practice, creditors often pledged to maintain existing exposure and in some cases to provide new monies. These agreements were intended to correct a trend noted in previous reschedulings: Banks had frequently continued to reduce their exposure during the immediate post-agreement period, thereby exacerbating the debtor countries' liquidity problems.[4]

Second, and more generally, the IMF served as a conduit of information between the debtor countries and their creditors. The Fund provided detailed information on the current and probable future state of the debtors' economies and in some cases also sought, with varying degrees of success, to organize debt information systems. The banks were thereby in a position to make more informed and rational decisions.

Third, IMF stabilization programs tried to begin to restore some confidence in the debtor nations' creditworthiness. The banks generally made reschedulings contingent upon the signing of an IMF stand-by arrangement. As the IMF noted, "negotiations with the banks and the Fund often took place simultaneously and in some of the major cases, their successful conclusions were closely interrelated."[5]

Fourth, official agencies in some cases provided "bridge" financing during the renegotiation period. Pending agreement on a medium-term financial package, industrial-country central banks sometimes provided short-term injections of liquidity to prevent an interruption in the developing countries' external payments. As the case of Mexico illustrated, the Federal Reserve Board and the U.S. Department of the Treasury worked with the commercial banks to stitch together the rescue package.

Fifth, public officials pressed banks to lower interest-rate spreads and rescheduling fees. In the wake of the debt crisis, banks had charged substantially higher spreads (over a reference market rate) on new and rescheduled loans and had tacked on fees amounting to 1-1.5 per cent of the rescheduled amounts. The banks argued that these charges were justified by the higher risk and the need to build reserves against potential losses. Public officials, however, noted that the cumulative effect was to make it more difficult for the borrowers to resume the growth required to meet future debt service. Moreover, the higher fees aroused deep resentment in the Third World against 'usurious' banks and their home governments. Acting in defense of the long-term economic and political interests of the banks themselves, as well as U.S. diplomatic interests, officials urged banks to reduce interest spreads and fees—advice that the banks began to heed during 1984. (The U.S. Congress had reinforced this advice in 1983 when it reduced the incentives to charge high fees by legislating that any loan fee exceeding the administrative cost of making a loan would have to be amortized over the life of the loan rather than taken in full up front.)

Sixth, public officials nudged banks to abandon their traditional preference for 'short leash' reschedulings and to undertake major, multi-year debt restructurings. In the past, banks had generally sought to avoid formal debt restructurings altogether and, when absolutely necessary, to limit the consolidation period to arrears and debts falling due during that year. However, the Communique issued by the heads of state of the seven leading industrial nations at their June 1984 summit in London forcefully encouraged "more extended multi-year rescheduling of commercial debts." Recognizing that the developing countries could not possibly repay principal falling due in the next several years, the assembled government leaders evidently felt that greater rationality and order could be achieved by tackling the problem head-on. Large-scale consolidations would relieve pressure on the banks and the debtors to continually renegotiate debts and would remove some of the uncertainties that were plaguing the financial markets and policy makers in developing countries. Shortly after the London Summit, the commercial banks and Mexico set the new pattern by agreeing to reschedule some $50 billion in principal payments falling due through 1990.

Thus official agencies have become deeply involved in many facets of the rescheduling process. They have provided essential information, offered short-term "bridge" financing, orchestrated the medium-term financial package, designed adjustment policies needed to restore the debtors' solvency, and advised changes in the terms for interest and principal payments. Some bankers were annoyed at these interventions, viewing them as usurpations of their managerial prerogatives, but many recognized that they might not have survived otherwise.

Government Regulation of Banking

Alarmed by the rash of reschedulings and the severe instabilities in financial markets, the U.S. Congress passed the International Lending Supervision Act of 1983 "to assure that the economic health and stability of the United States and the other nations of the world shall not be adversely affected or threatened in the future by imprudent lending practices or inadequate supervision."[6] The boom in international lending during the 1970s had caught the regulators napping. The regulatory system was fragmented among several agencies, and their guidelines for supervising international lending were archaic and unclear. Even when regulators did issue warnings regarding the Third World debt buildup, self-confident bankers often ignored them. Competitive pressures, inadequate market discipline, and in some cases careless management caused banks to "overlend," thereby jeopardizing the stability of the U.S. and international financial systems. Congress, therefore, decided to strengthen the regulatory framework in three major ways.

Congress mandated that the regulatory agencies establish minimum levels for bank capital. Observing low capital-to-loan ratios and high concentrations of lending to a few developing countries, Congress concluded that many banks had become overextended in relation to their equity and reserves. In the future, banks' ability to increase their lending will be tied to the size of their capital base.

Congress at the same time sought to stimulate more prudent lending and more realistic bookkeeping by requiring banks to set aside reserves against seriously troubled loans. The regulators will decide which loans require special measures as well as the timing and size of such provisionings against potential losses. The banks have thus lost some control over how they write their balance sheets.

Congress also required the banks to publish more information on international lending, including data that reveal country exposure in relation to bank assets and capital. The increased transparency of foreign operations should improve the ability of stockholders and depositors to judge the quality of the banks' portfolios and perhaps restrain banks from resuming "overlending" in the next global boom.

These new regulations could not stop the run by depositors on the Continental Illinois National Bank and Trust Company in May 1984. Concerned about the Chicago bank's lengthening list of troubled loans—mainly domestic but also international—U.S. and foreign depositors had been withdrawing their money at a rate that threatened to leave the bank illiquid. In response, U.S. regulatory agencies mounted the largest rescue operation in U.S. financial history (and comparable to that organized for Mexico two years earlier), providing Continental with $1.5 billion in capital (from the Federal Deposit Insurance Corporation) and over $4 billion in loans from the Federal Reserve system, while promising to protect all depositors and other general creditors of the Bank. Working closely with the regulators, a consortium of commercial banks injected $500 million in capital and opened a $5.5-billion line of credit. Once the panic had been squelched, the regulators moved in to reorganize the Bank and change its management. They demonstrated their willingness and ability both to act swiftly to contain a perceived threat to the domestic financial system and to work cooperatively with private banks to obtain a mutually satisfactory outcome.

Direct Foreign Investment

U.S. firms with overseas subsidiaries did not face the same sort of acute crisis that gripped the international credit markets. Nevertheless, U.S. direct investment in developing countries shared the same basic experience: The private sector retrenched and the public sector stepped up its activities.

The Reagan Administration instinctively favored foreign investment as beneficial both to U.S. firms and the host countries. Officials

were also aware that the tensions that had accompanied direct investment in the Third World had attenuated in many countries. Developing-country governments had learned how to protect their interests
through hard bargaining with interested multinationals, while many
firms had adopted more flexible investment strategies. The Administration also preferred direct investment to official assistance flows;
and as commercial bank credit became scarcer after 1982, the Administration began to point to direct investment as an alternative source of
finance for capital-hungry developing countries.

Despite its positive attitudes toward direct investment, the Administration did not introduce any major policy changes.[7] It concentrated
instead on expanding existing institutions—particularly the bilateral
Overseas Private Investment Corporation (OPIC) and, to a lesser degree, the multilateral International Finance Corporation (IFC) of the
World Bank—although it did advance three minor initiatives, two
targeted to increasing investment in the politically important Caribbean Basin.

OPIC is a government agency that stimulates U.S. investment in
developing countries by insuring firms against certain political risks
and, to a much lesser degree, by financing the early stages of projects.
The Administration appointed a dynamic new president, Craig Nalen,
to head an agency that had received heavy criticism from Congress in
the 1970s and had been somewhat neglected during the Carter years.
In 1981, the Administration persuaded Congress to lift the restriction
that had kept OPIC from doing business in middle-income countries.
OPIC was also authorized to issue a new category of political-risk
insurance covering "civil strife."

Taking advantage of more favorable attitudes in Congress and the
Administration, OPIC has each year issued record levels of insurance—
rising from $1.5 billion in FY1981 to $4.3 billion in FY1984. The
actual increase in U.S. investment was less, since a firm may take out
more than one insurance policy to cover different types of risk. Still,
the total amount of U.S. investment in OPIC-assisted projects rose
from $0.9 billion in FY1980 to $1.6 billion in FY1984 (see Table 2).

The IFC proved more sluggish. Neither the Reagan Administration nor the World Bank's management seemed to give it the priority
warranted by their rhetorical enthusiasm for direct investment. Despite annual variations, the IFC's investments and loans to private
firms (domestic and foreign-owned) in the Third World remained essentially stagnant at around $750 million a year (see Table 2). The
Bank blamed the IFC's disappointing activity levels on low overall
investment rates in new projects in the depressed Third World.[8] Nevertheless, the Reagan Administration and the World Bank believe that
the IFC can play a greater role in the event of a sustained global

Table 2. Official Support for Investment: Guarantees, Equity, and Loans, Fiscal Years 1979-84 ($ millions)

OPIC: Investment by U.S. Firms in OPIC-Assisted Projects

1979	1980	1981	1982	1983	1984
499	917	1,851	1,115	2,203	1,636

IFC: Authorized Equity Investment and Loans

1979	1980	1981	1982	1983	1984
425	681	811	612	846	696

Sources: Overseas Private Investment Corporation, *Annual Report* (Washington, D.C.: various years), and International Finance Corporation, *Annual Report 1984* (Washington, D.C.: 1984), p. 8.

recovery, and they agreed in 1984 to double the Corporation's capital (to $1.3 billion). This will permit the IFC to expand its level of real net investment at about 7 per cent annually over the next five years.

The Administration did conceive of three new initiatives to stimulate U.S. investment in developing countries. The Caribbean Basin Initiative originally included a tax credit for investment in the area, but Congress rejected it on the grounds that it would drain revenues from the U.S. Treasury without sufficient certainty that the tax credit would stimulate much additional investment.[9] Organized labor opposed the tax credit as fostering "run away" shops. The Administration also supported the creation, under the umbrella of the Inter-American Development Bank, of an Inter-American Investment Corporation (IIC) to provide equity and loans for small- and medium-sized private firms in Latin America and the Caribbean. At the end of its 1984 session, Congress approved the U.S. share of the initial capital stock of $200 million, enabling the Corporation to begin operating in 1986. This limited funding will prevent the IIC from having much impact in the larger Latin American countries, but it could play an influential role in the smaller economies of Central America and the Caribbean. Finally, the Agency for International Development created a Bureau for Private Enterprise to assist U.S. and indigenous investors in developing countries. However, on an annual budget of about $15 million and oversight authority on some $150 million in funds "set aside" under AID's regional and functional programs, the Bureau is not likely to have had a significant impact on the magnitude of U.S. direct investment flows abroad, although individual firms undoubtedly have benefited.[10]

The Administration's various efforts to stimulate U.S. direct investment failed to offset the disincentives being generated by the global recession. The contraction in markets in many developing countries, combined with foreign-exchange shortages and exchange controls, dampened investors' enthusiasm. Concretely, income on direct investment in developing countries fell from a 1979-80 annual average of $12.5 billion to an average $6.8 billion in 1982-83.[11] One survey of U.S.-owned affiliates operating in the four major sites of direct investment in Latin America—Argentina, Brazil, Mexico, and Venezuela— revealed a decline in employment from 215,000 in 1981 to 190,000 in 1984.[12] So dismal was the investment climate that the stock of U.S. direct investment in developing countries actually contracted, falling from $53.2 billion at the end of 1980 to $51 billion at year-end 1983. These U.S. Department of Commerce figures are somewhat misleading, since they include valuation adjustments and are reduced by the net borrowings from affiliates in the Netherlands Antilles by parent companies seeking to tap overseas capital markets. Nevertheless, even when these distortions are removed, net direct investment flows fell from $6.1 billion in 1981 to only $2.4 billion in 1983.[13]

The combination of this private retrenchment with the increase in public-sector insurance and loans suggests that a rising percentage of U.S. direct investment was receiving official support. Even if private-sector flows should increase as the investment climate improves in developing countries, this trend toward greater public-sector involvement may continue. Both OPIC and the IFC are planning to expand their activities, and the World Bank is actively considering—with Administration support—the establishment of a multilateral guarantee facility for private investors.

Government Expansion in Developing Countries

The shock waves emanating from the international economy penetrated deep into the interstices of developing-country economies and affected the balance between the private and public sectors. In many countries, the dismal economic environment hit the private sector particularly hard, and here too the public sector frequently had to intervene to steady markets and protect living standards. The same forces that drove the Reagan Administration to intervene in financial markets forced governments in the Third World to intrude more deeply into their own domestic economies.

In many countries, governments became voracious consumers of credit. Government deficits widened as expenditures expanded to offset the decline in private-sector employment and consumption, and revenues fell as the tax base contracted. The average ratio of government expenditure to gross domestic product (GDP) for all developing countries rose from 25.8 per cent in 1979-81 to 27.8 per cent in 1982 and 28.4 per cent in 1983.[14] To finance this relative increase in the size of the public sector, governments had to soak up a rising share of available credit, at the expense of the private sector.[15] Thus, the public sector's absorption of domestic credit in Brazil rose from 12 per cent in 1979 to 45 per cent in 1983; in Kenya, from 27 to 38 per cent; and in Sri Lanka, from 36 to 42 per cent.[16]

Many governments also slapped on exchange controls and imposed administrative mechanisms for determining trade flows. In some cases—as in Brazil, Chile, and Mexico—the crisis even forced governments to abandon recent efforts at trade or exchange liberalization. The IMF commented that "in developing countries, measures to restrict imports and current payments have increasingly been the response to severe balance of payments problems."[17] While pointing to certain trends toward liberalization in some countries, the IMF found "a general reversion to exchange controls" in developing countries experiencing balance-of-payments difficulties as well as the increased use of other restrictive practices, including the widespread buildup of arrears on debt-service obligations, the control of invisibles (such as personal travel allowances), and the use of administered, multiple-currency arrangements.[18]

Seemingly accepting the inevitability of such emergency measures, the IMF relegated its fundamental concern with market liberalization to a back seat as it gave greater priority to stabilization—narrowing current-account and budget deficits. Many IMF stand-by arrangements included "stand-still" clauses requiring governments not to introduce new interventions, but implicitly accepting, at least temporarily, many of the restrictions already in effect. Rather than be the vanguard of a new era of decentralized decision making, the IMF played a rearguard action to slow the rush toward administrative controls.

The private sector was most severely wounded in Latin America. As sales revenues slumped and debt-service costs rose sharply, profits fell, cash flows contracted, and bankruptcies multiplied. In Brazil, for example, business failures hit record levels. In Argentina, industrial production fell 16 per cent in 1981 and another 4.5 per cent in 1982.[19]

Severe recession also brought disaster to some domestic financial sectors. In Chile, the Pinochet government abandoned its version of free market ideology and took over eight major banks, three of which were liquidated. The Mexican government at one blow nationalized a banking sector reeling from massive devaluations, burdensome foreign debts, and capital flight.

The debt crisis adversely affected private firms in another way. Governments that controlled foreign-exchange allocation tended to give preference to debts owed by public-sector institutions. Private firms had to stand at the end of the queue, and some were forced to liquidate assets being held abroad in order to honor their debt-service obligations. Those international banks that had favored lending to government agencies precisely because of their superior access to hard currency had acted wisely. Paradoxically, the international private banks sometimes looked on benignly when governments nationalized their clients, content to have their credits transformed into sovereign risk.

To be sure, there were some contrary trends. The private sectors in many Asian countries benefited from the relative vigor of their national economies. Various socialist societies (especially China and Hungary) were experimenting with decentralized pricing and wider opportunities for private initiative. In some Latin American and Sub-Saharan African countries, the long-term trend toward increased public ownership of productive firms seemed to have peaked, and some governments were beginning to shed costly state enterprises. For the most part, however, efforts at denationalization were incipient and halting, facing the political constraints of vested interests and the financial thinness of private capital markets.[20] In Africa, some governments were decontrolling food prices to benefit agricultural producers, although progress was patchy and tentative.[21] In any case, these counter-trends should not blind us to the impressive shift of relative power and resources to the public sector that occurred in many Third World countries.

As the global recession ends, some emergency public-sector activities will recede. Thus, in 23 of the more important developing countries, government deficits as a percentage of GDP—which had jumped from 3.5 per cent in 1979 to 7.1 per cent in 1982—began to narrow slightly in 1983 to 6.9 per cent.[22] Throughout the developing world, governments were adjusting exchange rates and interest rates to reflect international realities. These corrections will eventually permit some relaxation of administrative controls in financial and foreign exchange markets. Nevertheless, the irony remains that the first Reagan Administration presided over a sharp expansion of public-sector activity in the Third World. For its part, the private sector in many

Latin American and African countries will take some time to recover from the traumas of recent years.

Conclusions

Rhetoric and reality sometimes can be far apart. Over the last four years, the U.S. government combined passionate faith in the free market with international financial policies that relied heavily on official action. Public-sector institutions mobilized their own resources and sought to coordinate private markets in order to manage a global financial crisis. This increased public-sector activity was required to steady credit markets and to reduce the costs of a deep economic recession. Similarly, governments in many developing countries intervened more decisively in their own credit and foreign-exchange markets.

In managing the debt crisis, public-sector institutions demonstrated their capacity to act quickly and effectively. Despite the tremendous size and complexity of the international financial markets, their workings proved not to be beyond the understanding or reach of wise functionaries. Their masterful crisis management enabled the commercial banks to avoid catastrophic losses, although some writeoffs were experienced in 1984 and more can be expected in the future. (The amelioration of the debt crisis in 1983-84 was also the result of economic recovery in the United States, itself the product of government action: the strong fiscal stimulus from the Administration's programmed budget deficit.)

The Reagan Administration succeeded politically as well. It avoided a financial collapse and generally won the grudging approval of the most immediately affected constituency—the bankers. It may have been politic not to broadcast its achievements, vulnerable as they were to being interpreted as a government bail-out for always unpopular 'Wall Street' bankers.

Some of the reforms have created new structures that ought to be institutionalized and strengthened. Through their inclusion in the IMF's General Arrangements to Borrow and their use of central bank swap lines of credit, the developing countries have been more fully integrated into the international financial system. New mechanisms and modalities have been created for the rescheduling of commercial debt. In the United States, as in other industrial countries, regulatory agencies have been permanently empowered to supervise international lending with greater vigor.

Other reforms that responded to the more momentary aspects of the crisis are unlikely to endure. The banks are anxious to make IMF-managed lending a matter of memory and to resume voluntary market decisions. But the creation by the banks of their own Institute for International Finance—to gather data on debtors' economies and debt positions and to discuss bankers' lending strategies—suggests a hesitancy to return completely to the decentralized market of the past. Whether the new private Institute will be able to perform some of the functions of the IMF adequately remains to be seen.

As developing countries adjust their economies to the new global realities, IMF stabilization programs will gradually end and the Fund will become a net recipient of capital flows from the Third World. Both the Reagan Administration and many developing countries favor such a withdrawal. The Administration wants to limit the Fund to emergency, short-term lending. At the same time, the IMF's stringent stabilization programs have won it few new friends in the developing countries; despite its role in preventing a financial collapse that would have caused great damage to creditors and debtors alike, the IMF is widely perceived as having captained a global adjustment process that provided the Third World little voice and a disproportionate burden.

Although considerable progress had been made, it would be a grave mistake to imagine that the debt problem has been definitively solved. Many debtor nations have only begun to readjust their development strategies; their debt-service ratios remain very high; and their ability to sustain rapid export expansion depends on many unknowns, including industrial-country growth rates and trade policies. Popular demand for relief from austerity could jeopardize export growth or could still interrupt debt service. Moreover, the sharp contraction in both private credit and investment flows that has occurred over the last three years has deprived developing nations of needed capital and has delayed their recovery. The commercial banks continue to behave with extreme caution, and net lending to the non-oil developing countries dropped to near zero during the first half of 1984. Even if direct investment becomes more robust, it will certainly not expand rapidly enough to offset the reduction in bank flows. Developing countries will have to struggle to raise internal savings rates to offset the reduced availability of external capital.

If the global recovery persists and officials decide that the debt crisis is over, the danger arises that ideology will actually determine policy. Yet the worlds of international finance and investment are still highly unstable. Among the more pressing issues are the following:

• During 1985-86, it will be decided whether the World Bank can try to step in where the IMF has left off. The Bank might assist developing countries making the transition from austerity and stabilization to structural adjustment and renewed growth and thereby also help strengthen the confidence of lenders and investors. But some Reagan Administration officials continue to view the Bank as a statist-oriented welfare agency.

• Industrial-country governments may have to dedicate greater efforts to stimulating direct investment if their positive rhetoric is to become reality. At the same time, developing countries will have to reexamine their own policies toward foreign investment, as many are already doing.

• Not presenting threats to systemic stability, the smaller debtor nations have received less attention from the international financial community. Yet some face a dim future if more external capital, or preferential debt relief, is not forthcoming. In addition, reductions in trade barriers (of the sort granted in the Caribbean Basin Initiative) could help them earn badly needed foreign exchange.

• Many developing nations are now paying more in interest than they are receiving in fresh commercial loans. If interest rates were to rise again, debtors would face a severe cash crunch. Under such emergency circumstances, it might be necessary to reschedule or "cap" interest payments, as Paul Volcker once suggested.[23]

The key to the successful management of these problems can be found in the lessons of the recent past: Changing circumstances demand a pragmatic adjustment in the relations between the public and private sectors.

Notes

[1] For their helpful comments on an earlier draft of this article, I would like to thank Paul Balabanis, Christine Bogdanowicz-Bindert, Gary Hufbauer, Kenneth Oye, and Ted Truman, as well as my ODC colleagues. Silvia Torres and Eugenio Diaz-Bonilla provided able research assistance.

[2] International Monetary Fund, *International Capital Markets: Developments and Prospects, 1984* (Washington, D.C.: 1984), Table 48; World Bank, *World Debt Tables, 1983-84* (Washington, D.C.: 1984), p. 2. The data for accumulated debts exclude private non-guaranteed debts.

[3] World Bank, *Annual Report 1984* (Washington, D.C.: 1984), pp. 23-24.

[4] International Monetary Fund, *Recent Multilateral Debt Restructurings with Official and Bank Creditors*, Occasional Paper No. 25 (Washington, D.C.: December 1983), p. 11.

[5] Ibid., p. 13.

[6] This section draws heavily on Karin Lissakers, "Bank Regulation and International Debt," in Richard E. Feinberg and Valeriana Kallab, eds., *Uncertain Future: Commercial Banks and the Third World* (New Brunswick, N.J.: Transaction Books, for the Overseas Development Council, 1984), pp. 45-68. For a discussion of the global trend toward increased government regulation of international banking, see *International Capital Markets: Developments and Prospects, 1984*, op. cit., pp. 12-21.

[7] The Administration released an "International Investment Policy Statement" on September 9, 1983, which basically reaffirmed traditional policies proclaiming that:

foreign investment flows which respond to private market forces benefit both home and host countries; "prompt, adequate and effective compensation" should be paid for expropriations; and foreign investors should be accorded treatment no less favorable than that accorded in like situations to domestic enterprises ("national treatment").

In May 1983, President Reagan appointed a task force, chaired by Dwayne Andreas, to identify new ways to use U.S. foreign assistance to promote private investment in developing countries. The report, issued in December 1984, implicitly criticized the Administration by urging a "substantial redirection" in U.S. policies toward greater activism and innovation to achieve that end. *The President's Task Force on International Private Enterprise: Report to the President* (Washington, D.C.: 1984).

[8] World Bank, *Annual Report 1984* (Washington, D.C.: 1984), p. 29.

[9] See Richard E. Feinberg and Richard Newfarmer, "The Caribbean Basin Initiative: Bold Plan or Empty Promise?," in Richard Newfarmer, ed., *From Gunboats to Diplomacy* (Baltimore: The Johns Hopkins University Press, 1984).

[10] See the essay by John Sewell and Christine Contee in this volume for a more extensive analysis.

[11] U.S. Department of Commerce, *Survey of Current Business*, Vol. 64, No. 8, August 1984, p. 27.

[12] Council of the Americas, "Debt, Economic Crisis and the United States Companies in Latin America," A Report of Responses to a Survey of 52 Companies, September 1984, mimeo.

[13] *Survey of Current Business*, op. cit., various issues.

[14] International Monetary Fund, *World Economic Outlook 1984* (Washington, D.C.: 1984), p. 51.

[15] Some of the resources captured by governments were used to meet service on the external debt. In that sense, governments gave preference to external creditors as against its own domestic borrowers. In this conflict of interest between the international banks and the indigenous private sector, Third World entrepreneurs lost out. At the same time, governments increasingly assumed some responsibility for the external debts of private borrowers, as discussed in Carlos F. Diaz-Alejandro, "Latin American Debt: I Don't Think We Are in Kansas Anymore," in William C. Brainard and George L. Perry, eds., *Brookings Papers on Economic Activity* No. 2 (Washington, D.C.: The Brookings Institution, 1984), pp. 377-80.

[16] IMF, *International Financial Statistics*, October 1984.

[17] IMF, *Annual Report on Exchange Arrangements and Exchange Restrictions 1983* (Washington, D.C.: IMF, 1983), p. 21.

[18] Ibid, pp. 6 and 46; and IMF, op. cit., 1982, p. 5.

[19] International Finance Corporation, *Annual Report 1984* (Washington, D.C.: 1984), p. 18.

[20] L. Gray Cowan, *Divestment and Privatization of the Public Sector: Case Studies of Five Countries (Jamaica, Kenya, Sudan, Indonesia, Bangladesh)*, prepared for U.S. AID, December 1983, mimeo.

[21] World Bank, *Toward Sustained Development: A Joint Program of Action for Sub-Saharan Africa* (Washington, D.C.: 1984), Chapter 4.

[22] Institute of International Finance, as cited in George J. Clark, "Economic Development: First Things First," in Khadija Haq and Carlos Massad, eds., *Adjustment with Growth: A Search for an Equitable Solution* (Islamabad, Pakistan: North-South Roundtable, 1984), p. 311.

[23] See Richard E. Feinberg, "Overview: Restoring Confidence in International Credit Markets," in Feinberg and Kallab, *Uncertain Future*, op. cit., pp. 11-14.

Chapter 3

Trade with the Developing Countries: The Reagan Record and Prospects

Steve Lande and Craig VanGrasstek

The Reagan Administration's trade policies have been a mixed blessing for the developing countries. Although the President has forcefully argued that the marketplace should set the national and international economic agenda, his attachment to laissez-faire principles has been subject to compromise with powerful domestic interests in some labor-intensive industries in which the developing countries have a comparative advantage.

This record should not be judged too harshly. Unemployment early in the first Reagan term, followed by a growing trade deficit, placed tremendous pressures on the White House. The President must be given credit for blunting many of the more odious protectionist initiatives attempted during his first four years.

This chapter examines how the Administration has dealt with three central trade policy issues[1]:

(1) textile restrictions negotiated under the Multi-Fibre Arrangement (MFA), in which case the Administration has collaborated with domestic textile interests by erecting new restrictions in the U.S. market;

(2) the application of import-relief measures to products from developing countries, in which case the President has exercised restraint (but generally has only limited discretion to intervene in decisions made on technical grounds); and

(3) tariff preferences for developing nations, in support of which the White House fought for renewal of the U.S. Generalized System of Preferences (GSP) and introduced the Caribbean Basin Initiative (CBI).

The chapter also discusses the prospects for bilateral and multilateral trade negotiations in the second Reagan term and the opportunities and dangers that these present to developing countries.

We argue throughout that the developing nations are not helpless bystanders in U.S. trade policy, but virtual participants in the policy process. Effective political pressure is best applied by convincing U.S. policy makers that it is in the interests of the United States to maintain open market access for the developing world. Individual countries rarely have enough power to influence U.S. trade policy through threats of retaliation (that is, threats to curtail American access to their markets), but they can coordinate action among themselves and can sometimes work closely with like-minded groups in the United States. The textile sector offers one example of how such coordination can be used to temper the power of protectionist interests in the United States.

Textile Restrictions Negotiated Under the Multi-Fibre Arrangement

With the possible exception of nuclear materials and sophisticated weapons, textiles and apparel are the most controlled items in world trade. They are also one of the most important industries in developing nations, both because the market is huge and because the industry represents a first step in many industrialization plans.

Developing-country manufacturers are frequently able to undercut the production costs of their industrial-nation competitors, who in turn have reacted by waging a defensive protectionist campaign. The political pressures brought by beleaguered textile interests in the United States and in Europe, together with the threat of unilateral market restrictions, led to the establishment of the Multi-Fibre Arrangement (MFA) and of its predecessors. Nearly all American textile imports from developing countries are governed by the bilateral agreements that the United States has negotiated with 28 nations under the auspices of the MFA.[2]

The U.S. textile industry has been far more successful in influencing the Reagan Administration's trade policy than have the footwear industry or other sectors that face import competition. Lobbyists have been particularly successful in reminding the President of a 1980 campaign promise to seek to relate total import growth to the rate of growth of the U.S. textile market and in using this pledge as a justification for new import restrictions. This rate was somewhat arbitrarily pegged by the textile industry at about 1.5-2.0 per cent annually. The President made this commitment to placate the textile industry's powerful congressional allies.

The MFA renewal negotiations of 1981 were the first major test of the Administration's textile policy. The European Communities approached these talks with restrictive proposals, including "rollbacks" (quota cuts) for the more advanced developing countries. Domestic textile interests hoped that the United States would join the Europeans in these efforts, but the Administration resisted the pressure. The U.S. negotiators satisfied the domestic interests with a pledge to reduce growth and quota limits for the three largest suppliers (Hong Kong, the Republic of Korea, and Taiwan). The United States was able to play the role of the 'honest broker' between the European Communities and the developing nations. The MFA was renewed through 1986 without any changes in the rollback rules or quota allocations. In view of subsequent events, this may have been a Pyrrhic victory for the developing world.

The year 1982 brought a sharp downturn in the U.S. economy, and the troubled textile industry did not hesitate to remind the President of his promise. U.S. textile negotiators concluded strict agreements with the three largest suppliers to the U.S. market in 1982 and 1983: Hong Kong, South Korea, and Taiwan. These countries' previous rates of export growth ranged from 3.7 to 4.0 per cent, but were limited by the new agreements to annual growth rates of only 0.5-1.5 per cent in most of their textile and apparel categories. The United States attempted to impose a similar regime on its fourth largest supplier, the People's Republic of China, whose previous rate of growth was 4.5 per cent, but the Chinese government effectively marshaled its retaliatory power against U.S. agricultural exports. With the assistance of the American agricultural community, the 1983 U.S.-Chinese textile agreement was reached on a compromise between the two nations' positions—a 3.8 per cent rate of growth.

Few developing nations possess China's enviable power to negotiate from a position of strength. This was demonstrated in 1983 and the first half of 1984, when the United States requested an unprecedented number of textile consultations with foreign suppliers. Restrictive actions were accelerated in December 1983 by the release of new textile guidelines. The Market Disruption Guidelines direct the inter-agency Committee for the Implementation of Textile Agreements to review cases of actual or threatened market disruption at relatively low thresholds.[3] This means that more textile exporters face bilateral consultations with the United States.

The U.S. Customs Service issued another set of interim regulations in August 1984 that tightened the country-of-origin requirements for textiles. Supporters of the new rules asserted that the larger textile exporters (especially Hong Kong and China) circumvent U.S. quota rules and limitations by shipping finished or semi-finished goods to other countries with underutilized quotas. The goods are given at least nominal processing there, and are then shipped to the United States under the intermediary's quota. The new Customs Service regulations attempt to halt these practices.

Opponents asserted that the rules a) violate existing textile agreements and GATT rules, b) would impose limits more severe than those established by the MFA or the bilateral accords, and c) would create inconsistencies in U.S. customs law. The Customs Service also came under fire for issuing the regulations without allowing adequate time for industry comments and thereby disrupting established patterns of trade. Following this criticism, the Customs Service exempted shipments contracted before the regulations were published and shipped before October 31. This special exemption was made to avoid disruption in the 1984 holiday season.

As of January 1985, it is unclear what will happen with these regulations. Some of the domestic interests that originally supported the rules, fearing that the regulations could actually create new loopholes, are beginning to have second thoughts. They now recognize that the regulations do not adequately answer the fundamental question of how one determines "origin" in an industry that is notable for its multiple stages of processing and transnational production. The Customs Service is reportedly considering the extension of the rules to other industries, which could have a stifling effect on some products now entering duty-free under the Caribbean Basin Initiative and the U.S. Generalized System of Preferences.[4]

It is difficult to predict how U.S. textile policy will develop in the second Reagan Administration. The textile industry notes that import penetration is rising rapidly despite the President's commitment and the restrictions he imposed, and it will persist in pressing for relief. The industry appears more likely to seek new restrictions for Far East suppliers than for newer producers in the Caribbean Basin. The Caribbean producers purchase much of their fabric from U.S. mills, and thus share common interests in keeping this market relatively open.

Still, there is reason to expect an improvement for the developing nations. The power of the American textile lobby is being challenged by an increasingly well-organized coalition of agricultural and retail groups that would suffer from any new restrictions. This domestic coalition is matched at the international level by a more united bloc of developing-country textile producers. The experience of China in 1983 is instructive. If producers cooperate among themselves and work closely with their American allies, they may be able to counter the influence of the U.S. textile interests. The tacit alliance between American interest groups and Third World textile exporters exemplifies the transnational benefits of free trade. The trade prospects for exporters in both the North and the South would improve if this experience could be repeated in other product areas.

It is also notable that during the 1984 race, the President resisted making any new promises to the domestic industry, and at the same time confirmed his basic commitment to liberal trade.

Application of Import Relief Laws

American firms that feel they have been injured by foreign competition may seek redress under several domestic laws described in this section. If the imports are alleged to benefit from unfair trade practices such as subsidization or 'dumping,' then the domestic industry may appeal to the government under the countervailing-duty (CVD) or anti-dumping (AD) laws. Imports that are not traded unfairly but that increase at a rate that causes or threatens to cause serious injury to U.S. industries may be restricted under an "escape clause." Three trade remedies have been used by domestic interests to restrict the U.S. market over the last four years.

Subsidies and 'dumping' are the two principal forms of unfair trade practices. American trade law takes a very dim view of any form of subsidization, and (unlike the GATT Subsidies Code[5]) does not recognize the principal that developing countries may offer subsidies to their exporters in order to overcome structural disadvantages. 'Dumping' is defined as import sales that are made in the United States at less than their fair market value.

The anti-dumping and countervailing-duty laws are administered by the Department of Commerce and the U.S. International Trade Commission (ITC); they are intended to be executed solely on the basis of factual considerations. When an American industry alleges that a foreign competitor benefits from one or both of these practices, the Department of Commerce determines whether or not the allegation is true. The ITC conducts an investigation to determine whether the imports actually cause or threaten material injury to U.S. industries or workers; this injury test is automatic in anti-dumping cases but is only applied to certain nations in countervailing-duty cases.[6] If both the Department of Commerce and the ITC reach affirmative decisions, then a duty is imposed to offset the dumping or subsidization margin.

During the first Reagan term, 50 anti-dumping cases were brought against developing-country exporters and 37 of these were decided. Twenty-one (over one-half) led to the imposition of anti-dumping orders, 9 were terminated or suspended, and 7 resulted in negative findings by the Department of Commerce or the ITC. The anti-dumping orders were issued for 7 countries: the Republic of Korea (5 orders), Taiwan (5), China (4), Brazil (3), Chile (2), Mexico (1), and Trinidad and Tobago (1). About half of the cases involved iron and steel products, with anti-dumping duties ranging from 0.8 to 39.6 per cent.

Countervailing-duty cases over the same period followed a similar pattern: 81 cases were brought, 56 final decisions rendered, 27 countervailing-duty orders issued, 24 cases terminated or suspended, and 5 negative decisions reached. The concentration of orders against certain countries was much higher than in the case of anti-dumping duties, with Mexico accounting for 12 of the 27 orders. Brazilian exporters received 6 orders, while 2 each were applied to the Republic of Korea, Argentina, and Peru, and one each to Pakistan, Uruguay, and Trinidad and Tobago. Well over half of the petitions alleged subsidization of iron and steel products. The countervailing duties imposed ranged from 2 to 77 per cent.

While the anti-dumping and countervailing-duty laws are supposed to be executed in an entirely technical fashion, the "escape clause" (Section 201 of the U.S. Trade Act of 1974) runs on both technical and political tracks. This is because the import relief granted under this law is usually broader than the country-specific decisions made under the unfair-trade remedy laws, and can have important consequences for U.S. relations with its trading partners.

The escape clause is invoked by domestic industries and/or unions when they feel that they are being injured by increasing foreign competition, even if the imports are being traded fairly. The ITC then investigates the allegation and—if it determines that imports are rising to a level that causes or threatens serious injury[7]—it recommends that the President provide import relief or adjustment assistance to the industry. The recommended relief may take the form of increased duties, quotas, tariff-rate quotas, adjustment assistance, or a combination of these measures. The President has complete discretion to accept, reject, or modify the ITC's recommendations.[8] He may also negotiate orderly marketing arrangements.

In the last four years, the ITC considered only eight escape-clause cases that had the potential for seriously restricting developing-country access to the U.S. market. The products involved included shoes, tuna fish, copper, and steel. The Commission reached only three affirmative decisions (specialty steel, carbon and alloy steel, and unwrought copper), and the President granted relief only in the steel cases. The copper and carbon steel cases were both filed by domestic interests in the hope that President Reagan would be forced to decide on them during the 1984 electoral campaign. The timing of the copper industry was correct, but its political calculations were wrong. The President rejected the ITC's recommendation that he either impose quotas or increase tariffs for copper, and he only approved a scaled-down import restraint program for the carbon and alloy steel industry.

The carbon and alloy steel case of 1984 was one of the most hard-fought cases in the history of the escape clause. The Commission had recommended that the President impose a five-year steel import quota system. Rather than approve such an all-inclusive relief program, President Reagan developed a more flexible plan. This alternative proposal was based on (1) establishment of an import-penetration goal of 18.5 per cent of domestic consumption for finished steel (or of approximately 20.2 per cent if semi-finished steel is taken into account), (2) vigorous prosecution of alleged unfair trade practices by foreign producers, (3) new "surge control" arrangements,[9] and (4) negotiation of new "voluntary" export-restraint agreements (VRAs) with some exporters.

Because the President's plan involved measures outside the scope of the escape clause, he was obliged to seek congressional approval. The Congress granted the authority to enforce any new "voluntary" export restraint agreements through Customs Service control at U.S. borders, but the Steel Import Stabilization Act of 1984 also required that the steel companies earn this import relief by devoting their net cash flow to modernization and worker retraining efforts.

As of this writing, the Office of the U.S. Trade Representative has completed its preliminary negotiations with the major developing-country steel suppliers. Mexico, South Korea, and Brazil have agreed to VRAs that bring their combined share of the U.S. market down to 3.06 per cent (or 3.91 per cent if semi-finished products are also included); this compares to their 4.58 per cent share of the U.S. market for all steel goods in the first ten months of 1984, and their 4.35 per cent share in 1983 as a whole.[10]

These agreements, together with the relief granted to the specialty steel industry in 1983, will be the only restrictions of developing-country exports to the U.S. market that were brought on by the escape clause during the first Reagan term.

The United States has shown restraint in the imposition of import relief measures over the last four years, particularly in the escape clause. This is quite notable in view of the tremendous pressures brought on by unemployment and the burgeoning trade deficit. It is frequently argued that the anti-dumping and countervailing-duty laws are not protectionist, but represent limited corrective actions taken against the unfair trade practices of foreign producers. The U.S. trade remedy laws provide for transparent procedures that allow all sides an opportunity to state their cases, and the domestic petitioners' success rate of about 50 per cent is taken by some observers as proof that domestic applicants have no undue advantage in the proceedings.

This sanguine view of the import relief laws is not, however, shared by all observers. Others argue that the U.S. statutes establish arbitrary standards that developing countries are hard-pressed to meet, and that they give American industries an opportunity to harass foreign competition. U.S. law does not prohibit industries from filing multiple petitions against the same product. Some industries abuse this privilege by bringing simultaneous anti-dumping and countervailing-duty cases—as well as other trade actions—against a foreign supplier. Even if cases do not lead to anti-dumping or countervailing duties, the developing-country exporter must pay substantial legal fees in its defense. Domestic importers may hesitate to purchase goods from a foreign supplier whose market access appears to be in jeopardy.

The number of trade remedy petitions may increase notably in the second term of the Reagan Administration, stimulated in part by enactment of the U.S. Trade and Tariff Act of 1984. This legislation makes a number of alterations in the statutes governing import remedies. Many of these modifications appear to represent nothing more than codifications of existing procedures in the Department of Commerce or the ITC, and are intended to avoid any future court challenges based on claims that the agencies went beyond their statutory authority. Other amendments rationalize the administrative and judicial review procedures, bring the anti-dumping and countervailing-duty laws into conformity with one another, and ease the administrative and investigative burdens placed on the government, the domestic petitioners, and the foreign respondents.

Some of the alterations, however, seem to tighten the operations of the trade remedy laws in ways that do not bode well for developing-country exporters. A detailed examination of the modifications in legislative definitions, administrative procedures, or investigative methods, is beyond the scope of this chapter, but a few examples should suffice to illustrate their implications.[11] One new clause in the anti-dumping and countervailing-duty laws will require the ITC to "cumulate" the imports from several suppliers when determining whether the imports are a substantial cause of material injury to U.S. industries. This will encourage petitioners to file against more than one country and is likely to increase the total number of anti-dumping and countervailing-duty orders. The Trade and Tariff Act also codifies an "upstream subsidization" practice under which the Department of Commerce may find that subsidies on principal components are passed through to the finished product. This may lead to countervailing duties for some imports that would otherwise be immune.

Other amendments that might work against the interests of exporters in the developing countries include a redefinition of "serious injury" that could assist petitioners in escape-clause cases, an expanded right of coalitions to petition in unfair trade cases, expanded coverage of the "presidential retaliation" authority,[12] increased authority for the Commerce Department to initiate anti-dumping investigations in cases involving persistent dumping, a stipulation that the party seeking revocation of a countervailing-duty or anti-dumping order must bear the burden of persuasion, and a provision that may increase the likelihood of retroactive duties in some cases.

We expect that these provisions will translate into more numerous findings against developing nations during the second Reagan term, but it would be premature to speculate on the magnitude of the increase. The regulations to implement these measures are not yet available, and even after they have been released, it will probably take months or years of experience before their impact can be assessed.

Preferential Tariff Programs

The President's firm belief in the superiority of market forces (trade) over government intervention (aid) has prompted him to support programs that provide the developing countries with duty-free access to the U.S. market. The Generalized System of Preferences (GSP) would have expired on January 3, 1985 if it had not been renewed, and the Administration successfully pressed the Congress for renewal in 1984. The one-way free trade area of the President's Caribbean Basin Initiative (CBI) provides even more favorable market access to its limited number of beneficiaries.

The Administration's support for these programs has not, however, been inspired solely by its attachment to liberal trade principles: The GSP renewal legislation carries with it *a new element of negotiability* that will be used by the United States to extract market access concessions from the more advanced beneficiary nations. And the CBI is widely regarded as having been motivated more by security and political concerns than by economic motives.

A Renewed U.S. GSP Program

The more important of the two programs, the GSP, was originally proposed by the secretariat of the United Nations Conference on Trade and Development (UNCTAD) during the 1960s. It was to be the embodiment of the 'trade, not aid' approach to economic development, with duty-free market access encouraging the growth of export industries in the developing nations. Most industrial countries agreed to institute these preferences; the U.S. program was the last to be implemented, in January 1976. But the actual GSP programs fell short of the expectations raised in the UNCTAD discussions, with all sponsoring countries establishing limitations such as product exclusions or strict customs procedures.[13]

Although the U.S. GSP is considered to be the most generous of these programs, it has been criticized for the statutory and administrative limits it places on product eligibility. Developing countries have not been alone in pointing out these limitations. A recent ITC report concludes that "GSP imports have not resulted in significant increases in the overall [developing-country] import share of the U.S. market," noting that actual GSP imports account for approximately 4.9 per cent of total non-petroleum imports.[14]

The ITC cited the GSP's 'safeguards' as one cause of the program's limited use. The United States defends safeguards as a means to assure that the most advanced developing countries do not reap exclusive benefits in certain product areas, but beneficiary nations often complain that the real aim of safeguards is to protect U.S. domestic industries from increasingly competitive industries in the newly industrialized countries. Whatever the rationale behind them, safeguards have been applied with increasing frequency during the last four years, and they are likely to play an even greater role in the second Reagan Administration. The principal safeguards are: (a) "rules of origin" that exclude many assembled products from GSP eligibility,[15] (b) statutory product exclusions,[16] (c) administrative exclusions of "import-sensitive" goods,[17] and (d) a "competitive need" clause (CNC) and a "graduation" procedure that keep in check rapidly rising GSP imports.

The last of these safeguards has been among the most controversial aspects of the GSP program. The competitive-need clause establishes a ceiling for the GSP exports of beneficiary countries, and any nation that goes above the ceiling in a given product area will lose its eligibility for that product in the following year. Exclusions are made during an annual GSP review conducted by the Office of the U.S. Trade Representative. The limits are currently set at 50 per cent of U.S. imports of the product, or $57.7 million (the dollar figure rises each year to account for nominal increases in U.S. GNP); imports that exceed either limit are excluded from the GSP. A product that has lost its eligibility due to competitive-need exclusions may be redesignated in a later review if a country's exports of the product drop below the ceiling. Redesignations are left to the discretion of the President (acting upon the recommendations of the Office of the Trade Representative), who in recent years has shown an increasing reluctance to redesignate the products of the major GSP beneficiaries (especially Brazil, Hong Kong, the Republic of Korea, Mexico, and Taiwan). A

Table 1. Results of the Three Annual GSP Reviews Conducted by the Reagan Administration ($ millions[a] and percentages)

	1981	1982	1983
Competitive Need Exclusions			
Exclusions in Force	$6,782	$7,108	$10,661
Eligible for Redesignation	810	1,012	1,181
Redesignated	213	207	155
(share of those eligible)	26%	25%	13%
Not Redesignated	597	805	1,026
(share of those eligible)	74%	75%	87%
Other Changes			
New Designations	$ 76	$ 10	$ 7
De Minimis Waivers:			
Eligible products	43	49	54
Waivers granted	41	47	52
(share of those eligible)	95%	97%	96%
Product removals	n.a.	73	33
Country-Specific Product Removal	$ 54	$ 95	$ 183

[a] All values are expressed in terms of the total products that the rule would have affected in the review year.

Source: Calculated by the authors from information supplied by the GSP Information Center of the Office of the U.S. Trade Representative.

product that is passed up for redesignation is considered to have "graduated" from the program. The scope of competitive need exclusions, redesignations, and graduations is shown in Table 1.

The annual reviews are based in part upon petitions from domestic firms, foreign industries, and the governments of developing countries, but the Office of the U.S. Trade Representative may also take actions on its own motion. Reviews may result in (a) designation of a new product for GSP, (b) waiver of the competitive need limit for a product that enters at a *de minimis* level,[18] (c) removal of a product from eligibility for all beneficiaries, or (d) removal of a product from eligibility for a single country. As Table 1 shows, product removals have far outweighed the value of new product designations and *de minimis* waivers in recent years.

Developing countries have been disappointed by the results of the U.S. GSP program, and (together with some domestic American supporters) have called for a restructuring of the system. Their suggestions have included proposals for eliminating or softening the competitive-need exclusions, extending the scope of product eligibility, and allowing for more flexible rules of origin.[19] These proposals have been countered by opposition from several American labor and industry groups, many of which view the program as a threat.

The conflicting demands of these two groups came to a head in the second session of the 98th Congress (1984), when the GSP program came up for renewal. Opposition from labor unions and others was strong enough to make the program's supporters in the House reluctant to bring it up for consideration for fear that products would be "graduated," that individual countries would lose their eligibility, or that the program would simply lapse. Despite these concerns, the GSP was renewed without significant opposition or crippling changes. No countries were directly graduated by statute; no products that are currently eligible were "graduated"; and the program is secure until mid-1993.

The Reagan Administration deserves most of the credit for shepherding this legislation through the Congress. The Administration proposed substantial changes in the fundamental nature of the program, and the renewal legislation incorporated the most important of these. The changes make the GSP walk the thin line between a non-reciprocal program[20] and one that induces the beneficiary countries to offer concessions to the United States.

The renewal act leaves the existing 50 per cent/$57.7 million competitive-need ceiling in place, but it also creates a lower competitive-need ceiling (25 per cent/$25 million) for "competitive" products. The President is directed to conduct a general review of GSP-eligible articles no later than January 4, 1987 (and periodically thereafter), in order to identify competitive products on a country-specific basis. There is no fixed standard established for determining what products are competitive, but one of the considerations will be the country's willingness to liberalize its trade—particularly for products of interest to the United States. In other words, U.S. trade negotiators will be able to use the threat of accelerated graduation as a tool in bilateral negotiations.

In addition to this 'stick,' the legislation also provides the renewed GSP program with a 'carrot' to induce liberalization. The carrot is a limited authority to waive the application of the competitive-need clause altogether. The total value of waivers that may be granted is limited by statutory restrictions, with a stipulation that the more advanced beneficiary countries may receive no more than half the total waivers.[21] The GSP renewal singles out the least developed countries for a special waiver.[22] Any country that is so designated by the President will be entirely exempt from the CNC for all of its GSP-eligible products. This waiver will not be counted against the limit placed on the President's use of discretionary waivers.

The President may still redesignate for preferential treatment nearly all products that have been excluded through the competitive-need clause. We calculate that, had the waiver authority been in effect during 1984, the President could have redesignated all but eleven of the 235 products that were then excluded by the competitive-need clause (nine of the still-excluded products would be from the more advanced beneficiary countries).[23] The waivers will not, however, be granted solely with a view toward redesignating the maximum number of products. The negotiating stance of the U.S. Trade Representative and the beneficiary countries' willingness to compromise will be more important considerations.

The new element of "negotiable eligibility" will clearly add to the uncertainty and conditionality of the program, especially for the more advanced beneficiary countries. It should be recognized, however, that the presidential waiver could actually make the program *more* liberal than it currently is for some countries, especially for the mid-level and least developed of the beneficiary nations. The developing countries also may reap collateral benefits from the negotiations conducted by the United States. Any tariff reductions that one developing nation grants will be extended to all other countries through the most-favored-nation principle, meaning that all the developing countries will gain increased access to one another's markets. This could be a boon to 'South-South' trade among the developing countries. Furthermore, the "uncertainty factor" may only rise in the near term. After the product-review and subsequent negotiations are completed, most developing countries should be reasonably certain of secure eligibility for the duration of the program.

The renewed GSP program includes other changes that could lead to further restrictions. The most important of these are the new "designation criteria" that the beneficiaries must meet. These require that a beneficiary (a) observe internationally respected workers' rights, (b) protect intellectual property rights, and (c) not engage in unreasonable export practices.[24] While these designation requirements do offer the Executive Branch new justifications to cancel a country's GSP eligibility, the Administration is not compelled to exercise this power.

The legislation also sets an income ceiling for the eligibility of beneficiary countries: Any nation with a per capita gross national product of $8,500 or more (as reported by the World Bank) will be 'graduated' from the program two years after it achieves this income level. The ceiling figure will be increased annually to reflect growth in the nominal GNP of the United States, but the figure will only grow at one half the rate of U.S. growth. The $8,500 limit is not likely to affect many beneficiaries. Brunei may have reached this level already, and Singapore's current income of about $6,000 per capita could grow beyond the limit by the early 1990s. No other countries are likely to be affected, however, especially since most OPEC countries are already excluded from the GSP.

The CBI Program

In contrast to the renewed GSP program, which is accompanied by some new restrictions, President Reagan's Caribbean Basin Initiative offers more than two dozen beneficiaries in Central America and the Caribbean a much more open access to the U.S. market. The CBI's one-way free trade area is similar to the GSP but offers several specific advantages.

The product coverage of the CBI is more extensive than that of the GSP. Both programs exclude certain products of interest to the beneficiary countries (for example, most textiles, footwear, and tuna fish). But while some CBI-eligible products are excluded from the GSP because of import-sensitivity or other considerations, virtually all GSP-eligible products are entitled to duty-free treatment under the CBI.[25] The CBI also offers much greater security of eligibility. Unlike the GSP, it has no built-in, limiting safeguards such as annual product reviews, competitive-need limitations, or graduation. Furthermore, the CBI "rules of origin" are more flexible than those of the GSP. Both programs require that eligible products contain at least 35 per cent local "value added" in order to qualify for duty-free entry. Under the rules of the CBI, however, this 35 per cent may be shared by any combination of beneficiary countries (thus opening up greater possibilities for regional co-production), and up to 15 percentage points may originate in the United States. Puerto Rico and the U.S. Virgin Islands are considered to be beneficiary countries when calculating the figures. The President has also pledged that, as part of the CBI, the United States will attempt to extend more favorable textile-quota treatment to the beneficiary countries.

The U.S. government has taken a very active interest in the success of the CBI, and the tariff exonerations of the program are complemented by a wide range of promotional activities designed to attract and assist private investment in the region. This includes government sponsorship of investment missions and feasibility studies, technical assistance to local businesses, inter-governmental cooperation in export promotion programs, and increased financial assistance for governments and development agencies.

It is still too early to assess the CBI's impact on investment and trade in the region. Total U.S. imports from the beneficiary countries during the first six months of operation (January-June 1984) were 17 per cent higher than in the previous year,[26] but this increase may be due more to the value of the dollar and to the U.S. recovery than to the influence of the CBI. The CBI beneficiary countries are still in the process of adjusting to the program, including a gradual shift from GSP exports to use of the CBI. The real fate of the program lies in the hands of American, European, and Japanese investors, who must decide whether the new benefits of investment in the Caribbean make it an attractive area in which to start new ventures.

The GSP will continue to be the dominant tariff preference program for developing countries during the second Reagan term. Its future will be intimately tied to the prospects for bilateral and multilateral trade negotiations. As the next section shows in greater detail, the new conditionality of product eligibility—the 'carrot and stick' approach—will make the GSP an important element in any such negotiations, particularly any bilateral talks held with the more advanced, newly industrializing developing countries (NICs).

Possibilities for Future Bilateral and Multilateral Negotiations

The Reagan Administration is currently gearing up for tough trade negotiations during the second term, and the more advanced developing nations are near the top of the U.S. agenda. Armed with new authority by the Trade and Tariff Act of 1984, the U.S. trade negotiators have drawn up an ambitious agenda that includes so-called new issues such as trade in services (banking, communications, and insurance, for example), trade-related investment, high technology products, and intellectual property rights, as well as 'traditional' issues of market access for manufactures and agricultural exports. Whether the United States approaches developing countries with threats of retaliation or with offers of *quid pro quo*, negotiations will be unavoidable for many of the NICs.

The U.S. agenda items are all likely to encounter opposition from developing countries, which appear to have a great deal to lose but little to gain. Previous rounds of multilateral trade negotiations (MTNs) have been criticized for dealing almost exclusively with products and sectors of interest to the industrial countries, for eroding the

GSP preference margins that developing countries enjoy, and for frustrating developing nations with vague and unfulfilled promises of special and differential treatment.

The U.S. Trade Representative, Ambassador William Brock, has called for a new MTN round to be held under the auspices of the GATT. World Bank President A. W. Clausen has expressed his support of such a round, stating that he would "like to see the next GATT round focus on non-tariff barriers and on products of special concern to the developing countries."[27] The developing-country members of the GATT are not likely to share President Clausen's optimism, given the U.S. objectives and past experience with MTNs, but a new round would still be preferable for them to bilateral negotiations based on threats of unilateral U.S. retaliation. The developing nations would find better safety in numbers—although this would not necessarily mean joining a new MTN round *en masse*.

An alternative to MTNs would be negotiations with the United States in various 'plurilateral' forums composed of regional developing-country blocs. For example, the Latin American states could present a united front by reviving the Special Committee for Consultations and Negotiations of the Organization of American States (OAS). Other regional organizations that could operate this way might include the Association of South East Asian Nations (ASEAN), the Caribbean Community (CARICOM), the Organization of African Unity (OAU), the Latin American Development Association (ALADI), or the Andean Pact. Plurilateral forums could also be used by developing countries to prepare unified positions before the MTN round begins.

If multilateral or plurilateral negotiations are not feasible, the United States can be expected to pursue its interests on a bilateral basis. It is prepared to force the more advanced developing countries into negotiating—even if this means applying unilateral sanctions. The new negotiability of the GSP program has already been discussed as one such sanction, and the Trade and Tariff Act of 1984 also broadens the power of the Executive Branch to retaliate through other forms of market restriction. The White House has had a broad 'presidential retaliation' power since 1974, including the authority to unilaterally raise tariffs or establish quotas for countries that engage in unfair trade practices not covered by other trade remedy laws. The 1984 legislation clarifies that this authority covers unfair trade practices involving services and trade-related investment, and this expanded retaliatory power is likely to be applied to an increasing number of developing countries.

Bilateral negotiations do not need to be coercive; the Trade and Tariff Act of 1984 presents another option that may be more attractive for the more advanced developing countries. The Act authorizes the Executive Branch to conclude a free-trade-area (FTA) agreement with Israel, and also to conduct similar negotiations with other countries. While an FTA is similar to the GSP or the CBI, in that it offers duty-free access to the U.S. market, there is one major difference: An FTA is reciprocal. Any developing country that negotiated such an agreement would be expected to offer equally free access to the United States. Sectoral agreements are limited to individual sectors (e.g., automobiles) and would also be reciprocal.

The authority might also be used to conclude agreements on a product-specific basis, provided that the Congress approves. This could be supplemented by the authority that the Executive Branch already possesses to conclude non-tariff agreements with other countries. One welcome feature of this tariff and non-tariff authority is its expedited procedures for congressional ratification. The Executive Branch is required to inform the trade committees of the House and Senate of any such negotiations. If the committees do not object, any subsequent agreements can be submitted on a 'fast track.' The fast track is an expedited ratification procedure that requires a congressional decision within 60 days and does not allow for amendments. This ensures that any liberal agreements would not be loaded down with protectionist amendments in Congress.

The United States and the developing countries have many options as to how to proceed with negotiations. Talks can be bilateral, multilateral, or plurilateral; they can encompass issues ranging from tariff rates to investment rules; and they may be based on mutual accommodation or on threats of unilateral retaliation. No matter how they are pursued, the developing nations will be in a much better position if they adopt pragmatic positions rather than resort to rhetorical flourishes. They should also prepare their common positions well enough in advance to have a meaningful impact on the proceedings. The United States has taken the initiative thus far, but the developing countries should not remain idle.

Prospects for the Second Reagan Term

Although developing countries clearly met with some new restrictions in the first Reagan term, any assessment of the Administration's performance must weigh these developments against the pressures directed at the White House. High unemployment, a growing trade deficit, and the pressures of election-year politics conspired to line up many powerful interests in favor of protectionist initiatives. The President must be given credit for his efforts to hold back these proposals.

The White House did give in to demands for the textile industry, but it succeeded with its CBI and GSP initiatives and exercised restraint in import relief programs.

The trade deficit shows no sign of abating. Although a deficit may be superficially heartening to the developing countries—for a U.S. trade deficit is matched by growing surpluses abroad—it also increases pressures for new market restrictions. The burdens of any new protectionist measures are likely to fall disproportionately upon the shoulders of the developing nations because their products compete with the most troubled industries in the United States, their trade policies appear more interventionist than those of industrial nations, and they rarely have the retaliatory strength to influence the United States.

The President's commitment to liberal trade principles may help fend off protectionist initiatives in the next four years, but the experience of the recent past shows that he is ready to compromise these principles when necessary. His willingness and ability to avoid restrictive policies will vary according to the issue involved in each case. The President is in a strong though not commanding position vis-à-vis new trade legislation. The 98th Congress granted him nearly all that he requested, and he now has little reason to approach Congress on any new matters. If special interests succeed in getting any significant new restrictive legislation passed, the White House should be in a good position to veto the proposal.

Textiles will nevertheless continue to be a problem area in U.S. trade relations with the developing countries. Domestic producers, arguing that import penetration is increasing despite the relief they have already received, will press for more market restrictions. The President may, however, be more reluctant to support these proposals in his second term than he was in the first; he made no binding commitment to the textile interests during his 1984 reelection campaign, and free trade was part of his electoral plank. The emergence of a liberal trade coalition composed of U.S. retailers and agricultural interests should also temper the relative power of the textile lobby. Farmers and merchants share common interests in free trade, and are beginning to work together to block further restrictions in U.S. textiles trade. Such restrictions also would not be in the interest of U.S. consumers and firms that export to the Third World. Moreover, many U.S. textile producers themselves have a stake in more open market access for the fabric they sell to foreign producers and for the finished goods produced in their off-shore assembly plants.

It is also likely that the U.S. trade remedy laws will prove a growing source of tension between the United States and the developing countries in the next several years. Because the anti-dumping and anti-subsidy laws are administered on semi-autonomous technical tracks, there is little room for political intervention from the White

House or foreign capitals. The President has much more opportunity to control import relief imposed under the escape clause and the 'presidential retaliation' statutes, and should continue to resist pressures to apply these trade remedies. He should also continue to oppose protectionist revisions of these laws by Congress.

At a more fundamental level, the United States should be more tolerant of government subsidies and other export promotion measures undertaken by developing countries. The GATT Subsidies Code recognizes that subsidies and other forms of government intervention are sometimes necessary to overcome the structural disadvantages of developing countries. Ideally, U.S. trade law should reflect this principle instead of applying identical standards to countries of manifestly unequal competitive status. It would be quite difficult, however, to reverse the political momentum in the United States for creating the proverbial 'level playing field.'

The area in which the Executive Branch has the most control in the period ahead is in negotiations with other governments. The Reagan Administration now has authority to negotiate on a broad range of issues. In the next MTN round, the United States will seek international agreements on the 'new issues' of trade in services, trade-related investment, and high-technology trade. Any agreements that are reached in these areas should take into account the special needs of developing countries. For example, many developing nations restrict foreign investment in certain service industries, such as communications and banking. The legislative intent of these restrictions is to encourage the development of nascent Third World industries rather than to protect established industries. They are qualitatively different from similar restrictions imposed by industrial countries. If the United States attempts to impose conditions of equal competition on countries of unequal development, this is likely to stunt the growth of the developing-country economies.

The U.S. position in any upcoming trade negotiations should be based more on offers of mutual concessions than on threats of unilateral retaliation. Moreover, the United States should not demand absolute reciprocity in trade concessions. Demands for *quid pro quo* from the developing countries should be commensurate with their relative levels of economic development and industrial sophistication. Because trade reciprocity runs counter to the still-valid philosophical underpinnings of the GSP program, which were intended to help advance development in the poorer countries, the new 'carrots and sticks' of the GSP are tools that should be used sparingly, with more frequent resort to the carrots than to the sticks.

To a greater extent than in past MTN rounds, whether the negotiations are based on promises of mutual concessions or on threats of unilateral retaliation depends on the developing-country negotiators themselves. Developing countries, especially the NICs, are not helpless bystanders in the negotiating process. If they develop a coherent and unified position and, where possible, work together with U.S. domestic interests desiring the same outcomes, they can do a great deal to maintain their access to the U.S. market.

Notes

[1] This paper deals with questions of market access and does not cover international commodity agreements, which have not been an important aspect of the Reagan Administration's trade policy. The Administration is generally hostile to any arrangements that interfere with natural market forces. For this reason, it has refused to adhere to the International Cocoa Agreement and the International Tin Agreement. The only notable actions that the United States has recently taken in this area are the negotiation of a new coffee agreement in 1983, fruitless discussions relating to a new sugar accord, and ratification of the International Jute Agreement. This last arrangement includes no market-intervention mechanisms and thus does not conflict with the Administration's free-market position.

[2] The United States has concluded bilateral textile agreements with Brazil, China, Colombia, Costa Rica, the Dominican Republic, Egypt, Haiti, Hong Kong, Hungary, India, Indonesia, Japan, the Republic of Korea, Macao, Malaysia, Maldives, Mauritius, Mexico, Pakistan, Peru, the Philippines, Poland, Romania, Singapore, Sri Lanka, Taiwan, Thailand, and Yugoslavia.

[3] These guidelines provide that the CITA will review a country's imports for their market-disruption effects on a product-specific basis when (1) the total growth in imports in that product or category is more than 30 per cent in the most recent year, or the ratio of total imports to domestic production in that product or category is 20 per cent or more; and (2) the imports from the individual supplier equal 1 per cent or more of the total U.S. production of that product or category.

[4] See "Customs May Expand Textile 'Rule of Origin' Policy," *Inside U.S. Trade*, December 7, 1984 (Washington, D.C.: Inside Washington Publishers).

[5] The GATT Subsidies Code provides special consideration for the developing countries by recognizing that these nations must sometimes provide subsidies to offset their structural disadvantages. The Code generally allows developing-country subsidies as long as they are consistent with the country's competitive and development needs, do not prejudice the trade or production interests of other countries, and do not result in any developing country's receiving a more-than-equitable share of the world market. The practical implication of this provision is that while subsidies offered by developing countries may run afoul of domestic countervailing-duty laws (such as that of the United States), they are unlikely to be the object of dispute-settlement procedures under the Code.

[6] While the ITC injury test is granted to all countries in anti-dumping cases, in countervailing-duty cases it is restricted to countries that are signatories to the GATT Subsidies Code, are members of the GATT (when the case involves duty-free goods), or other countries with which the United States has assumed such an obligation.

[7] "Serious injury" is a more difficult standard to meet than the "material injury" requirements set under the anti-dumping and countervailing-duty laws.

[8] If the President chooses not to impose the ITC's recommended relief, the Congress may override his decision through the use of a joint resolution. The President may, in turn, veto a joint resolution, and the Congress can override the veto with a two-thirds majority.

[9] In reaction to a surge in imports that the United States perceives to be rapid, "excessive," and "unfair," the Office of the U.S. Trade Representative can pressure foreign suppliers to negotiate such controls by threatening to resort to unilateral retaliation (under Sec. 301).

[10] *Washington Tariff & Trade Letter*, Vol. 4, No. 51 (December 24, 1984), p. 2.

[11] For a detailed discussion of these changes, see Steve Lande and Craig Van-Grasstek, "The Trade and Tariff Act of 1984" (forthcoming).

[12] Section 301—also known as the "presidential retaliation" law—is a catch-all statute designed to fight foreign unfair trade practices that do not fall under other statutes such as the anti-dumping law. It is administered by the Office of the U.S. Trade Representative, which is given the authority to raise tariffs or cut off access to the U.S. market. The Trade and Tariff Act of 1984 clarifies that the law is not restricted to trade in goods, but also covers services and trade-related investment. Developing countries have not been subject to many Section 301 cases in recent years, but the service and investment amendments should increase the number of 301 cases involving Third World nations.

[13] For a description of the various GSP programs instituted by 20 developed nations, as well as a review of their performance, see Secretary-General, Organisation for Economic Co-operation and Development, *The Generalized System of Preferences; Review of the First Decade* (Paris: OECD, 1983).

[14] International Trade Commission, *An Evaluation of U.S. Imports Under the Generalized System of Preferences* (Washington, D.C.: U.S. Government Printing Office, 1983), pp. v-vi.

[15] The rules of origin stipulate that, to qualify, an export (1) must be a product wholly of the eligible country, or be substantially transformed into a different article of commerce; (2) must be directly imported into the United States; and (3) must originate in the beneficiary country for at least 35 per cent of their appraised value.

[16] Congress has explicitly excluded the following product categories from GSP eligibility: textiles and apparel articles that are subject to textile agreements; watches; import-sensitive electronic articles; import-sensitive steel articles; most footwear; and import-sensitive glass products.

[17] The Executive Branch has deemed the following products to be import-sensitive in the context of GSP: handbags, luggage, flat goods, work gloves, and leather wearing apparel; tuna fish; petroleum and petroleum products; processed agricultural goods; rum; and tobacco.

[18] GSP imports that exceed the 50-per cent rule but enter at less than a certain dollar figure may (at the discretion of the U.S. Trade Representative) be kept on GSP through a *de minimis* waiver. The dollar figure for the most recent review (effective March 30, 1984) was $1.37 million. Under the terms of the GSP renewal legislation, the *de minimis* level will be increased to the equivalent of $5 million in terms of the 1979 U.S. GNP. This would have been equal to $6.8 million in 1983, had the new *de minimis* level been in effect at that time.

[19] For two examples of complaints and recommendations, see Organization of American States, Inter-American Economic and Social Council, *Report of the Technical Meeting on the United States Generalized System of Preferences* (Washington, D.C.: June 1983), and Stuart Tucker, "The U.S. GSP Program: Trade Preferences and Development," Overseas Development Council, *Policy Focus* No. 6 (September 1984).

[20] Because the GSP program runs counter to the most-favored-nation (MFN) principle, the United States and other industrial countries were required to obtain a special GATT waiver before they implemented these programs in the 1970s. If the United States were to make the program blatantly reciprocal, the GATT waiver would be put in jeopardy.

[21] The President's waiver authority is circumscribed by the legislation in three ways. First, he must consult with the ITC on whether any industry in the United States is likely to be adversely affected by such a waiver. The President is only required to "receive the advice" of the ITC, and the Commission is given no veto over the waiver. Second, the total value of such waivers is limited, with their distribution governed by the development level of the beneficiaries. The "least developed beneficiary countries" are entirely exempt from the CNC. The waiver authority for all other countries is limited to a total of 30 per cent of the value of all GSP imports in the previous calendar year. Only one half of the value of these waivers may be granted to the more advanced beneficiary countries. These countries have per capita incomes of $5,000 or more (as reported by the World Bank), and/or account for more than 10 per cent of total GSP imports. The countries that currently fulfill one or both of these criteria are Brunei, Hong Kong, Israel, Republic of Korea, Singapore, Taiwan, Trinidad and Tobago.

[22] The USTR intends to use the U.N. definition of least developed countries when making these designations. There are some 36 nations that the United Nations now considers to be least developed countries, 32 of which are currently GSP beneficiary countries. The majority are African nations.

[23] As of the most recent GSP review (effective March 30, 1984), the competitive-need exclusions in force applied to $10.7-billion worth of total trade. We calculated that this figure includes $5.6 billion in marginal exclusions. The total GSP trade in 1983 was $10.9 billion, so the 30 per cent cap means that had the waiver authority been in effect in

1984, the President could have granted waivers worth up to $3.27 billion. This is about $2.37 billion shy of what he would have needed in order to grant waivers for all excluded products. If, however, these waivers were granted in an optimal distribution (that is, one in which waivers were granted to the greatest number of products while still staying within the 30 per cent limit), then all but eleven of the 235 products excluded by the CNC could have been restored.

[24] The Trade and Tariff Act of 1984 loosely defines "internationally recognized workers rights" to include (1) the right of association, (2) the right to organize and bargain collectively, (3) the prohibition on the use of any form of forced or compulsory labor, (4) a minimum age for the employment of children, and (5) acceptable conditions of work with respect to minimum wages, hours of work, and occupational safety and health. These criteria will be further defined in regulations that will be drafted through inter-agency consultations. The intellectual property rights covered in the designation criteria are patents, trademarks, and copyrights. This criterion was added out of concern that some beneficiary countries permit their nationals to engage in pirating, counterfeiting, and other illegal practices. The "unreasonable export practices" criterion is not defined in the legislation, but the legislative history of the Act indicates that this refers to copper exports from Chile and other producers.

[25] Due to statistical discrepancies, there are several categories of textiles and apparel that are eligible under the GSP but that were inadvertently excluded from the CBI.

[26] Lavonne Trueblood, "Caribbean Basin Initiative—Trade Results for the First Six Months," *International Economic Review* (Washington, D.C.: International Trade Commission, September 1984), p. 8.

[27] A. W. Clausen, President, World Bank, "The World Bank in Mexico: A Continuing Partnership," Remarks before the U.S.-Mexico Chamber of Commerce, Washingon, D.C., October 4, 1984.

Chapter 4

U.S. Foreign Aid in the 1980s: Reordering Priorities

John W. Sewell and Christine E. Contee

The last four years have been a time of considerable ferment in the U.S. aid program. Four major Executive Branch commissions have been appointed to examine various aspects of U.S. aid. Three major regional initiatives have been proposed. U.S. contributions to multilateral institutions have been a topic of considerable debate. And a new set of policy guidelines for U.S. development assistance has been superimposed over the existing aid legislation. Yet none of the recent initiatives or discussions has succeeded in creating a coherent set of foreign aid objectives capable of generating legislative and public support.

U.S. foreign aid[1] has always been used to achieve a broad range of often conflicting goals: meeting the emergency needs of the world's poorest people, satisfying U.S. strategic and political interests, fostering long-term development in the Third World, and expanding U.S. commerce. The multiplicity of goals has been the price paid for political support of the total aid program. There is no agreement between Congress and the Executive Branch—and certainly not a broad public consensus—on the overall purpose of the program, or even on the preferred pattern of development that the United States should support. In recent years, contradictory pulls on the U.S. aid program have led to frequent political stalemate, with the repeated failure of Congress and the Administration to agree on programs and with *ad hoc* funding of aid through the use of continuing resolutions instead of new legislation.

Current trends in the U.S. aid program raise serious questions about the continued feasibility of addressing such a wide range of divergent interests in one program. The primary goal of U.S. development assistance has been defined by Congress as the alleviation of the worst aspects of poverty affecting the world's poor majority. The Reagan Administration's policies have generally downplayed this objective. A strong security thrust now characterizes the aid program, and there have been significant shifts in both program philosophy and implementation. Bilateral economic aid has become increasingly oriented toward short-term security and political interests while both poverty alleviation and longer-run political or economic interests receive greatly reduced priority.[2] Although these changes have, in effect, contributed some measure of coherence to the program, inasmuch as they all point to a greater effort to achieve perceived U.S. strategic and political aims in the developing countries, they are detrimental to other objectives of the program, and they have generated considerable controversy among the traditional aid constituencies.

The enormous increase in security aid designed to meet U.S. short-term strategic and political concerns is making it increasingly difficult to combine these programs in the same legislation with programs designed to improve human well-being and to further U.S. commercial interests; different countries demand priority for one or the other of these objectives, and budgetary stringency forces competition for resources between them.

The premise of this chapter is that it is nevertheless possible to reconcile these objectives and the tools to achieve them provided that debate on current and future aid policies takes into account the changes that have taken place in U.S.-Third World relations. First, in the last three decades, developing countries have emerged as important participants in the international economy, particularly in terms of trade and finance. Today these countries are major markets for U.S. exports, important suppliers of an increasingly sophisticated range of relatively low-cost goods, major customers (and profit centers) for U.S. banks, and the locus of a considerable amount of American private investment. Renewed growth in the developing countries is, moreover, one requirement for a full, sustained U.S. recovery.[3] Second, perceptions of a "Soviet threat" to the United States tend to be exaggerated in many areas of the developing world. Although instability and civil strife in the Third World sometimes offer the Soviet Union the opportunity to increase its influence, they are frequently due to indigenous causes and may be an inevitable part of the development process. This is particularly true given the current economic recession in the Third World, which makes it increasingly difficult for leaders to meet the needs and demands of their people. Finally, where the threat is real, U.S. military programs often are only one possible policy response among many. In contrast to the Soviet Union, which concentrates its assistance programs on military aid, the United States, like other industrialized countries, offers the Third World a great deal in trade and investment as well as development assistance. The real strengths of the United States lie in its economic power, in the desire of developing countries to attract American investment, finance, and technology; and in its democratic traditions.

This chapter analyzes U.S. aid policies over the last four years and makes some recommendations for policy change. The discussion focuses on bilateral development assistance, the Economic Support Fund (ESF), and U.S. support of the multilateral development banks.[4] Military assistance is here of concern only to the extent that it forces budgetary trade-offs within the total aid program.

The Current Program

The Reagan Administration entered office in 1981 with strong views both on the changes needed in American foreign policy to restore U.S. primacy and ensure American security and on the set of economic policies needed to lower inflation and restore economic growth. As reflected in the Administration's prescriptions for development cooperation with the Third World, these views have resulted in policies that represent a marked shift from U.S. aid programs developed over the last decade under both Democratic and Republican leadership.

Security Assistance

The centerpiece of the Reagan Administration's foreign policy is the restoration of U.S. global power vis-à-vis the Soviet Union. This emphasis on a single, over-arching theme has had a detrimental effect on U.S. development cooperation,[5] overshadowing the country's interest in fostering equitable economic and social development. In the 1970s, it was widely believed that equitable development was in the long-term U.S. interest, not only on humanitarian or commercial grounds, but because inequity and poverty contributed to political instability and regional tensions. Now the overriding concern is Soviet intervention or influence, which is perceived to be the major cause of Third World unrest. The East-West emphasis of U.S. foreign policy has also relegated other American interests in Third World development—such as trade and financial linkages—to a distant second place.

The priority accorded to security is apparent in the emphasis given to particular programs, regions, and countries. Military aid is favored over economic aid. Within the bilateral program, security-oriented economic aid is preferred over development assistance. And bilateral programs are considered more useful than multilateral contributions. Assistance is also heavily concentrated in countries where U.S. politi-

Table 1. Changes in the Regional Emphasis of U.S. Bilateral Aid
($ millions current)

Region	Development Assistance[a]			Security Assistance[b]		
	1977-1980 Average	1983	Percentage Change	1977-1980 Average	1983	Percentage Change
Sub-Saharan Africa	397.0	518.4	+ 31%	137.8	402.9	+ 192%
Middle East and N. Africa[c]	117.3	141.5	+ 21	602.9	1,147.1	+ 90
Israel and Egypt	193.0	255.1	+ 32	3685.4	4,561.9	+ 2.4
East Asia	395.2	237.3	− 40	364.1	422.5	+ 16
South Asia	527.5	559.4	+ 6	1.0	461.3	+4,603
South America	151.0	194.7	+ 29	34.5	10.2	− 70
Central America[d]	232.5	417.8	+ 80	21.7	639.1	+2,845
Other	56.8	38.0	− 33	450.5	827.1	+ 84

[a] Development assistance includes bilateral development assistance, P.L. 480, and other bilateral development programs.
[b] Security assistance includes all military assistance programs and the Economic Support Fund. Inter-regional programs are excluded.
[c] Excludes Israel and Egypt.
[d] Includes Central America, the Caribbean, and Mexico.
  Source: Agency for International Development, *U.S. Overseas Loans and Grants,* various issues.

cal and strategic interests are perceived to be threatened by the Soviet Union or its proxies (Table 1).

Total U.S. foreign aid grew from $10,600 million to $19,200 million between 1981 and 1985 (Table 2). But this increase was not evenly shared among programs. Assistance related to security concerns grew from 55 per cent of total aid in FY1981 to 67 per cent in FY1985, while the share of development assistance in total aid dropped from 45 per cent to 33 per cent. As reflected in the budget submitted to Congress in February 1985, the Administration apparently plans to continue this security-oriented trend.[6] If this budget is approved, security assistance will comprise 72 per cent of total U.S. aid by FY1988.

From FY1981 to FY1985, the Economic Support Fund alone grew by $1,700 million. Although the Foreign Assistance Act requires that the ESF be used in a manner that is consistent with development "to the maximum extent feasible," it is first and foremost a tool to address U.S. strategic and political objectives.

Table 2. The Foreign Aid Balance,[a] 1981-85 ($ millions current and percentages)

Account	FY1981	FY1982	FY1983	FY1984	FY1985
Security Assistance					
	($ millions and percentages)				
Amount	5,800	7,200	8,500	9,000	12,900
Percentage of total assistance	54.7%	58.5%	62.0%	61.6%	67.2%
Military[b]	3,700	4,300	5,500	5,600	9,100
Economic Support Fund	2,100	2,900	3,000	3,400	3,800
Development Assistance					
Amount	4,800	5,100	5,200	5,600	6,300
Percentage of total assistance	45.3%	41.5%	38.0%	38.4%	32.8%
Multilateral	1,300	1,500	1,800	1,600	1,900
Bilateral	2,300	2,600	2,400	2,500	2,900
P.L. 480 (Food for Peace)	1,200	1,000	1,000	1,400	1,500
Total Foreign Aid	**10,600**	**12,300**	**13,700**	**14,600**	**19,200**

[a] Budget authority. Figures for FY1981-FY1984 are actual; figures for FY1985 are estimates.
[b] Includes MAP, PKO, IMET, anti-terrorism assistance, and on- and off-budget FMS.
  Sources: Agency for International Development, "Summary Tables: FY1985" (Washington, D.C.: A.I.D., 1984; Executive Office of the President, *Budget of the United States Government* (Washington, D.C.: Office of Management and Budget, various issues).

The rapid growth in ESF levels is due largely to the increased emphasis on security and political issues. This trend began with the Camp David accords and was spurred by the Soviet invasion of Afghanistan and by the Iranian revolution. Most recently, ESF has been used in attempts to bolster stability in Central America, the Caribbean, and Southern Africa, and to ensure access to the Indian Ocean and the Persian Gulf region.

Beyond the ideological bent of U.S. policy makers, the growth in ESF also is a result of the harsh international economic environment of the late 1970s and the 1980s. The ESF program provides both direct cash transfers to developing-country agencies and financing of U.S. exports to developing countries through the Commodity Import Program. Thus ESF is one of the two major bilateral aid tools (Food for Peace, or P.L. 480, is the other) through which the United States provides balance-of-payments support to developing countries.

The resurgence of perceived security interests in the Third World, coupled with the balance-of-payments problems of developing countries, has also led to an increase in the number of countries receiving ESF. In FY1981, twenty-one countries received ESF funds; by FY1985, thirty-nine states will participate in the program.[7]

What does this growth in ESF mean for the aid program? Some effects of the expansion seem positive. First, while most ESF is allocated to the more advanced developing countries, the expansion of the total aid 'pie' is incrementally advantageous to some of the poorer countries. In FY1985, some $259 million in ESF was allocated to countries with per capita incomes below $419.[8] And about 40 per cent of ESF (25 per cent if funds earmarked for Israel are included)[9] is used to finance projects, some of which are largely indistinguishable from development assistance projects in design and implementation. Thus the growth in ESF has expanded the resources available for development-oriented projects (although it is important to note that development assistance itself has actually declined slightly in real terms since 1981).

Some A.I.D. missions actually prefer working with ESF because it is easier to use than development assistance. Over the years, a variety of implementation regulations have been applied to development assistance; ESF, in contrast, is relatively free of such restrictions. Finally, some observers claim that ESF "protects" development assistance. Without a separate fund for politically oriented aid, it is argued, support for high aid levels would not be forthcoming and scarce development assistance would be further diverted from long-term development projects to meet short-term U.S. political objectives.

Despite these possibly positive aspects, using ESF in lieu of development assistance presents some serious problems. The first of these is country allocation of the funds. The $259 million allocated to low-income countries in FY1985 represents only 7 per cent of ESF. In contrast, five middle-income countries are slated to receive 59 per cent of that year's ESF: Oman (per capita GNP, $6,090), Spain (per capita GNP, $5,430), Israel (per capita GNP, $5,090), Turkey (per capita GNP, $1,370), and Egypt (per capita GNP, $690).[10] Since all these countries are of strategic interest to the United States, it is perhaps understandable that they receive the bulk of economic security aid; yet since ESF now accounts for 45 per cent of total bilateral economic assistance—which comprises ESF, development assistance, and Food for Peace—the result is to shift the whole program away from the poorer countries and toward the more advanced nations of the Third World (Table 3). This concentration of aid is not a new development. But it remains an issue of concern to those who, in keeping with the Foreign Assistance Act, view the improvement of the well-being of the majority in the

Table 3. U.S. Bilateral Aid, by Income Group and Region,[a] FY1983

	Countries In Category	Countries Receiving Aid[b]	Total Aid	Aid Per Capita[c]
			($ millions)	($)
Low-Income Countries	**40**	**36**	**1,171.6**	**.50**
Africa	27	27	344.2	1.55
Asia	12	8	781.2	.37
Latin America	1	1	46.2	7.35
Lower-Middle-Income Countries	**40**	**24**	**2,182.7**	**4.05**
Africa[d]	16	14	1,494.2	6.50
Asia	7	4	272.2	1.00
Latin America	11	4	414.7	13.94
Oceania	5	2	1.6	.28
Europe	1	0	0	0
Upper-Middle-Income Countries	**39**	**24**	**982.5**	**1.61**
Africa	7	4	28.1	.45
Asia	10	3	73.1	.55
Latin America	18	15	575.3	1.72
Oceania	1	0	0	0
Europe	3	2	306.0	3.81
High-Income Countries	**23**	**5**	**816.7**	**11.65**
Africa	3	1	1.5	.29
Asia[e]	9	2	800.1	34.36
Latin America	6	1	.1	.01
Oceania	2	0	0	0
Europe	3	1	15.0	.63
Total	**142**	**89**	**5,153.5**	**1.45**

[a] Developing countries, regions, and income group as defined by ODC plus Israel (see Statistical Annexes, Table E-1).
[b] Aid includes bilateral development assistance, P.L.-480, and the Economic Support Fund. Regional bilateral programs are not included.
[c] Indicates U.S. aid per capita for all countries in column 1.
[d] If Egypt is excluded, lower middle-income Africa receives $2.65 aid per capita.
[e] Includes Israel.

Source: Agency for International Development, *U.S. Overseas Loans & Grants*, July 1, 1945-September 30, 1983 (Washington, D.C.: 1984).

poorest countries as the major objective of both development and the aid program.

The second problem posed by emphasizing ESF relates to how monies are spent. In many cases, the level of annual funding is determined at the political level, and the recipient country may come to expect a certain level of funding each year. There are no criteria for phasing out ESF recipients. And because ESF is generally offered in return for the political *quid pro quo*, projects using these funds are often designed to be immediately visible and quickly disbursable. In Egypt, many problems have arisen as A.I.D. has tried to spend enormous sums of money each year in project form. In the Philippines, almost 65 per cent of ESF allotted under the base-rights agreement is spent around the bases, often on projects that can be completed rapidly and that are easily identifiable as U.S. supported.[11] Omani officials chose to have their ESF funds expended on projects because they wanted to provide tangible evidence of the U.S.-Omani relationship.[12] These types of projects are not necessarily designed or implemented in any relation to the needs of the poor.[13]

Approximately 60 per cent of ESF (75 per cent if Israel is included) is delivered through cash transfers or the Commodity Import Program.[14] This kind of assistance also does not necessarily benefit the poor. While ESF cannot be used for military purposes, it does free up domestic resources, possibly for military use. Cash transfers and CIP may also be used to import goods—whether luxury items or industrial equipment—that do not directly or even indirectly benefit the poor.

In addition, most of this type of ESF funding is, at least in theory, meant to foster a policy dialogue between the United States and the recipient country and to support policy reforms. As will be discussed below, A.I.D. has neither the scale of financial resources nor the number of appropriately trained personnel necessary to carry out policy dialogues, and these problems are exacerbated when ESF funding is the available tool. First, the political objectives of ESF funding prevent A.I.D. from pressing too hard for development objectives for fear that this might cause political friction. (For example, a General Accounting Office study of the aid program in Jamaica concluded that the United States had not pressed for policy reforms in some instances "because Jamaican resistance was strong and for political reasons the State Department did not want to require the reforms even though they would enhance development."[15] This problem also appears to have arisen in Egypt, where the attempt to shoehorn large amounts of money each year into development projects has led to growing U.S.-Egyptian political friction.) Moreover, because country allocations are made on political grounds, funds cannot be switched by A.I.D. from one country to another where policy change may be more promising— although occasionally A.I.D. can hold back funds to encourage policy change (as was done with programs in Kenya and Zaire). Paradoxically, it is precisely in those countries where U.S. aid looms large that the ability to promote policy change is limited simply because the overriding goal is political or strategic rather than economic.

Unfortunately there have been few solid assessments of whether these programs even meet their purported strategic and political goals.[16] (This contrasts sharply with development aid programs, which have been exhaustively evaluated by A.I.D., by Congress, and by outside specialists.) Judgments of results are relatively clear where security aid is direct compensation for base rights or some other facility (although observers question, for example, whether the price paid for base-rights in the Philippines is not inflated); they are far less clear when the desired policy outcome is less concrete.

The United States will continue to have a range of foreign policy interests in the developing world, including security interests, that require financial support of particular countries and regimes. That being said, however, the current foreign aid program's emphasis on security and short-term political purposes at the expense of longer-term economic and development purposes raises serious questions about the balance of objectives.

The United States should be far more selective in providing financial support for particular regimes on political grounds. Even where such support is essential, it should not be considered a substitute for financing longer-term economic and development efforts. And in all cases, the political goals must be more clearly defined. Where ESF is used to compensate for U.S. military facilities, for example, it would be better to transfer these programs to the defense budget, where priorities among programs can be decided on the basis of their contribution to national security.

Setting aside security-related funds for a limited number of clearly justified country programs might also remove some of the ambiguities in the current program that serve to undercut the expected political and development returns. As already noted, the attempt to impose development performance criteria on funds allocated for political ends can make the political relationship more difficult. Conversely, the existence of American political goals often makes economic and development aims a secondary priority for the United States in some countries. It is probably wiser to establish a political aid program limited to a few carefully selected countries. Some aid observers may be disturbed by the idea of losing whatever development benefits security assistance does provide; however, the trade-off between political and developmental impact is not an issue that can be avoided.

Using political aid more selectively might also make funds available for non-project development assistance. Currently most development assistance is provided in the form of projects. Yet both project and non-project lending is needed, depending on particular country circumstances. Moreover, the need for non-project assistance will grow as developing countries work their way out of the current debt crisis. Especially in smaller countries, even small amounts of balance-of-payments support can be very beneficial. A development program that has the authority to provide both project and non-project funds to countries on the basis of their particular development situation would be far preferable to one that continues to rely heavily on a tool that is allocated largely on the basis of political aims.

Bilateral Development Assistance and the "Four Pillars"

While the overall security orientation of the program is largely a result of the Administration's ideological proclivities, the currently preferred strategy for approaching economic development is in part a reaction to perceived shortcomings of development assistance in the 1970s. In the late 1960s and early 1970s, U.S. foreign aid was the target of heavy criticism by both the public and policy makers. The program was closely associated with U.S. involvement in the Vietnam war and thus became equated with American military intervention in the Third World. At the same time, those concerned about the impact of U.S. aid on human well-being in developing countries began to attack the program as ineffective. In the 1950s and 1960s, it was widely believed that the benefits of economic growth would automatically, if gradually, flow to the majority of the people, and development efforts therefore focused on stimulating growth. With a few exceptions, however, this theory, later labeled "trickle-down," proved to be wrong—at least within any politically relevant timeframe; growth in many countries was impressive, but its impact on the poor majority was often marginal.

Faced with growing opposition to the foreign aid program, Congress rewrote the U.S. aid legislation. The Foreign Assistance Act of 1973 established the current goals for U.S. bilateral development assistance: a) alleviation of the worst physical manifestations of poverty among the world's poor majority; b) promotion of conditions enabling developing countries to achieve self-sustaining economic growth with an equitable distribution of benefits; c) encouragement of development processes in which individual civil and economic rights are respected and enhanced; and d) integration of the developing countries into an open and equitable international system. This "New Directions" focus called for targeted, long-term development assistance, primarily through projects carried out at the local level, to improve the lot of the poor majority.

The emphasis on poverty-oriented development resulted in a host of important changes aimed at enabling poor people within developing countries to meet at least the basic requirements for human life and dignity through a combination of economic growth and programs designed to deliver social services by direct means. More effort was directed toward the agricultural sector, the linchpin of most developing economies as well as the sector in which the poor are concentrated. In many countries, programs in health and education produced dramatic results. In the course of the 1970s, however, the international donor community came to realize that—just as economic growth alone would not alleviate poverty in many instances—local-level projects could not be self-sustaining in the midst of economic recession and in the absence of strong indigenous institutions and recipient-country economic policies conducive to growth and efficiency.

The Reagan Administration did not seek to change the basic legislation governing U.S. bilateral aid programs. Instead, it added an overlay to the existing programs in an effort to correct perceived problems. Described by A.I.D. Administrator M. Peter McPherson as program instruments, the new 'four pillars' include (1) policy dialogue, (2) private sector initiatives, (3) technology transfer, and (4) institution-building. Unfortunately, it is difficult to analyze the full budgetary impact of these four instruments on A.I.D.'s activities, since the agency does not keep track of projects or expenditures by these categories.

Two of the policy instruments—institution-building and technology transfer—are relatively non-controversial programs that usefully re-emphasize A.I.D. activities of the 1960s. A.I.D.'s institution-building focus responds to the need for strong, efficient, indigenous institutions and managers to plan and implement self-sustaining development programs. A.I.D. policy has stressed the need to upgrade a variety of local institutions, such as schools, voluntary organizations, agricultural extension services, cooperatives, agricultural research centers, training institutes, and health care delivery systems. The emphasis on technology transfer strives to foster "an indigenous capacity to adapt, create, and apply a continuing stream of usable technologies."[17] A.I.D. currently spends approximately $250 million a year on research activities. Agricultural research is heavily concentrated on pest and disease control, techniques of cultivation, and the development of hybrid crop varieties; in the health field, A.I.D. is currently placing a great deal of emphasis on developing a malaria vaccine and on expanding the use of oral rehydration therapy—a simple and inexpensive technology that could dramatically reduce infant mortality in the developing world. The United States has a long-standing comparative advantage in research and technology, and several of A.I.D.'s activities show promise of having a major impact on the world's poorest people.

The other two instruments are more controversial and warrant closer examination. The emphasis on 'policy dialogue' is based on the generally accepted view that the domestic economic policies of developing countries are the prime determinant of development progress; in the absence of good policies, economic growth and efforts to improve human well-being cannot be fostered efficiently. In the words of A.I.D.'s FY1985 presentation to Congress, "policy dialogue with recipient governments can initiate needed reforms, and our assistance can smooth the path of such reforms in some countries."[18] Emphasis on policy dialogue is not new to A.I.D.; prior to the New Directions legislation, the agency was involved in program lending for *sectoral* policy reforms. Neither is the current emphasis on policy dialogue unique to the U.S. aid program. Most major bilateral and multilateral donors are urging similar changes in response to the lessons of the 1970s.

It is far from clear, however, that A.I.D. can play a useful role in *macro-economic* policy reform. The amount of U.S. aid to most countries is no longer significant enough to make recipient governments change established macro-economic policies, particularly if such changes involve significant economic or political costs. For example, in 1970 the United States provided approximately 54 per cent of India's total official development assistance; in 1980, only 11 per cent of India's aid came from the United States. Aid that carries with it conditions considered too onerous can be rejected without too high a cost.

It is almost impossible to separate the instruments of ESF funding and macro-economic policy dialogue, since ESF is one of A.I.D.'s key tools for attempting to facilitate and encourage policy change. Yet, as indicated earlier, it is difficult if not impossible for A.I.D. to press hard for reforms when a recipient country knows that, for political reasons, the United States is highly unlikely to exercise the ultimate condition of assistance withdrawal. In addition, aid funds that are not obligated in the year they are appropriated must be returned to the U.S. Treasury. The fact that recipient countries are well aware of this need to commit funds further weakens A.I.D.'s leverage.

Nor is A.I.D. well equipped to participate in discussions of macro-economic reforms—either in Washington or in its field missions. Although its large and experienced field organization does provide an opportunity rare among bilateral donors for closer dialogue on program and sectoral policy matters with the developing countries (having focused during the 1970s on project and key sectoral aid), the agency is insufficiently staffed with economists to provide the data and analyses for sophisticated macro-economic policy discussions. More economists are being recruited by A.I.D., but such staffing changes take time.

This is not to argue that A.I.D. has no role to play in urging policy reform. First, policy dialogue has had some useful effects with respect to micro-economic or sectoral policy reforms. For example, A.I.D has successfully worked in Senegal to change policies toward user fees in health-care projects, lowering the recurrent costs of primary health care. In Bangladesh, the agency played a significant role in the phased elimination of fertilizer subsidies and the privatization of the marketing system—reforms that have resulted in record fertilizer distribution. Such reforms are also important building blocks in the direction of encouraging broader, macro-economic changes. Second, A.I.D.'s policy dialogue efforts have had an influence on the general discussion of development strategies and have therefore reinforced the messages being conveyed by the World Bank and the International Monetary Fund.[19] Coordination by the United States, the world's single largest bilateral donor, with multilateral organizations and other donors on the policy matters of specific countries is crucial. However, the multilateral agencies are better suited than A.I.D. to take the lead in macro-economic dialogue, and A.I.D. would do better to work where possible on micro-economic or sectoral reforms.

The emphasis on private-sector initiatives, like that on policy dialogue, is not a new element in U.S. aid programs; all legislation since the program's inception has sought to involve the private sector. While A.I.D.'s private-sector efforts diminished during the 1970s, due to the emphasis on projects targeted directly at the poor, the agency's focus on small farmers remained a constant theme throughout the 1970s.

The philosophy behind the re-emergence of interest in the private sector was perhaps best expressed by President Reagan himself when he stated, in an October 1981 speech in Philadelphia, that "free people build free markets that ignite dynamic development for everyone." The President's faith in the 'magic of the marketplace' gave rise to great concern about two issues: Is the emphasis on growth through the private sector a return to the "trickle down" theory of the 1950s and 1960s? and to what extent is A.I.D.'s program to be devoted to promoting American commercial interests?

The emphasis on economic growth was—and, given recent global economic conditions continues to be—necessary. In the aftermath of the oil price increase of 1979, growth dropped precipitously in almost all developing countries. Adverse economic conditions presented major problems to donor and recipient countries attempting to implement poverty-oriented projects in the late 1970s and early 1980s. Developing countries were unable to maintain completed projects (such as roads or water and sewage systems), to meet recurrent costs in schools and health care, or to provide counterpart funding requirements for new projects. As a result, many donors, national and international, have begun to focus on projects that generate both local and foreign currency quickly. However, the experience of the 1960s demonstrated that economic growth does not necessarily assure, as the President has said, "development for everyone." Nor is it entirely clear that the private sector in developing countries can single-handedly generate equitable growth. Shortages of capital and human resources, as well as market imperfections, often require the public sector to play a more active role.[20] The key issue is the proper mix of the two.

Still, there is not necessarily a conflict between poverty-oriented development and projects focusing on the indigenous private sector. Private enterprises often can help meet basic needs in ways that over-extended public sectors cannot. For example, much of the private sector in developing countries consists of small-scale farmers or entrepreneurs who are themselves part of the poor majority. One area in which A.I.D. has apparently experienced considerable success is in creating or expanding intermediate financial institutions; the programs that make credit available to previously excluded groups can inject much-needed capital into small-scale farms and private enterprises. In the family planning field, to cite another of type example, A.I.D. efforts to foster private marketing of contraceptives in Bangladesh have widened their distribution and stabilized their prices.

To direct and focus the private-sector initiative, A.I.D. created the Bureau for Private Enterprise (PRE). While the PRE budget has grown from $7.5 million to $30.0 million in the last four years, it still receives only about 1 per cent of A.I.D.'s budget. The impact of the initiative extends beyond the PRE, however. In addition, A.I.D.'s regional bureaus programmed $200 million in 1984 for private-sector projects.

One aspect of the private-sector initiative that differs from past A.I.D. experiences is the current attempt to evaluate ways in which private sector involvement can be useful in all kinds of development projects. An A.I.D. policy paper on health assistance[21] illustrates how emphasis on the private sector can be integrated into the functional accounts: Health care practitioners, such as midwives and pharmacists, can be supported by fostering private distribution channels for drugs and medicines, by encouraging local drug manufacturers to produce generic drugs (which cost less than imported ones), and by instituting private contributions and user fees for health services.

It is not yet possible to determine who the ultimate beneficiaries of the private-sector projects will be. The projects are limited in number and are only in the early stages of implementation. It is important to recognize, however, that this approach carries with it the danger that project beneficiaries may turn out to be largely the better-off segments of populations in developing countries. This could happen if private-sector targeting were to divert resources away from necessary public-sector projects such as health care, rural roads, or primary schools. Similarly, the desire to focus on the commercial private sector—to stimulate jobs and exports—may result in a neglect of the non-commercial private sector. As described by A.I.D., the private-sector initiative does not seem to run counter to the main purposes of the U.S. bilateral assistance program's mandate. But those concerned with ensuring the use of U.S. aid for fulfilling the legislative mandate need to monitor trends within the program.

It should also be noted that the private-sector initiative and the emphasis on policy dialogue are integrally related. The agency's policy paper on private enterprise development states that "the primary emphasis of A.I.D.'s efforts to promote private enterprise development will be to encourage policy reform and to improve the ways markets function."[22] A good deal of effort has been focused on the importance of agricultural pricing, the devaluation of foreign exchange, the creation of credit institutions, the removal of food subsidies, and a re-evaluation of private investment regulations. Although much of this emphasis on greater reliance on market forces is useful, it raises once again the issue of A.I.D.'s role in macro-economic policy reform.

A second major concern about the renewed stress on private sector initiatives is that it may focus on the promotion of U.S. commercial interests in the Third World rather than on development needs. Perhaps the most disturbing development in this area is the recent appearance in the U.S. aid program of mixed credits—so called because concessional assistance is mixed with commercial financing to lower the overall interest rate for U.S. exports. The increased use of such mixed credits by European and Japanese competitors in recent years has spurred American business to pressure the U.S. government follow suit. In 1983, Congress passed the Trade and Development Enhancement Act, which requires A.I.D. to draw on funds allocated for the Commodity Import Program to finance mixed credits under certain conditions and in cooperation with the Export-Import Bank. The first U.S. mixed credit—beyond an experimental program in Egypt—was recently approved.[23]

The United States has traditionally opposed mixed credits because they distort trade by encouraging countries to purchase goods they would not choose without the concessional element. A.I.D. Administrator McPherson has fought hard against mixed credits on the grounds that they divert scarce development aid and use it for the commercial purpose of stimulating exports. The introduction of mixed credits into the program could also have a negative effect on the ability of A.I.D. to undertake its stated aim of policy dialogue. Like economic support (ESF) funds, mixed credits obfuscate the objectives of aid; in this case, the purchase of American goods becomes the requirement for receiving assistance. The Administration maintains that the use of mixed credits is a defensive measure and that the United States will resort to them no longer than other industrial-country governments. But even a defensive program will require a considerable amount of money. The United Kingdom, for example, has estimated that, over the next two to three years, its mixed credits program could cost $1 billion.[24] From what sources can such amounts be drawn in the United States? Although there is considerable support within the business community and in Congress to place the administration of mixed credits (should their volume increase further) under the jurisdiction of the Export-Import Bank, the 1983 Act clearly expresses a willingness to use aid for commercial purposes.

U.S. Multilateral Assistance

The Reagan Administration entered office suspicious of multilateral institutions. Many political appointees, particularly in the Department of the Treasury, believed that the multilateral development banks tend to favor government solutions to development problems over reliance on market forces or the private sector. This belief persists, despite the findings of a 1981 Treasury Department study that few projects undertaken by multilateral institutions could be seen as displacing the private sector and that, in most instances, the multilaterals have been strong proponents of market-oriented development.[25]

The Administration's emphasis on security also caused it to cast a baleful eye on multilateral organizations. Conservatives, arguing that the World Bank has grown too powerful and does not sufficiently promote U.S. political interests, point to the number of times that U.S. votes against proposed World Bank projects have been overriden in recent years.[26] This type of criticism entirely overlooks the fact that the de-politicization of aid is one of the strongpoints of institutions like the World Bank. As the above-mentioned 1981 Treasury Department study concluded, "U.S. bilateral and multilateral aid have different comparative advantages. . . . multilateral assistance primarily serves long-term U.S. interests, can be very cost-effective, and promotes a stable international economic environment through the encouragement of market-oriented policies."[27]

The Reagan Administration's stance has softened toward some of these institutions. The importance of the International Monetary Fund to global financial stability became apparent to the Administration with the onset of the debt crisis in 1982, and it subsequently pressed for an increase in the IMF's resources (although the funds were approved in Congress only with considerable difficulty). The Administration has also favored general capital increases for some of the smaller multilateral institutions, such as the Inter-American Development Bank. It has, however, continued to oppose proposals for greater expansion of the World Bank's lending capacity.

The effects of the Administration's attitude have been most marked in the case of the World Bank's International Development Association (IDA), which provides long-term concessional loans to the poorest countries. The sixth 'replenishment' (the three-year pledge of funds from Bank member governments) totaled $12 billion. Most major donor countries agreed that the seventh replenishment of IDA should provide resources at a level at least equal in real terms—and preferably somewhat higher—than that of the last replenishment. In a decision reportedly made by the President himself, however, the Administration agreed upon an annual U.S. contribution of $750 million a year, or $2.25 billion over three years. Under the complex formula governing contributions, this effectively held the total capitalization of IDA-VII at $9 billion, representing a 40-per cent cut in real terms, since other industrial-country donors were unwilling to raise their contributions without a corresponding U.S. increase.

The Administration's opposition to increased resources for IDA-VII certainly is not in keeping with its expressed objective of assisting the poorer countries. A lower level for IDA effectively means a loss of some $3 billion in development resources for the world's low-income countries. Diminished support for IDA, and for the multilateral development institutions in general, is also inconsistent with the Administration's current concern with policy change and increasing the role of the private sector. The multilateral institutions, particularly the World Bank, have played a central role in advising and assisting developing-country governments through the process of changing policies to give greater emphasis to efficiency and growth. Over the last two decades, these institutions have emerged as the pre-eminent development institutions, outweighing individual bilateral programs in terms of resources and influence on developing-country policies. Their 'clout' stems not only from their available funds, but also from the caliber of their staffs and the widespread perceptions that multilateral institutions are much less politically motivated than bilateral agencies.

In many countries, A.I.D. has worked closely with the World Bank to support policy changes. Current U.S. policy, however, has sought to diminish the Bank's role and influence. The result has been to limit the utility of an institution that has a major impact on, and provides support for policy changes by, developing countries. The seriousness attached by the Administration to policy changes is therefore undercut by the greater priority awarded to accomplishing such changes bilaterally rather than multilaterally.

Multilateral organizations also have a crucial role to play in improving coordination among the growing number of bilateral and multilateral donors. Three decades ago the United States was practically the only major provider of development assistance; the other OECD countries were not yet in the business, and the multilateral development institutions were very small. Today, some forty official donors (not counting the programs of the centrally planned economies) are active in the developing world: seventeen OECD-country bilateral agencies; ten Arab or OPEC development funds; several OPEC and other governments; and the multilateral aid agencies. In addition, there are some 150 private voluntary organizations in the United States alone. Yet at the moment, very little operational coordination is taking place among either donors or recipients, and no serious attempts are being made to simplify and standardize donor procedures. The importance of these issues is rapidly increasing, particularly in relation to the Sub-Saharan countries, where the number of donors often overwhelms seriously understaffed governments.[28]

A Program for the Future

If the developing countries as a group are to regain long-term economic and social progress, two conditions must be met: The countries themselves must choose internal economic policies that will support their own goals for growth with equity, and their efforts must be supported by industrial countries. This support will have to include forms different from those of the past in trade, finance, and technology; foreign aid, however, will continue to be an important component, and its uses and levels in the future must be rigorously reassessed by the Executive Branch and by Congress.

Reaffirming the Mandate

The current mandate of the U.S. aid program—"to help the poor majority of people within developing countries to participate in a process of equitable growth"—must be reaffirmed. The sum effect of the Reagan Administration's aid policies, regardless of their intent, has been to undermine this goal. The country allocation of aid funds has been dominated by security concerns. The heavy focus on aid to the middle-income countries continues. And support for multilateral development institutions, particularly for the World Bank, has diminished considerably. These trends are especially disturbing in light of the recent global recession, which has forced most developing-country governments to adopt painful austerity policies; the impact of these policies, in turn, is an overall decline in the standard of living, with particularly grave effects on the poorer groups within those countries.[29]

The emphasis of U.S. aid must now begin to shift from the middle-income countries to where the need is greatest: to the low-income countries—and particularly to Sub-Saharan Africa. The dire condition of these countries is the greatest development challenge of our time. Long-term development prospects in these countries are not necessarily bleak, provided that both recipients and donors can reshape their policies; whatever approaches are tried, however, concessional assistance will continue to be necessary for investment in training and infrastructure-building—which are essential to the success of both official and private-sector-initiated development programs.

To a certain extent, the book is still open on the impact of A.I.D.'s current four-pillar approach to development and poverty alleviation. Any policy innovation takes at least two years to permeate the bureaucracy and foster change in program planning and implementation. Thus the Administration's policy changes are only now beginning to be translated into actual projects within developing countries. (The same lag was evidenced in the implementation of the 1973 New Directions changes in the foreign aid program.) But there is a danger that the effort to tap the development potential of the private sector will lead to neglect of the poorest segments of the population or of necessary public-sector programs, and that over-estimation of A.I.D.'s capacity to influence and support policy reform will result in marginal long-term improvements.

The obvious need for economic growth and efficiency—even more crucial now, given the particularly adverse economic conditions facing most developing countries—must be reconciled with the long-standing goal of enabling the world's poor majority to obtain at least the most basic physical essentials. Economic growth, market forces, and private enterprise are not necessarily antithetical to the address of poverty. But the development goals of the 1970s, which emphasized meeting basic human needs, urgently need to be reaffirmed. It is also important to learn from the experience of the last decade, instead of dismissing it as the international equivalent of supposedly failed domestic welfare programs. The key issue is to meld the two, and that task remains to be done.

U.S. Support for the Multilateral Development Banks

The international financial institutions—particularly the World Bank and the International Monetary Fund—all have a crucial role to play in responding to the needs of the developing countries. They are essential providers of capital for the middle-income countries, of concessional resources for the poorer countries, and of much-needed advice on overall policy changes and specific sector programs to promote efficient growth and meet human needs. All current assessments, whether conducted by the U.S. government or by outside sources, give these institutions high marks for their programs and for their alignment with U.S. interests. The low priority they currently receive in U.S. policy needs to be reversed.

Program Lending Through Development Assistance

Aid programs also could be made far more effective if development assistance were more readily available in *program* rather than *project* form. Merging a portion of the economic support (ESF) fund with the development assistance account for program lending would give A.I.D. decision makers increased flexibility and resources. They would be able to choose a mix of program and project assistance that meets the needs of a particular developing country, rather than having to rely largely on ESF—allocated primarily on security grounds—to provide balance-of-payments support. Such a program would take full advantage of A.I.D.'s considerable experience, its large and knowledgeable staff, and its useful sectoral expertise on issues such as population growth and intermediate credit. In addition, it would provide additional financial and technical resources to allow A.I.D. to work more closely with the multilateral institutions to support policy reforms.

What Can the United States Afford?

Pressures to cut federal expenditures in the United States will be a fact of life in the years ahead. With a projected budget deficit of over $200 billion and a defense budget seemingly immune to all but minor cuts, locating resources to support development becomes politically very difficult. Therefore the key issue for those concerned about the U.S. foreign aid program is how to allocate very scarce resources—among programs, institutions, and countries—to make their use more congruent with the fundamental foreign policy objectives of the United States. At the same time, it should be recalled that foreign aid is such a relatively small fraction of the federal budget (less than 2 per cent in FY1985) that overall resource constraints are not a credible justification of the program's low level. If the political will existed, the aid budget could be raised significantly without doing any real violence to the deficit. The issue is not how much foreign aid the United States can afford, but how important it perceives it to be to U.S. and global interests.

The budget submitted to Congress in January 1985 shows expenditures in the foreign aid program rising from $14 billion in FY1984 to $18.7 billion in FY1985, and then declining to $14.4 billion by FY1988 (Table 4). However, neither the increases nor the subsequent declines

Table 4. Foreign Aid Budget Authority, FY1984–FY1988 ($ millions)

Foreign Aid	1984[a]	1985[b]	1986[b]	1987[b]	1988[b]
International security assistance					
Foreign military sales credit:					
On-budget under current law	1,315	4,940	5,655	5,779	5,901
Off-budget under current law	3,503	3,147	1,311	524	262
Military assistance	712	805	949	970	991
Economic Support Fund	3,389	3,841	2,824	2,883	2,941
Other:					
Existing law	110	214	108	110	112
Proposed legislation				145	278
Offsetting receipts	−86	−93	−99	−105	−161
Subtotal, international security assistance	8,943	12,854	10,748	10,306	10,324
Foreign economic and financial assistance					
Multilateral development banks	1,324	1,548	1,348	1,348	375
International organizations	315	359	196	200	204
Agency for International Development	2,013	2,286	2,113	2,133	2,171
Public Law 480 (food aid)	1,377	1,540	1,307	1,296	1,286
Peace Corps	117	128	125	128	132
Refugee assistance	336	350	338	340	334
Compact of Free Association (Micronesia)			299	146	148
Other	80	95	96	99	101
Offsetting receipts	−493	−459	−479	−604	−660
Subtotal, Foreign economic and financial assistance	5,069	5,847	5,343	5,085	4,093
Total, Foreign Aid	14,012	18,701	16,091	15,391	14,418

[a] Actual.   [b] Estimate.

Source: Executive Office of the President, *Budget of the United States Government: FY1986* (Washington, D.C.: Office of Management and Budget, 1985), pp. 5-18.

are shared equally across programs; 69 per cent of the FY1985 allocations are devoted to international security assistance. The budget indicates both security and economic assistance shrinking over the next three years, but with security aid declining 20 per cent (according to a budget which does not include any economic support funds for Israel after FY1988) while economic assistance drops 30 per cent. By FY1985, security assistance is to total 72 per cent of foreign aid funds.

Thus the important question is whether the priorities assigned to various programs grouped under the rubric of 'foreign aid' match U.S. interests in the Third World. In FY1985, for instance, some $7.5 billion of a $18.7-billion total in foreign aid will go for military assistance, rental of military bases, or transfers to countries with annual per capita incomes of $2,500 or more. In many cases these expenditures are justified on the ground that they add to U.S. military security, with little effort devoted to assessing their returns to either U.S. strategic or political interests. Policy makers need to seriously consider whether some portion of the amounts to be spent on security programs would not yield greater returns for the United States if they were instead expended on programs fostering long-term economic development. The budget as presented shows no U.S. contributions to the International Development Association, the Asian Development Fund, the African Development Bank, or the African Development Fund after existing commitments are fulfilled in FY1987.

The federal budget also indicates that in FY1985 the United States will receive some $550 million in repayments from past foreign economic and military assistance and sales. Until the mid-1970s, these funds were re-programmed for development purposes (with congressional approval), but now they are returned directly to the U.S. Treasury. In a period of scarce development assistance resources, restoring these repayments to A.I.D. is logical; the funds available were originally appropriated for development and their repayment should be used to continue to support the program. The funds available for re-programming could total over $820 million in FY1988—an amount that could, for example, raise the U.S. contribution to IDA-VII to an adequate level.

The United States can afford to increase its support for the long-term development of the Third World—a goal that is very much in its own interest. Moreover, based on the projections cited, the United States can afford a considerable *increase* in development support without materially affecting current budget levels. The real challenge is to reorder priorities to harmonize expenditures on foreign aid with the long-term interests of the United States and with Third World development.

Notes

[1] The term "foreign aid" is used here as it is in the federal budget. It includes, therefore, not only traditional bilateral and multilateral programs but also international security assistance and military aid, on one hand, and refugee and Peace Corps programs on the other. This definition was chosen because it includes a range of policy instruments and choices available to U.S. decision makers concerned about relations with the developing countries. The data used here should not be confused with that issued by the OECD. For the OECD definition of "official development assistance," see the Glossary of this volume, p. 00.

[2] Ironically, this conclusion is echoed by the Heritage Foundation's recent report, *Mandate for Leadership II*, which suggested, "If AID is to continue as a separate agency, its statutory authority, objectives, and focus should be changed to reflect the fact that much of its work is really security-related." Stuart M. Butler, Michael Sanera, and W. Bruce Weinrod, eds., *Mandate for Leadership II* (Washington, D.C.: 1985), p. 372.

[3] A study by the Organisation for Economic Co-operation and Development concluded that the forty richest developing countries had added as much to the increment in gross world product in the 1970s as did the United States or Japan and West Germany combined. *World Economic Interdependence and the Evolving North-South Relationship* (Paris: OECD, 1983).

[4] The P.L. 480 Program, popularly know as "Food for Peace," is not analyzed here; the problem and potential of using food aid either for political or development purposes is a complicated subject distinct from other U.S. aid programs and beyond the scope of this chapter. P.L. 480 is, however, included in the tables of this chapter.

[5] John P. Lewis, "Can We Escape the Path of Mutual Injury?" in John P. Lewis and Valeriana Kallab, eds., *U.S. Foreign Policy and the Third World: Agenda 1983* (New York: Praeger, for the Overseas Development Council, 1983), p. 20-21.

[6] See Table 4.

[7] Another factor contributing to the dispersion of ESF was a 1981 change in aid legislation that had previously prohibited the use of development assistance and ESF in the same countries.

[8] A.I.D., Section 653(a) Report, *"Program Allocations—FY1985"*, mimeographed, November 1984. Includes $200 million for Pakistan.

[9] 1979-1983 average.

[10] A.I.D., *Program Allocations*, op. cit.

[11] General Accounting Office, *Economic Support Funds in the Philippines* (Washington, D.C.: GAO, January 27, 1984) p. 6.

[12] General Accounting Office, *Political and Economic Factors Influencing Economic Support Funds Programs* (Washington, D.C.: April 18, 1983), p. 30.

[13] For instance, one study estimates that in 1982, 19 cents out each ESF dollar were spent on a project that fulfilled the current legislative mandate; in 1985, only 7 cents of every dollar will be used on these kinds of projects. Roy Prosterman, *The Quality of Foreign Aid*, RDI Monograph on Foreign Aid, and Development No. 1 (Seattle: Rural Development Institute, 1984), p. 4.

[14] 1979-1983 average.

[15] General Accounting Office, *AID's Assistance to Jamaica* (Washington, D.C.: GAO, April 19, 1983) p. 8.

[16] The Carlucci Commission, for example, simply worked from the premise that these programs were effective, but did not evaluate them. A recent examination of security assistance programs undertaken by the Center for Strategic and International Studies showed that in many cases their relationship to American *military security* is at best tenuous. The study concluded that security assistance "cannot be defended primarily on military grounds. . . . both the Congress and many within the Executive Branch tend to perceive the security assistance programs as meeting U.S. *international political objectives* [emphases added]." (Franklin D. Kramer, "The Government's Approach to Security Assistance Decisions," in Ernest Graves and Steven A. Hildreth, eds., *U.S. Security Assistance: The Political Process* (Lexington, Mass.: Lexington Books, 1985), p. 123.

[17] A.I.D., *Congressional Presentation FY1985* (Washington, D.C.: 1985), p. 5.

[18] A.I.D., *Congressional Presentation, FY1985* (Washington, D.C.: 1985), p. 4.

[19] Congress, however, has reservations about the link with the IMF. Last year, an amendment attached to the appropriations resolution stated that U.S. aid should not be linked to IMF requirements for economic reform.

[20] For a full discussion of this point, see Chapter 1 of this volume.

²¹ A.I.D. Policy Paper, *Health Assistance* (Washington, D.C.: December 1982), pp. 9-10.

²² A.I.D. Policy Paper, *Private Enterprise Development* (Washington, D.C.: 1982).

²³ The government of Botswana rejected the U.S. offer of $4.2 million to finance the purchase of General Electric locomotives when it discovered that the funds would not be additional, but would come out of A.I.D. funds already allocated to the country; Botswana instead accepted a Canadian offer that did represent additional aid.

²⁴ Nicholas D. Kristof, "Foreign Aid by U.S. is Tied to Exports," *New York Times*, November 24, 1984.

²⁵ U.S. Department of the Treasury, *United States Participation in the Multilateral Development Banks in the 1980s* (Washington, D.C.: 1982), pp. 161-62.

²⁶ *Mandate for Leadership II*, op. cit., p. 374.

²⁷ U.S. Department of the Treasury, *United States Participation*, op. cit. p. 42.

²⁸ John P. Lewis, "Development Assistance in the 1980s," in Roger Hansen, ed., *U.S. Foreign Policy and the Third World: Agenda 1982* (New York: Praeger, for the Overseas Development Council, 1982), pp. 119-21.

²⁹ Unfortunately, no overall data or analysis is available to assess the impact of these changes on human well-being or on the incidence of poverty within developing countries. Some examination of this issue has been undertaken. See, for example, "The Impact of World Recession on Children," *World Development*, Special Issue, March 1984.

Chapter 5

Wrestling with Third World Radical Regimes: Theory and Practice

Anthony Lake

There is a dangerous moment, at conferences and in a writer's mind, whenever the question is asked: What do we *mean* by development? by national security? by human rights? Too often, a heated and time-consuming debate ensues, with various doctrines being offered in the guise of definitions. In the end, one is usually left with only a slightly more elegant version of the justice's comment about pornography: One knows it when one sees it. And much depends on the eye of the beholder.

So it is with the term 'radical regime.'[1] One common thread runs through the numerous definitions, explicit or implicit, encountered in such discussions: Radical regimes show a consistent immoderation in their behavior. For most, this means that their actions regularly and grossly violate those principles of international and national behavior enshrined (if all too inconsistently observed) in the United Nations Charter and the Universal Declaration of Human Rights. In essence, such regimes either seek rapid change in the existing order (abroad or at home) or use radical means to preserve that order within their societies.[2]

The immoderation can take many forms. The regimes may be radical in policies domestic but not foreign, or vice versa. They may be of the left (Vietnam) or of the right (Iran), or of both in bewildering mixture (Libya); they may be radical in their principles, in their actions, or in both. They may be hostile to the United States (in many cases) or prefer not to be (South Africa, Angola). They may or may not be 'radical' in what was once the prime American definition of foreign radicalism: disrespect for U.S. property.

All radical regimes, however, have one thing in common. They are the objects of suspicion in American eyes and of attack in U.S. political rhetoric. In many cases, these regimes came to power through the overthrow of a pro-American government whose own venality and incompetence could not be offset by U.S. protection.[3] In just about all cases, U.S. policy makers—of all administrations—have failed to deal effectively with radical regimes. Indeed, from Korea to the Bay of Pigs to Vietnam to Iran and now Nicaragua, these regimes have, in one way or another, posed some of the most damaging challenges to the United States.

The failures have been conceptual as well as practical. Indeed, beyond noting sporadic efforts to punish or remove such regimes throughout most of this century, it is hard to describe a coherent, much less a consistent, U.S. policy approach to them. During the past eight years, we have, however, witnessed two successive administrations come to office espousing the two chief and competing American views of how to deal with radical regimes in the Third World. This provides an opportunity to assess their practice of what they professed—bearing in mind two cautions. First, four years is not enough time, the world being what it is, to test conclusively almost any foreign policy proposition. Second, constrained by pragmatic impulses and sometimes by domestic politics, neither the Carter nor the Reagan Administration always pursued the theoretical approaches it espoused.

Nonetheless, a review of U.S. relations with a number of radical regimes over the past eight years offers a number of lessons—about the efficacy of seeking to change the domestic behavior of such a regime or even to change the regime itself, about moderating its foreign policies, about the value of both 'carrots and sticks' as instruments of U.S. leverage, about literally 'bleeding' radical states as a lesson for other radicals, and about the ways in which U.S. domestic politics impels and constrains Washington's international policies.

Conflicting Concepts

The two predominant strains in American thinking about this issue go by many names: conservative or liberal, globalist or regionalist, or— more invidiously—accommodationist or aggressive. Most policy makers, having once tried to come to grips with the issue, stray from pursuing one or the other view in its pure form. But even when not pursued as doctrine, the two schools of thought represent clearly distinct predispositions that have shaped mainstream political debates of the issue for the last generation.

There has been little disagreement at the level of basic U.S. interests, except when the argument has been carried on through partisan caricature. Both camps believe that radical regimes tend to pose threats beyond their borders and to the political rights of their own citizens. Both are in favor of limiting Soviet influence in the Third World. Both say they prefer democratic, pluralistic systems and societies. There is strong disagreement about priorities when these interests collide, but agreement that U.S. foreign policy should serve them all. Indeed, these numerous shared assumptions lead others who believe that economic and social progress can be made only through revolutionary change and the radical restructuring of Third World societies to lump the two mainstream schools together before dismissing them both.

The disagreements between liberals and conservatives concern methods and priorities. But these are not mere tactical debates. They reflect profound differences over the nature of Third World radical regimes, the severity of the threat such governments pose to U.S. interests, the extent of and reasons for their ties with the Soviet Union, the limits to U.S. influence with or against them, and the legitimacy of the means that can be employed in dealing with them. Much of the difference comes down to an argument about whether U.S. interests in the Third World lie primarily in the competition there with the Soviet Union or in the Third World itself.[4]

If you hear someone say that radical regimes in the Third World generally are not really Marxist—and even if they are, we can work with them on many issues—you will probably also hear this: Such regimes tend to be highly nationalistic and can thus be weaned from the Soviet Union. The problems of the Third World tend to be particularistic; a radical regime is thus not necessarily the spearhead of a Soviet thrust into the Southern Hemisphere. Revolution can seldom be exported by radical regimes; it can only be supported by them. It is best to focus not on the wickedness of the radical regime but on the social and economic inequities of its neighbors that create those revolutionary possibilities. According to this view, since most radical regimes seek economic ties with the West, they may be induced to trade in their Mao jackets for pinstripe suits.[5] Therefore, from this perspective, we should pursue a path of "constructive engagement" with radical regimes,[6] using economic aid and trade not only to moderate their international behavior but also to promote pluralism and even a little more respect for human rights within their borders. Military pressure, economic sanctions, or harsh words tend only to drive these regimes into a defensive shell or into the arms of the Soviets.[7]

Indeed, the radicalism of such regimes may reflect a failure of sympathy and even support by the United States in the early stages of

their existence. Where such governments are actively engaged in conflicts beyond their borders, military aid to their opponents may be
appropriate—but the United States should also pursue active diplomatic efforts to resolve the conflict itself. Thus Cuba: Castro became a
Marxist largely because he was spurned by the United States. Yes, he
probably still would have been a radical—but not a Soviet client, and
not our enemy. U.S. sanctions drove him further into his dependency
on the Soviet Union. He supports revolutionary change in the Hemisphere but cannot create it. We still can work with him—not only on
bilateral issues but also on resolving the conflicts of Central America
and even Africa. He pursues a foreign policy that is occasionally independent of Soviet strictures, when this serves Cuban interests; he
would like to be still more independent.

If, on the other hand, you hear someone speak of Third World
radicalism as almost synonymous with Marxism, you will almost certainly hear this as well: The spread of radicalism in the Third World
has a clear pattern and at the center is the Soviet Union. Revolution
can be and is exported. The existence of radical regimes thus poses a
severe threat to U.S. interests. It is best not only to oppose such efforts
by shoring up threatened neighbors but to 'go to the source.' And
radical regimes, by their very nature, are both unrelentingly hostile to
the United States and insusceptible to liberalizing reform through
economic ties to the West.[8] In this view, we should pursue a path of
active opposition to radical regimes. Constructive engagement only
strengthens these regimes[9] and offers them legitimacy. They cannot be
reformed; we should therefore work for their removal. Instead of offering economic blandishments, we should look to economic and other
pressures to deter their foreign adventures and even to defeat them at
home as well. Thus, Cuba: Castro became a Soviet client not because of
U.S. failure to woo him, but because of a failure to prevent the consolidation of his Marxist state before it had become strengthened by
Soviet aid and arms. What allows him to act in a hostile manner is not
his lack of love for America but his lack of fear of the United States.

In this debate, one also hears, sometimes only implicitly, an argument not only about the nature of Third World radicalism and the
efficacy of different U.S. policies but about *values*—about the legitimacy of certain tactics. At what point, in adopting the tactics of the
enemy, does one defeat one's own purpose? Is it legitimate to destabilize
a regime because it seeks to destabilize others? To oppose a revolution
while it is still popular because it opposes democratic values? To use
terrorist tactics against terrorists? To act in an undemocratic fashion in
the making of our own policies for the sake of acting more assertively
in the foreign defense of our democracy? To contravene international
law in acting unilaterally against those we charge with undermining
it?

Both sets of questions—concerning the nature of Third World radicalism and the values we bring to dealing with it—can and should be answered by analysis of foreign realities and by philosophical inquiry (although the latter seldom gets further than the ambiguities illuminated in the soul-searching of John Le Carré's George Smiley). But we also can test the approaches of the two camps, in at least a limited way, by taking as objective as possible a look at how effectively each has been able to *apply* its views over the past eight years.[10] Have radical regimes responded with more moderate foreign or domestic policies to U.S. efforts at positive economic and political engagement? to U.S. threats or use of force? Do regional strategies focusing on conflict resolution fare as well as, or better than, concentration on support for friends and opposition to the radical state?

These questions about *means* are tied to judgments about the practicality of possible U.S. *objectives* in such situations. Can either approach work effectively to moderate the external behavior of radical regimes? Can we also change their domestic policies, or remove them altogether? Are these two objectives mutually reinforcing or antithetical in practice? Alternatively, should we simply seek to make life harder for radical regimes, at home and abroad, as an object lesson for others about the costs of radical behavior?

Putting Theory Into Practice

The classic case is that of the People's Republic of China, which was for so long and with so little success treated in U.S. policy circles as a nonstate. That record of futility leads liberals to place its lessons on their side of the ledger; but conservatives may argue that without those years of U.S. opposition, Chinese internal and external policies would never have evolved to the point at which normalization of relations could be considered. Some, indeed, believe that point has not yet been reached. In any case, China presents less interesting contrasts between the approaches of the last two administrations than the cases reviewed in this chapter; after surmounting the views on the Taiwan issue with which he entered the presidency, Ronald Reagan has pursued policies toward the People's Republic that are remarkably similar to those of his three immediate predecessors.

It is more instructive to review the recent histories of six other cases: Nicaragua, Afghanistan, Indochina, Southern Africa, Libya, and Iran. In all of these cases, the policy approach of each administration can be tested by the results it achieved. The six regimes involved fall within the loose definition of "radical" suggested earlier. They differ greatly from one another in character and the challenges they pose, and in the past eight years, they have been the object of contrasting U.S. approaches.

The Carter Approach

Of the three objectives U.S. policy might pursue—(1) seeking moderation of a radical regime's behavior, (2) removing the regime, and/or (3)
'bleeding' it as a warning to others—the Carter Administration concentrated almost solely on the first. The primary focus was on seeking
to influence the external policies of radical regimes—to gain their
cooperation on regional diplomatic issues, to make progress on economic and other bilateral issues, and to weaken their ties to the Soviet
Union. While espousing human rights and criticizing its violation by
these regimes, the Carter Administration in most cases did not make
internal actions the touchstone for its approach. At least initially, the
means employed in pursuit of this goal emphasized diplomatic and
economic blandishment. Force or the threat of its use was seldom
employed.

Nicaragua

After failing to prevent a Sandinista victory in Nicaragua in the
summer of 1979 either by gaining reform of the Somoza regime or (at
the last moment) by stitching together international efforts at a moderate resolution of the fighting, the Carter Administration concentrated on gaining leverage with the new regime. A $75-million aid
program was instituted, after frustrating delays by Congress. The
program was designed to: (a) allow the United States to compete on the
ground with the Soviets and the Cubans, who were sending a small
number of military advisers and thousands of civilian teachers, medi-
cal workers, and the like; (b) strengthen the position of the middle
class, which had provided much support for the Sandinistas but might
also be an important force for economic and political pluralism under
their rule; and (c) encourage moderation in Nicaraguan foreign policy,
especially with regard to El Salvador. Seeking either to overthrow the
victorious new Sandinista government or to sever completely the long-
standing ties between its leaders and their friends in Cuba seemed
unrealistic.

Despite evidence during 1980 that modest amounts of arms were
flowing from Nicaragua to the rebels in El Salvador, President Carter
in September 1980 provided Congress with the required certification
that Nicaragua was eligible for continued U.S. aid, since it was not
exporting violence to its neighbors. The Nicaraguan government had
assured him that any arms that passed the country's borders were
carried by smugglers whose actions contravened Nicaraguan policy.
The concern in Washington was that a denial of aid would lead to less
rather than more restraint by the Sandinistas with regard to El Salvador and would damage the prospects for some degree of pluralism in
a still evolving political system.

In November and December 1980, however, U.S. intelligence agencies reportedly found evidence of a significant increase in the arms flow into El Salvador—and of Sandinista involvement in the smuggling operation. In its last month in office, the Carter Administration suspended (but did not cancel) the aid program, one-fifth of which had not yet been provided. Those are the facts. Interpretations of them vary widely. Some argue that the Carter approach was a success. The Sandinistas were receptive to U.S. and other Western economic ties and as a result acted only within careful limits in expressing their support for the revolution in El Salvador. Only the November 1980 election led the Sandinistas to conclude that Reagan's anticipated hostility called for preemptive action of their own. They therefore gave more aid to the Salvadoran rebels in preparation for the rebels' January 1981 offensive.

Others view the same facts very differently. Increased Sandinista aid to revolutionaries in El Salvador was inevitable in any case; its growth was a function of events in El Salvador and allowed by U.S. complacency. The Carter Administration's efforts to improve relations with Castro, which bore fruit on some bilateral issues, only encouraged Cuban meddling in both Nicaragua and El Salvador.

Without better knowledge of the policy debates that went on within both Nicaraguan and Cuban councils, it is hard to resolve the difference in the two interpretations. Score it as a *possible*, and in any case *limited*, success for the liberal approach. Arms flows were restrained until Carter's defeat. The Sandinista government was clearly prepared to pursue accommodation with Washington on issues beyond Nicaragua's borders. At the same time, the degree to which U.S. aid and diplomatic engagement were encouraging economic, social, and political pluralism there is ambiguous. What is clear is that human rights within Nicaragua fared worse in later years; it is also evident that within the United States, there was little success in the Carter approach on this issue when it came to the politics of 1980. Reagan and his supporters used Nicaragua in the campaign; it was hardly a central point in Carter's speeches.

Afghanistan

To a far more limited degree, the same approach was pursued with regard to Afghanistan during the period between the establishment of a Marxist regime there in April 1978 and Soviet occupation of the country of December 1979. Until the assassination of U.S. Ambassador Dubs in February 1979, a policy of active engagement was pursued in the hope that the new regime would act more like 'national communists' than like Soviet clients. Existing economic aid ties were maintained; Ambassador Dubs met frequently with the Foreign Minister. After his murder, however, a distinct coolness set in. Dubs was not replaced by a new ambassador, for understandable reasons. Human rights abuses and growing Soviet influence were denounced in official statements, and after an April 1979 policy review in Washington, U.S. sympathy for a burgeoning insurgency deepened. Nonetheless, there were continued statements in Washington about an American desire for "normal and friendly relations," and a chargé d'affaires remained in Kabul to represent U.S. interests.

It has been argued that if policies of engagement had been pursued as firmly after February 1979 as before, President Nur Mohammed Taraki—or, more likely, his successor, Hafizullah Amin—might have become, if not a Tito, then at least a Ceaucescu. After all, as the bloody events of December were to show, the Soviets did find in Amin a strong streak of independence. Why could Washington not have played more effectively on this?

But, as with Nicaragua, this is a hard thesis to prove. We cannot know how important the American connection was in the calculations of Afghan leaders. In any case, it is not clear that Washington had much choice. As the insurgency grew, it would become ever harder for U.S. policy to avoid a choice between it and the Marxist regime it opposed, whether or not a sympathetic policy were translated into practical support for the rebels. And the events of December suggest that to the degree a consistent American policy of constructive engagement had succeeded, Soviet repression might only have come sooner—assuming that it was Amin's independence as well as domestic unpopularity that led the Soviets to intervene.

While Nicaragua may have provided an actual if mixed success for the liberal approach, Afghanistan thus provides argument only for a *mixed and potential* but unrealized success. In the event, after the bloody Soviet intervention, both the goals and tactics of the Carter approach shifted. From containing the damage of the April 1978 revolution, it turned to active opposition against the regime through economic sanctions and covert but publicly reported aid to the rebels.

Carter did not claim that there could be immediate results either in terms of a Soviet withdrawal or the defeat of their client regime by the insurgency. But the policy was not one of merely 'bleeding' the Communists. Active efforts were made to design and pursue a diplomatic, compromise settlement to the conflict. Such attempts were important to our European allies as they considered whether or not to join in the U.S. sanctions; they also reflected a genuine desire in Washington to see the fighting ended. The efforts failed, however, at the conceptual as well as at the practical level. No one could design a political process that might provide the people of Afghanistan some freedom of choice yet prove so attractive to the Soviets and their unpopular clients that they might be tempted to compromise.

Indochina

During the first two years of the Carter Administration, American policy toward Vietnam was of a design any regionalist would applaud. As Cyrus Vance had written to Carter in a lengthy foreign policy memorandum even before the 1976 election, the road to normalization of relations with the Vietnamese government should be explored, since normalization "would give the U.S. an opportunity to have more influence with a nation which obviously will play an important part in the future development of Southeast Asia." It would be welcomed by the Vietnamese, he argued, because it would reduce their dependence on the Soviet Union.[11]

Normalization was explored at a series of meetings with the Vietnamese during 1977 and 1978, but without success. Initial failures came as a result of Vietnamese insistence on U.S. aid—to be called reparations—as a condition of normal relations. By the summer and fall of 1978, the Vietnamese were moving toward greater flexibility, but they found the Carter Administration moving in the opposite direction for a variety of reasons: Congressional and political opposition, Vietnamese human rights abuses and the agony of the boat people, growing ties between Hanoi and Moscow, and the quickened pace of movement toward normalization of U.S. relations with Beijing. The issue was settled by the Vietnamese venture into the Cambodian quagmire in early 1979. So long as Vietnamese troops were occupying their neighbor, diplomatic relations were deemed to be impossible in both policy and political terms. Negotiations on such bilateral issues as an accounting for Americans missing in action and the orderly departure of refugees were pursued. A policy of constructive engagement was not.

Many liberal critics of the Carter Administration's Indochina policy have argued that a great opportunity was needlessly missed. The nationalistic Vietnamese, who have always chafed under dependency on any foreign power, were interested in an American connection as a counterweight to the Soviets. Either through incompetence or by giving the Chinese connection unnecessary priority over the Vietnamese, the argument goes, the Carter Administration helped create the very ties between Hanoi and Moscow that then became a political barrier to normalization. Indeed, it is argued, progress on the American front might have led the Vietnamese away from an attack on the Cambodians. In short, this was, in the breach, a sad but clear demonstration of regionalist wisdom.

It is true that the Vietnamese were willing to normalize relations, and that this might have reduced their economic dependence on the Soviets. But though willing, they were hardly so anxious to do so that they could resist a diplomatic fishing expedition along the way. One

senior Vietnamese official involved in the issue recently told some
American visitors to Hanoi that, "as diplomats," the Vietnamese "had
to try" to get the reparations—i.e., to test the limits of American
accommodation. Nor should one believe that normalization would have
prevented the invasion of Cambodia or precluded increasing Soviet
military ties. Those have little to do with Hanoi's relationship with
Washington; they have almost everything to do with Hanoi's fear of
China and Vietnam's historic designs and disputes in Indochina.

Thus in the Indochina case as in that of Afghanistan, one finds
only *potential success* for the liberal view—in the limited sense of
possibly competing with the Soviets and more easily pursuing our
bilateral concerns with Hanoi. The Vietnamese did want to deal and to
diversify their ties to external powers. But neither Washington nor
Hanoi would strike a bargain on terms acceptable to the other.

Southern Africa

The Carter approach did bear tangible fruit in Southern Africa. Policies of engagement with Mozambique, and to lesser degree with Angola, proved invaluable in British and U.S. efforts to produce settlements in Zimbabwe and Namibia. Indeed, it was the successful effort of
the government of Mozambique to persuade Robert Mugabe and his
followers to participate in British-held elections that finally allowed an
agreement in Zimbabwe. This followed a series of meetings, over the
course of the long Zimbabwe negotiations, between U.S. and Mozambican officials. In 1980, President Carter waived the congressional
prohibition of aid to Mozambique and initiated a small program of
assistance.

President Carter refused to extend diplomatic recognition, much
less aid, to Angola until Cuban troops were withdrawn from that
nation, despite State Department recommendations that he offer normalization but not assistance. Neither his National Security Council
staff nor the winds of domestic politics favored such a course.

Nonetheless, there was a pattern of improved relations, with benefits for both sides. Close consultation with the Angolans regarding the
Namibia negotiations helped produce agreement on compromise measures to be offered to South Africa. An evident Angolan interest in
closer ties with the West was promoted. In the end, the Carter Administration encouraged growing American business interests in Angola
and authorized $152.4 million in Export-Import Bank loans and guar-
antees.

Both liberals and conservatives tend to reverse their prescriptions
when it comes to South Africa. The Carter approach on apartheid met
with barely mixed success. Threats of sanctions did occasionally produce South African tactical flexibility on Namibia, but never the fun-

damental concessions that could have produced a settlement. An arms embargo imposed after the death of Steve Biko in a South African prison may well have led to a period when fewer South African political prisoners died in jail. But stern talk and a threatened deterioration in relations with the United States did little to achieve progress toward an end to apartheid.

Thus in Southern Africa: Small carrots produced some success in gaining Angolan and Mozambican cooperation on regional issues (although such cooperation was in their interest, in any case); and small sticks conveyed some small tactical results, but nothing more, in South Africa.

Libya and Iran

In contrast to these cases of partial or potential success of the regionalist approach, the cases of both Libya and Iran convey only failure. The Libyan case goes back to 1970, when the Nixon Administration essayed a policy of accommodation to the new regime of Muammar el-Qaddafi. Washington quickly agreed to his request that the Wheelus Air Force Base be evacuated. It is said that Qaddafi was even warned by the Americans of a coup plot against him. The friendly gestures proved fruitless, however. Qaddafi continued to put pressure on American businesses operating in Libya, enthusiastically joined in oil price hikes, and regularly denounced Washington and its works. By 1972, U.S. representation had been reduced to the level of a chargé d'affaires. Relations remained poor in subsequent years.

Libya was not given great attention in the first years of the Carter Administration. A Libyan threat against the life of the U.S. Ambassador to Egypt was firmly but privately dealt with. An improvement in relations was, at first, carefully left open. But Qaddafi nonetheless regularly denounced American imperialism, and Washington increasingly accused him of supporting terrorism and abusing human rights. An aircraft embargo was implemented. In December 1979, after Americans were taken hostage in Teheran, a government-backed mob burned the American Embassy in Tripoli. By May of 1980, the last U.S. diplomat had been removed from Libya.

While the oil trade from Libya had remained healthy throughout this period, by the end of 1980, the United States was represented in Tripoli only by remaining American business people, former CIA officials on unsavory business, and the President's brother in his embarrassing visits. It is hard to judge the Carter policy a failure, at least in its own terms, since it attempted so little. But the deterioration of U.S.-Libyan relations and Qaddafi's intemperate behavior hardly suggest much in the way of success. The score after a decade: Qaddafi, 1, sporadic 'regionalism' in Washington, 0.

One need not rehearse the sad story of the Carter Administration's efforts to develop some kind of relationship with the Khomeini regime in Iran. Its efforts to prevent the emergence of this regime, first by seeking to reform the rule of the Shah while supporting him, then by backing a moderate alternative to Khomeini, may have loaded the dice against such an effort in any case. But Washington's persistent efforts to develop some kind of working relationship with Iranian officials in the first months of Khomeini's reign were overwhelmed by the hostage outrage.

The Results

Neither President Carter himself nor certainly some of his advisers were pure 'regionalists.' But the thrust of his policies, at least in the early years, was in such a direction. Regionalism as practiced by the Carter administration achieved some limited success in affecting the *international*—but not the *domestic*—behavior of some radical Third World states: Mozambique, Angola, and perhaps Nicaragua. It is also at least arguable that, had the Administration pursued such policies in other cases, some further success might have been achieved—in Vietnam and in Afghanistan, for example—although in very limited ways in the first case and with a Soviet invasion still the likely result in the second. The approach failed in Iran and was barely attempted in Libya. In no case could 'regionalism' be considered a success in U.S. domestic politics.

The political difficulties encountered by the Carter policies are not surprising. Liberal regionalist approaches are not only vulnerable to the charge of being 'soft on radicalism,' but also are inherently difficult to explain in a *political* context, where the simple argument will always destroy the complex. In contrast, globalist arguments about the Soviet threat can be made consistently in explaining all cases; the anti-Soviet message is a clear one that lends itself to the headline or the thirty-second spot on the evening news. Regionalist policies, on the other hand, rely on case-by-case analyses that defy easy generalization and can all too easily seem inconsistent if not incoherent. Indeed, liberals face a fundamental dilemma here: Regionalism calls for heavy reliance on the judgment of regional experts, which is at odds with the liberal instinct in favor of public debate of foreign policy issues.

The Reagan Approach

Ronald Reagan came to office promising a very different approach. The Carter years, he said, had been a time of retreat and weakness. His own administration would stand up to foreign challenges, working not only to prevent the emergence of radical regimes (a separate but closely related issue) but requiring those that already existed to behave themselves. During the 1980 campaign, he used President Carter's problems in Iran, Nicaragua, and Afghanistan to telling effect.

A more 'muscular' U.S. approach would not necessarily involve the actual use of force, however. By building up American strength, a Reagan Administration would recapture respect for the United States. This in turn would deter others from challenging our interests. Simply having new military strength would be enough. In debating President Carter during the campaign, Reagan said "I don't ever want to seen another generation of young Americans bleed their lives into sandy beaches in the Pacific or jungles in Asia or the muddy, bloody battlefields of Europe."

But the radicals of the world, who also tend to be its hard cases, are not so easily cowed, and during his first years in office, President Reagan found it necessary in almost every case to use force—indirectly and by proxy. One reason for this was that with the muscular stance came an escalation in goals.

In contrast to the Carter emphasis on moderating the behavior of radical regimes, there was now at least an ambiguity about going beyond their containment to efforts at their removal. For Reagan's theoreticians, who saw Moscow and radical ideology as the root of the problem, it followed that there was little hope for encouraging moderation among radical regimes (except South Africa). Unwavering, ideological hostility toward the United States called for unwavering, ideological hostility in return. Most notably in the case of Nicaragua, the Reagan Administration seemed either to believe that there is a continuum between containment and "rollback"—that pressures applied for the purpose of containment might lead also to the destabilization of the adversary—or to be unable to decide through its internal debates which was the primary goal.

In any event, there was a real contrast to the Carter approach—at least ambiguity about rolling back radicalism as well as containing it, a refusal in almost all cases to consider economic inducements, a quicker reliance on force, and a predisposition toward letting radical regimes and their people be bled in various conflicts.

Nicaragua

The tough new U.S. approach was applied most consistently in the case of Nicaragua. After an initial period of uncertainty, the Reagan Administration pursued two sets of goals: *containment*—that is, halting Nicaraguan aid to the El Salvador rebels, limiting the Nicaraguan military buildup, and inhibiting ties between Managua, Moscow, and Havana; and *rollback*—at least internal 'democratization' and, for some officials, the forced removal of the Sandinista regime. According to press accounts, the internal debates and occasional bureaucratic purges that took place over Central American policy pitted relative moderates (mostly in the State Department and among the military) promoting the first set of goals against hardliners (mostly in the White House and the CIA and among Defense Department civilians) insisting on the second set as well, with the hard line generally prevailing.

The problem with this expansion of goals was twofold. First, no foreign policy will be judged fully successful if its accomplishments fall short of the goals that are set for it. And in Nicaragua, the number of President Reagan's goals was beyond the reach of his means. Second, the two goals of containment and rollback do not lie on a continuum; efforts at destabilization help persuade a regime that there is no point in agreeing to limit its foreign actions or to moderate its behavior at home. If American hostility is unrelenting, why concede on any point? Why be "contained" if this will not alter Washington's approach? Thus assumptions of hostility on both sides become self-fulfilling.

Pressure against the Sandinistas took a number of forms. At the end of 1981, the President authorized the most overt covert operation since the Bay of Pigs. As it evolved over more than thirty months, the program entailed support for paramilitary operations within as well as beyond Nicaragua and was aimed at economic as well as military targets. In addition, a series of U.S. military exercises in Honduras and off Nicaragua's shores seemed clearly designed to intimidate the Sandinistas. The Administration sought to do further economic damage by opposing loans from the multilateral development banks and discouraging bilateral aid donors.

In regional political councils and in speeches at home, President Reagan and his representatives pursued efforts to isolate the Sandinistas. In American rhetoric, Nicaragua was a "totalitarian dungeon"; the United States would not let it become a "platform for terror and war." Such rhetoric not only reduced American flexibility should the Administration ever have wished to adopt more moderate policies. It also implied that the ultimate goal of U.S. policy was precisely that held by the hardliners in the White House and at the CIA: the overthrow of the Sandinistas. And indeed the pattern of operations of the anti-Sandinista guerrillas as well as their obvious intentions cast doubt on the Administration's assertions that it did not seek the destabilization of the Nicaraguan regime. The infamous CIA manual developed for the guerrillas was clearly designed not only to encourage repellant methods but also to promote the overthrow of the Nicaraguan government.

Not all of the Reagan Administration's approach was purely punitive, however. Sporadic efforts were made at engaging the Sandinistas in negotiations; the State Department pushed the efforts while the hardliners reportedly preferred the sporadic. In any case, here, too, U.S. policy makers seemed to see a continuum between the goals of gaining international moderation and internal change. With increasing rigidity, the United States insisted that without "democratization" inside Nicaragua, there could be no agreement on issues between the two nations. By the fall of 1984, diplomatic maneuvering was again picking up. But no progress on substantive issues seemed possible so long as Washington insisted on rearranging internal Nicaraguan affairs.

When goals seem to lie beyond the power to achieve them, three courses of action are possible. First, the unsatisfactory position may simply be continued. Second, more power may be threatened or applied. But in late 1984, increasing threats seemed only to be creating closer ties between Managua and Moscow and tighter controls within Nicaragua. Third, more moderate goals may be introduced. The experiences of early 1981 and late 1983 suggest that more modest goals— external containment and agreement to limit the Soviet and Cuban military presence—might have been achievable. During the spring of 1981, the Nicaraguan government seemed to be acting out of fear of the 'sticks' that Reagan had said he would use and out of hope for economic-assistance 'carrots.' The Sandinistas reportedly closed a clandestine radio beaming rebel broadcasts into El Salvador, gave assurances that they would refrain from further aid to the rebels, and actually began to cut back on the flow of weapons. This was not enough for Washington, however, and the U.S. aid program was definitively canceled. Talks were initiated by the State Department in the summer and continued into the fall, but what little progress they made was destroyed by increasingly acerbic rhetoric on both sides.

Similarly, in late 1983, U.S. threats and pressures had apparently helped convince the Nicaraguan government to seek a regional settlement along lines proposed by third parties. Washington responded with terms that had become even more demanding than in 1981, especially with regard to Nicaragua's internal politics. The Sandinistas considered this a call for their surrender, not a settlement, and the opportunity was lost.[12]

To judge the success of the Reagan approach *in its own terms,* let us look at the goals listed previously. With regard to containment: There was a failure in the first years to keep arms flows down to the levels of most of 1980 and early 1981; by 1984, ties to the Soviets and Cubans were stronger than ever; the Nicaraguan military buildup continued. It appeared that the U.S. position was only strengthening the hard-line faction in Managua, which could argue that any concession on such issues would only encourage Washington in pursuit of its other goal— their destruction.

As for rolling back the Nicaraguan revolution: Economic damage had been inflicted, but there were few signs that the U.S.-supported attacks had hurt the Sandinistas politically. Although Nicaraguan economic problems hurt their popularity, American pressure gave them an explanation and an issue against their adversaries. While elections were held in the fall of 1984 (perhaps partly in response to international pressure) and some opponents of the regime were allowed to campaign against the Sandinistas, the terms of the election did not satisfy Washington nor much of the Nicaraguan opposition, who withdrew from the campaign. The anti-Sandinista guerrillas seemed to be making little progress, and Congress had at least temporarily denied them U.S. funding. All in all, not a litany of success.

Libya

The initial approach of the Reagan Administration toward Libya was in some ways very similar to its Nicaraguan policies. Just as Nicaragua was used to dramatize the threat in Central America and the difference in approach from that of the Carter years, so Libya and its leader were used to demonstrate both the threat of international terrorism—a major theme of early speeches by Secretary of State Haig and others—and, again, the contrast with Carter's policies. No more Billy Carter visits to Tripoli; now, Qaddafi would be brought to heel.

Again, a policy of pressure against the offending government was implemented. In May 1981, Libyan diplomats were expelled from the United States following revelations of attacks against Libyan students in this country. Washington announced that it considered travel by Americans to Libya to be hazardous. In August 1981, two Libyan aircraft were shot down in a dogfight over the Gulf of Sidra. A policy review within the Administration considered complete sanctions against Libya.

The Administration apparently intended to pursue containment, rollback, and 'bleeding' all at the same time. Military aid to Libya's threatened neighbors would be increased. Economic sanctions would reduce Qaddafi's ability to make trouble abroad while creating economic difficulties that might imperil his rule at home. Encouragement for Hissène Habré in Chad might help increase the cost for the Libyans of their adventure there.

But the initial impulse was tempered by a concern for U.S. economic interests. The review culminated in a decision in December 1981 to go only for partial sanctions. A step-by-step approach, it was decided, made more sense both in terms of effectiveness with Qaddafi and, of course, for U.S. businesses in Libya. The legal complexities encountered by the Carter Administration in pursuing sanctions against Iran were also an inhibiting factor. The decks were cleared for further action, however: After announcing (but never offering evidence) that the Libyans had sent a hit squad to the United States with the President as its target, the Administration asked all Americans to leave Libya. In March 1982, all oil imports from Libya (by then down to less than 1 per cent of U.S. consumption, in any case) were banned, as were high-technology exports.

Perhaps because Secretary of State George Shultz customarily spoke in a lower key than his predecessor, or on account of the Reagan Administration's concern about the damage that further sanctions might do to U.S. corporations, or because our European allies were most unenthusiastic about economic sanctions, or because Qaddafi moderated *his* behavior during 1983, or because of a realization that rhetorical or any other kind of attention is what the Qaddafis of the world most crave—whatever the reasons, the focus during most of 1982-84 was more on support for threatened neighbors than on further public pressure against Libya itself. When Libyan troops invaded Chad, the French were urged to respond militarily. American words as well as deeds were surprisingly muted. The 'step-by-step' approach to economic sanctions had effectively stopped with the single step of March 1982.

Did the "toughness" of 1981 and the relative pragmatism of 1982-84 produce results? If so, was it more muscle or reason that did so?

Qaddafi clearly went through a period of relative moderation during 1982 and much of 1983. He withdrew his forces from Chad, reportedly put a halt to any targeting of Americans, and stopped attempting to assassinate Libyan dissidents abroad. It may well be that his restraint was caused by fear of Reagan's wrath and the loss of Libyan jets to American firepower over the Gulf of Sidra. But his adjustment in Chad was clearly related to his hopes of currying favor within the Organization of African Unity while maneuvering for its chairmanship. It is not clear that the threat to President Reagan was in fact real. And Qaddafi's campaign against Libyan dissidents was earning him a well-deserved hostility abroad that he apparently did not enjoy.

In any event, in the summer of 1983, Qaddafi sent forces back into Chad, and in 1984 attacks on Libyan exiles began again. If Qaddafi remained deterred from attacks on Americans, in August the blood of a British policewoman in London showed that the Libyans had not yet adopted international Marquis of Queensbury rules. The end to Qaddafi's moderation may have been the result of a diversion of U.S. attention (and warships) to Lebanon, as conservatives would argue. Liberals would suggest that it had to do more with events in Chad and with the May 8, 1984, coup attempt inside Libya. Did Qaddafi start to attack his opponents in the preceding months because he had sniffed a plot in the wind? Did he tighten up at home and become less moderate abroad because he believed, whatever the facts of the case, that there was an American hand in the plotting?

By late 1984, while Qaddafi was pursuing an active diplomacy in the Arab world (including a startling liaison with Morocco) and encouraging European investors to expand their Libyan operations, he did not seem to be entering a new period of moderation. His promises of a new military withdrawal from Chad were not being kept. The lid on opposition within Libya remained tightly in place. Allegations of Libyan intent to bomb the Aswan Dam and of complicity in the mining of the Red Sea suggested that Qaddafi's appetite for trouble-making remained large. In mid-December, the Reagan Administration again asked Americans to leave Libya.

With as unpredictable a character as Qaddafi, it is not surprising that a case can be made either way about the role of threats and rewards in influencing his behavior, or even about what that behavior would be. One thing seems clear: A towering ego loves attention, and the modest American rhetoric of 1983-84 seemed better calculated to encourage moderation than the rhetorical bluster of 1981, which probably had only appealed to his vanity.

Iran

The Reagan Administration's approach to the Khomeini regime in Iran was much closer to the quiet of the latter stages of its Libyan policies than the flurries and sound of the early campaign against Qaddafi. Iran was of course a major item in Reagan's bill of particulars against Carter during the campaign, and many expected him to use Khomeini as a symbol of the world's evils, much as he used Qaddafi and the Sandinistas. But perhaps Reagan and his advisers had no desire to repeat the Carter mistake of playing up Khomeini even more than his actions warranted. More important, the Administration likely saw that attacking a non-Marxist, indeed an anti-Marxist, regime would only play into the hands of the Soviets. More concerned about the threat to Iran from the north than about the threat posed by Khomeini to his south, the Administration for once was led by its anti-Soviet preoccupations to a relatively relaxed policy against an anti-American radical. Paradoxically, ideological calculations produced pragmatic policies.

This is not to say that U.S. attitudes and actions toward Iran were in any way friendly. American policy tilted somewhat toward Iraq in its conflict with Iran, although the tilt was limited by Iraq's reported use of chemical warfare, its ties to the Soviets, and the fact that the regime in Iraq almost matches its neighbor in unsavory domestic behavior. After allegations of Iranian complicity in the terrorist attack against the Marines in Lebanon, the President properly added Iran to the list of nations that have "repeatedly provided support for acts of international terrorism." Administration officials also are said to have met quietly with some key Iranian exile leaders.

Yet consider what the Administration *might* have done but did not. Despite initially toying with the idea, it did not renounce the financial arrangements made by the Carter Administration in gaining the release of the hostages, and it allowed modest economic intercourse to continue. It did not make a major public issue of Khomeini and the brutality of his regime, although some specific human rights abuses were criticized. It did react with verbal warnings and enhanced support for friendly Persian Gulf states in response to Iranian threats and actual attacks on shipping there—but it avoided direct military involvement. It did not, at least so far as one can tell, support anti-Khomeini exiles through a covert action program. While moving in late 1984 to normalize relations with Baghdad, it did not tilt toward Iraq nearly as far as it might have or as much as some Arab friends wished it to. And it did not retaliate against Iran for the terrorist attacks against American personnel in Lebanon, despite the possibility of Iranian involvement. Washington reportedly decided that such retaliation might only produce further attacks.

It would be unfair to emphasize that the Reagan policies toward Iran did not accomplish much. There was not much that they could have accomplished. The policies were reactive and pragmatic where pragmatism was called for. There was, perhaps, too easy an acceptance of the advantages of letting Iran and Iraq have at it when the human costs are so high. But the way to achieve a diplomatic solution to that conflict was not immediately apparent. In short, it was a situation in which there were more opportunities to make things worse than openings to make them better—and the Reagan Administration, to its credit, showed restraint.

Afghanistan and Indochina

While Nicaragua and Libya—and Iran in the first days of January 1981—were used to demonstrate differences with the Carter approach, Reagan's policies toward Afghanistan and Indochina were similar to those of his predecessor. These were the two cases, of course, in which Carter, after attempting policies of diplomatic engagement, had ended up indirectly supporting the use of force. Indeed, in ending the grain embargo against the Soviet Union, Reagan took a somewhat less muscular approach than had his predecessor on one aspect of his Afghanistan policies. Remarkable parallels can be found between the Reagan approaches to Afghanistan and Indochina. His policies in the two cases were similar in their goals, in their reliance on force, and in their reactive diplomatic stances.

In both cases, the Reagan Administration sought the removal of an offending regime—the Babrak Karmal regime in Afghanistan and that of Heng Samrin in Cambodia. The American position was that there should be self-determination for both peoples—constituting, in effect, a call for the removal of unpopular regimes then in power.

In both cases, the position of working for the removal of a Marxist regime was different in fact and legality from calling for the removal of regimes that had gained power through revolutions that were primarily indigenous. Both regimes had been brought to power and sustained there by the military forces of powerful neighbors, the Soviet Union and Vietnam.

In both the Afghanistan and the Cambodia cases, some form of economic sanctions was pursued against a neighboring aggressor nation, although the sanctions were much stronger against Vietnam, where they hurt U.S. economic interests less.[13]

In both cases, although in different ways, American support was given to rebels fighting against the radical regime—rebels supplied or based in neighboring countries friendly to the United States (Pakistan and Thailand). Under Reagan, support for the insurgency in Afghanistan was channeled, as under Carter, through a covert CIA program that soon became public knowledge. Support for the coalition of forces fighting against the Heng Samrin regime in Cambodia reportedly has not involved the U.S. provision of military supplies. But it has involved diplomatic support in various forms as well as approval of Beijing's provision of military supplies to the rebels.

In both cases, Washington was accused of political error in its selection of the rebel groups with which it became associated, although its support of forceful resistance to aggression was not widely criticized.

Under Reagan as under Carter, U.S. policy was to support the former regime of the genocidal Pol Pot as the legitimate claimant to Cambodia's seat in the United Nations—but to oppose his return to actual power in Cambodia. American sympathies lie with Pol Pot's uneasy allies, Prince Norodom Sihanouk and former Premier Son Sann. But by acquiescing so easily in Chinese support of Pol Pot, and through its position at the United Nations, the United States allowed itself to become associated with one of the most loathsome figures of modern history and a useful symbol for the Vietnamese and their client government.

In Afghanistan, Washington reportedly directed its aid to those rebel groups most favored by the Pakistan government. Partly for internal political reasons, the Pakistanis are said to prefer Muslim fundamentalist guerrilla leaders, although their political support within Afghanistan may not be as deep as that of the local chieftains who have traditionally ruled the countryside. In the long run, Islamic fundamentalism also may not be the best trend to encourage from the point of view of U.S. interests.[14]

In both Afghanistan and Indochina, neither Carter nor Reagan officials held out much hope for military success in any foreseeable future. And in both cases, the Reagan Administration left the diplomatic going to regional friends. Washington was generally passive, if supportive, as the Pakistanis in the first case and the Association of Southeast Asian Nations in the second offered diplomatic solutions to the conflicts. This made sense in terms of short-run U.S. interests. Relations with regional friends were strengthened, and the prospects for negotiated settlements in any case were not bright—despite Hanoi's indications in late 1984 that it sought to negotiate a Cambodian settlement. The U.S. position of insistence on self-determination as part of a solution was inherently unattractive to regimes dependent for their existence on the presence of foreign military forces.

But in the long run, diplomatic passivity could lead to opportunities for settlement being missed when the participants in the fighting were ready to move to serious talks. In the case of Indochina, the Reagan Administration did do well to welcome Hanoi's statements in 1984 about the desirability of a settlement. And progress toward a bilateral agreement on the emigration from Vietnam of thousands of Amerasian children and prisoners held in Vietnamese 're-education' camps was to be praised. But there was more that could be done to promote a regional peace: It would serve a number of U.S. interests to urge China and the ASEAN nations to remove Pol Pot and his chief lieutenants as the leaders of the Khmer Rouge. Such a step would not only strengthen the political position of the coalition within Cambodia and in world opinion, but could also improve the prospects for diplomatic progress—since the Vietnamese claim that the major sticking point in any compromise is the possibility of Pol Pot's return.

Southern Africa

The Reagan approach to Southern Africa was an exception to the pattern of behavior shown in the other cases. Here, the Administration pursued a policy of diplomatic engagement not only with South Africa but also with its neighbors who have proclaimed Marxist ideologies. U.S. diplomats were very active in pursuing a settlement in Namibia, although with little evident progress, and improved relations between Pretoria and its neighbors—with apparent results in the achievement of a non-aggression pact between South Africa and Mozambique and a cease-fire between South Africa and Angola along the Namibian border. Indeed, State Department officials argue both that such diplomatic activism is in the U.S. interest and that only the United States is in a position to deal with both sides along the racial faultline in the region.

This activism is not the only difference between this case and the others. While there was, again, resort to the use of 'sticks'—not directly, but in taking a neutral position on South Africa's use of force against its neighbors—there was also the provision of 'carrots.' After Mozambican and South African leaders signed a non-aggression pact at Nkomati in March 1984, the Reagan Administration for the first time submitted a waiver to Congress and announced an economic assistance program for Mozambique, in addition to generous emergency food supplies. At the beginning of 1985, it went further, requesting $1 million from Congress for non-lethal military aid.

There was also remarkably little concern about the ideological makeup of the Angolan and Mozambican governments. Despite these regimes' espousal of radical philosophies, Secretary of State Shultz met with the Angolan Interior Minister in April 1983, and in July the Administration restored relations with Mozambique to the ambassadorial level. To be sure, the Administration was clearly sympathetic to Jonas Savimbi and his guerrillas in their struggle against the Angolan government, refused recognition of the Angolan government, and wished to see Mozambique join the International Monetary Fund in order to encourage its pragmatic moves away from a government-directed economy. But in general, the Administration pursued its diplomacy without letting ideological differences bar professional exchanges of views.

The regional issue on which the Reagan Administration did act in the most ideological manner was the one on which it achieved the least: Namibia. By insisting that Cuban forces be withdrawn from Angola at the same time that any settlement was implemented in Namibia, rather than as its consequence, Reagan greatly complicated an already complex issue and earned the disapproval of both African states and some of our European partners in the Namibian negotiations. A settlement remained possible even on those terms, but it had apparently been delayed by this linkage.

Some have argued that the success of the accords between South Africa and its neigbors was no real success at all. Angolan and Mozambican agreements with Pretoria had been forced not so much by U.S. diplomacy as by South African pressure and the devastating effects of regional drought. Furthermore, they argue, the United States had only achieved complicity in the temporary codification of South African dominance of weaker states along its borders. And its policy of constructive engagement with South Africa had, in its softened stand on apartheid, earned the anger of Africans across the continent.

But in his own terms, Reagan's policies in this region had largely succeeded. All but the South Africans had accommodated themselves, at least in part, to U.S. goals. And the Soviets were clearly displeased by what happened. Indeed, officials in Moscow were telling American visitors that Southern Africa had been moved down in their scale of priorities. The irony was that the greatest success had been achieved where the Administration had acted least according to form—by providing carrots while leaving the sticks more or less to others, by pursuing an activist diplomacy, and by dealing with the radicals in a relatively unideological fashion.

Why had such policies been pursued in Southern Africa but not in Nicaragua? The answer would seem to lie in propinquity and politics. The farther an issue was from the United States and from its political debates, the easier it was for the pragmatists in the Administration to hold sway.

Implications for Future Policy

What do the Carter and Reagan experiences in all these cases tell us about the most practical approaches that the United States might in the future take toward radical regimes in the Third World? More specifically, which of the three objectives—moderation of their behavior, their removal, or 'bleeding' them—have been most nearly achieved? Which tactics—carrots or sticks—have been most effective? Are efforts at their isolation or policies of diplomatic engagement more productive?

These six cases provide clear differences between the Carter and Reagan approaches: Under Reagan, there has been more emphasis on the removal of offending regimes, a higher tolerance or even encouragement of conflicts that impose costs on radical regimes and their people, a less activist diplomacy, more reliance on the threat or use of force, and less reliance on economic blandishments. And as seen in the case of the CIA Nicaraguan pamphlet, Reagan seems to have been less concerned with the dilemma of how one competes with an ideological opponent in ways that do not contradict U.S. values and begin to erode the quality of our own democracy.

But neither approach has been notably successful. Perhaps the more important lessons to be drawn are found not in a competitive comparison, but by looking for instructive patterns in the experiences of both administrations. Ten such patterns seem to emerge:

1. It is interesting that *in no case, in either period, was there any success in removing a radical regime or even significantly affecting its internal behavior*. This does not mean that it is impossible, as the case of Allende demonstrated.[15] It does suggest that efforts either to prevent

the consolidation of revolutions (in states less vulnerable than Grenada) or to induce such regimes to liberalize in their early stages may be more difficult than either globalist or regionalist rhetoric has seemed to imply. The lesson here is clear: The limits of U.S. leverage are narrower than either liberals or conservatives like to believe.

2. *It may well be that there are opportunities to encourage trends toward pluralism within revolutionary states once they have had full experience with the difficulties of trying to manage their economies through central (and generally inefficient) bureaucracies.* It is clear that pragmatic impulses are on the rise in, for example, China, Vietnam, Angola, and Mozambique. *But in their first years in power, revolutionary regimes may be the least receptive to external efforts to influence their internal policies*, perhaps because of the very fragility of the infant institutions they seek to protect and build.

3. *There were, however, some partial successes, either potential or real, in affecting the foreign policies of these regimes*: in Southern Africa in both periods, in Nicaragua in 1980 before November and again in 1981, perhaps in Libya in 1982-83, and potentially with Vietnam during both the Carter and Reagan Administrations.

4. However, *when the goal of rollback was pursued at the same time as efforts to induce foreign moderation, the former seemed to interfere with the latter.* Such was the case in Nicaragua, and perhaps in Libya in May 1984.

5. *It is not difficult to stand by and allow, or even to encourage, the 'bleeding' of a radical regime in some local conflict—as in the later Carter years and under Reagan with regard to Afghanistan, Iran and Iraq, and Indochina. In some cases, it is also practical to impose economic costs on such regimes, as a warning to revolutionaries elsewhere.* But do such policies truly serve American interests in the long run? The danger to regional friends of being involved in such conflicts is very real and also involves dangers to the United States. How far, for example, is Washington prepared to go in helping defend Pakistan from possible Soviet moves? Nor are the economic consequences of such conflicts insignificant, as in the case of the Iran-Iraq war. And beyond the issue of U.S. interests, there is the fundamental issue of morality. 'Bleeding' a radical regime is not an abstract metaphor: It means the blood of Iranian children, villagers and soldiers, and other human beings. The political ends of the 'bleeding' must consciously be weighed against the economic suffering inflicted on a people who may not be responsible for the actions of their government.

This is not to say that in these cases the United States could have produced a diplomatic miracle. It is to argue that inflicting, or being indifferent to, such a situation as an end in itself serves neither American interests nor American ideals.

When it comes to the *means* employed, the record is mixed:

6. *The blandishments preferred by liberal theorists have apparently had some limited impact*: in Southern Africa, in Nicaragua in 1980, and in the reported desire for improved relations expressed by Hanoi and, from time to time, by Havana. As noted, a policy of 'carrots' has also, in some cases, failed.

7. *Similarly, the 'sticks' wielded by Reagan have sometimes influenced the behavior of radical regimes*: in Nicaragua in late 1983 and perhaps in Libya during the period of Qaddafi's moderation in 1982 and early 1983.

8. *The greatest successes or opportunities came, however, when carrots and sticks were combined*: in Southern Africa and in Nicaragua in early 1981. (Similarly, the success of the Carter Administration in helping the British achieve a settlement of the Rhodesian conflict came through a policy of pressures and promised rewards.)

9. *A policy of diplomatic engagement paid off for both the Carter and Reagan Administrations* in the case of Southern Africa. *Efforts to isolate radical regimes do not seem to have worked*, as seen in the cases of Libya (early under Reagan) and Nicaragua.

10. *Where there has seemed little possibility of either carrots or sticks inducing significant change in the behavior of a regime* (as in Iran or Libya), the *low-key policies of 1982-84 served the Reagan Administration better*, in both foreign and domestic political terms, than a barrage of hostile rhetoric.

Judging by the events of the past eight years, it would seem clear that no single theoretical approach always, or even almost always, works. This does not mean that debating the issue at a broad level of generality is useless, nor that these archetypical approaches have no value. Through such debates, important attention is given to questions about the fundamental goals and values that the United States should be pursuing when facing the challenges posed by Third World revolutions. But it seems clear that whether a nation's goals are primarily global or regional in character, neither regionalist nor globalist doctrine can by itself provide consistently effective policies.

Policies can best be shaped, therefore, by asking questions about each situation rather than by pretending to know the theoretical answers even before the questions are posed. Radical regimes vary widely in their governing structures. It is not surprising that these different folks respond to different kinds of strokes. In each case, policy makers would do well to ask such questions as: How deeply are U.S. interests involved? What is the nature of the regime in question? Do its decisions reflect internal discussions that might be influenced (as with the Sandinistas) or the private impulses of an individual, like Qaddafi, within whose mind the decision-making process is not entirely clear? What is the true scope of potential American influence? What do our allies and regional friends think, and what are they prepared to do? If policy fails, is our exit clear?

The answers to such questions may be very different in each case. This suggests, in turn, that U.S. policy toward radical regimes should be characterized more by flexibility and patience than by doctrinal purity. The difficulty of dealing with such regimes also suggests that there is seldom value to rhetorical holy wars, to promising easy results, and thus to turning our policies in these cases into public tests of American foreign policy as a whole. Rhetorical excess in Washington only leads to political embarrassment at home, diplomatic rigidity abroad, and expanded egos for the objects of American diatribes. A Khomeini or a Qaddafi is not shocked or hurt when attacked by Washington; he only knows that the United States understands his importance. A Sandinista is not moved to accommodation; he becomes convinced that accommodation might be a fatal weakness. And, in the long run, the American voter is not impressed when results fall short of rhetoric.

But is such pragmatism in Washington really possible? A policy of flexibility and patience depends, finally, on the flexibility and patience of the American public. Radical regimes and their leaders make wonderful targets in domestic political speeches and produce exciting images on the evening news. They easily become major figures in the American mind. It is thus not surprising that from the Bay of Pigs to the Iranian rescue mission, American presidents have felt impelled by public impatience as well as other concerns toward ill-advised action. Yet since the Vietnam war polls have generally shown that while the public wants success (the defeat of these regimes), it must come at little cost to the United States (that is, involve no great losses through intervention, grain embargoes, or other actions).

Both Henry Kissinger with his intricate policies of détente and Cyrus Vance with his efforts to engage a complicated world through complex American policies discovered the difficulty of building public support for a sophisticated American stance abroad. Some might therefore turn to the cynical course of sacrificing effectiveness abroad for popularity at home, making policy through simple slogans. Others might despair and turn away from policies of complexity because they can so easily be attacked as policies of incoherence or conciliation. Surely we can afford neither course. The first requirement is for an understanding that a policy of pragmatism depends on leadership in Washington that consistently elucidates and educates, thus giving itself the political room it needs for maneuver abroad.

Notes

[1] The analysis of these cases owes much to the contributions, written and oral, of the participants at a conference held on this subject at the Overseas Development Council on July 31, 1984: Lisa Anderson, Dick Clark, Selig Harrison, Zalmay Khalilzad, Paul Kreisberg, William LeoGrande, Herbert Levin, Elaine Morton, Robert Pastor, Anthony Quainton, Barry Rubin, Gary Sick, Raymond Smith, Marianne Spiegel, and Sanford Ungar. The author would also like to thank Richard Feinberg, Vincent Ferraro, and Kenneth Oye for their comments on a draft of this article.

[2] For an interesting discussion of his own and Henry Kissinger's concepts of legitimate behavior within the international system, see Stanley Hoffman, *Primacy or World Order* (New York: McGraw-Hill, 1980), pp. 37-40.

[3] The question of how U.S. policy can best work to prevent the emergence of radical regimes is not considered in this essay; here we are concerned with policies toward entrenched governments. The two issues are, however, closely linked, since the processes by which the regimes came to power and the attitudes of the United States at that time may well affect their subsequent policies.

[4] Some in both camps assert that there is less of a difference on these issues than meets the eye—that a concern for regional realities need not interfere with a concern about the global competition with the Soviets. But very different versions of the point emerge in these assertions. The liberal focus is on effective U.S. regional policies that act to limit Soviet influence by addressing the indigenous problems of which the Soviets might take advantage; the conservative view has it that by deterring troublemaking by the Soviets, regional realities can be altered in our favor.

[5] There are important differences in emphasis within the liberal camp. 'Neo-realists' tend to argue that economic ties are the most important *immediate* interest of the United States in dealing with radical regimes; affecting their behavior on political and military issues is difficult and less important, in the short run, than is commonly believed, since over time economic intercourse will encourage moderated political behavior. And in any case, they argue, neither the Soviets nor their radical clients are as influential as conservatives or even many liberals are wont to suggest. 'Neo-realism' has not apparently become the majority view in the liberal camp, however, since it de-emphasizes the ways in which the actions of radical states may immediately affect regional issues of war and peace, tends to reduce the importance of pursuing the human rights that liberals hold dear, and, not least, flies in the face of dominant domestic political concerns about the radical ideology of, and Soviet ties to, many such regimes. The thinking of both 'neo-realists' and more traditional liberals (reflecting a direct tradition of thought going back to Richard Cobden and Sir Norman Angell) sees trade and aid both as useful in themselves and as a means to the end of improved political relationships. The neo-realist would rely on those relationships to work their way through over time; the traditional liberal would be more likely to use them for leverage in the short run.

[6] Except in the case of South Africa. I use the term "constructive engagement" advisedly; the negative connotations it now has in this context for a liberal are precisely the connotations it would have in the mind of a conservative when applied to a leftist regime.

[7] Except in the case of South Africa.

[8] See, for example, Jeane Kirkpatrick, "Dictatorships and Double Standards," in *Commentary*, November 1979, pp. 34-45.

[9] Except in the case of South Africa.

[10] Pure objectivity is impossible and its assertion can be dishonest. The author, who worked on some of these issues in the Carter Administration, claims here only to be attempting to step back from partisan and ideological loyalties in order to learn.

[11] Cyrus Vance, *Hard Choices* (New York: Simon & Schuster, 1983).

[12] For a detailed history of diplomatic contacts between the two sides in both periods, see the fascinating account by Roy Gutman, in "Nicaragua: America's Diplomatic Charade," *Foreign Policy*, Fall 1984.

[13] While Carter piled on the sanctions partly for the sake of appearing tough in an election year, Reagan also acted politically in removing the grain embargo that offended American farmers.

[14] Similarly, in Nicaragua, the trend toward support not only of disaffected former Sandinistas but also of former supporters of the unpopular Anastasio Somoza created difficulties both within Nicaragua and among the rebel forces.

[15] This is not to imply that destabilization is thus a desirable goal; the human suffering during Chile's years under Pinochet hardly argue that it was.

Statistical Annexes

Stuart K. Tucker

Special thanks are due to Andy Baird and Michael Miarecki for assistance with statistical compilation.

Statistical Annexes

Statistical Note

Whenever practicable within the Statistical Annexes, countries are treated consistently, with the classification set out in Annex E, Table E-1. This table identifies 171 geopolitical entities according to income and region and according to whether they are developed or developing. "Low-income" countries are those with a 1982 per capita GNP of less than $420; "lower middle-income" countries are those with a per capita GNP of $420 to $1,059; "upper middle-income" countries have a per capita GNP of $1,059 to $3,699; "high-income" countries have per capita GNP of $3,700 or more. Table E-1 also identifies the thirty-six countries on the U.N. list of "least developed countries" and the thirteen members of the Organization of Petroleum Exporting Countries.

Countries are classified as "developed" or "developing" on the basis of their per capita GNP and their PQLI. The PQLI—Physical Quality of Life Index—was developed by the Overseas Development Council in response to the need for a non-income measurement that summarizes many aspects of well-being. It is a composite index of three indicators— infant mortality, life expectancy at age one, and literacy. Each of the components is indexed on a scale of 0 (the worst performance in 1950) to 100 (the best performance expected by the end of the century). For life expectancy at age one, the best figure expected to be achieved by any country by the year 2000 (77 years) is equivalent to 100 and the worst performance in 1950 (38 years in Guinea-Bissau) is 0. Similarly, for infant mortality, the best performance expected by the year 2000 (7 per thousand) is rated 100 and the poorest performance in 1950 (229 per thousand in Gabon) is set at 0. Literacy figures (as percentages) are automatically on a 0 to 100 scale. The composite index, the PQLI, is calculated by averaging the three indexes (life expectancy, infant mortality, and literacy), giving equal weight to each component.[a]

The "developed countries" are those having both a 1982 per capita income of $3,700 or more *and* a PQLI of 90 or above. On the basis of these criteria, not all "high-income" countries qualify as developed countries: those thirty which do are so specified in Table E-1.

The term "developing countries" refers to the 141 countries in Table E-1 with 1982 per capita incomes of less than $3,700 and/or PQLIs of less than 90. Although Cyprus, Romania, and Trinidad & Tobago each have a per capita GNP in excess of $3,700 and a PQLI of at least 90, they have been included in the "developing" category. The three countries are considered by the ODC to be in a transitional stage of development and are classified as "advanced developing countries."

The various agencies that are the source of the data provided in the Statistical Annexes differ in their classifications of countries. The World Bank, the U.N. Conference on Trade and Development, the U.S. Agency for International Development, and the Development Assistance Committee of the Organisation for Economic Co-operation and Development do not agree in all instances on whether to call particular countries developed or developing. Inclusion of a country in one category or the other often depends upon the purposes of the compiling organization. For example, the DAC list of developing countries includes all countries, territories, or other geopolitical entities that receive official development assistance or other resource flows from DAC members. Thus while Portugal was a member of DAC, it was considered "developed"; however, since it has left DAC and itself become a recipient of aid from DAC members, it has been considered by that body to be "developing." Similarly, U.N. trade data are compiled according to the statistically more convenient breakdown of "developed market economies," "developing market economies," and "centrally planned economies" (which is followed for the most part in the second half of Annex C).

Greece, Portugal, Spain, Turkey, Yugoslavia, and Israel are examples of countries that are variously defined as developed or developing. UNCTAD considers them all developed, except Turkey. With the exception of Spain, the World Bank and DAC designate them as developing.

The classification of countries may also differ by region and analytical group. In terms of regions, the World Bank, for example, includes Cyprus and Turkey in Europe, while the Population Reference Bureau considers them part of Asia. Also, the Annexes refer to South America, Central America, the Caribbean, and Mexico collectively as "Latin America." In terms of analytical groups, for example, both DAC and the IMF classify some nations as "non-oil developing countries." The two organizations differ, however, on the country composition of this group. DAC's group of non-oil developing countries is comprised of all non-OPEC developing nations. However, inclusion in the IMF's non-oil group is determined by whether or not a country meets certain oil export criteria—one of which is that its oil exports must have accounted for at least two-thirds of its total exports during 1978-80. Countries which are "net oil exporters" but which do not meet these criteria are included in the IMF's non-oil group. Mexico is one of these countries, as are some members of OPEC. The Statistical Annexes adhere to the IMF's classification of non-oil developing countries.

Small statistical discrepancies in the tables, unless otherwise explained, are due to rounding of data. An entry of "n.a." signifies that information was not available. Dashes (—) signify that amounts are negligible or less than the smallest unit.

---

[a]For a more extensive discussion of the PQLI, see Todd R. Greentree and Rosemarie Philips, "The PQLI and DRR: New Tools for Measuring Development Progress," ODC Communique No. 1979/4, and Morris D. Morris, *Measuring the Condition of the World's Poor: The Physical Quality of Life Index* (New York: Pergamon Press, for the Overseas Development Council, 1979).

Glossary

Agency for International Development (AID). The U.S. government agency that administers the U.S. bilateral economic assistance program.

Balance of Payments. A summary of all international transactions (the sum total of the current account, capital account, and errors and omissions) undertaken by a country during a given period of time, resulting in either a surplus (an excess of earnings over outflows) or a deficit (an excess of payments over earnings).

Bank of International Settlements (BIS). Established in Basel, Switzerland, in 1930, to aid in the handling of German reparations and loan payments and in fostering cooperation among major central banks.

Bilateral Assistance. Economic or military assistance provided directly from one country to another. The U.S. bilateral economic aid program, for instance, consists primarily of development assistance, Economic Support Fund aid, and P.L. 480 food aid.

Capital Account. A component in the balance of payments that measures net flows of international assets, such as bank and other loans, purchases and sales of foreign stocks and bonds, and foreign direct investment.

Centrally Planned Economies. Those nations where government ownership and control are decisive and primary. For the purposes of these statistics and following the U.N. Statistical Office's classifications, the centrally planned economies are: Albania, Bulgaria, Czechoslovakia, Democratic Republic of Korea, the German Democratic Republic, Hungary, Mongolia, People's Republic of China, Poland, Romania, U.S.S.R., and Vietnam.

Current Account. A component in the balance of payments that measures net exports and imports of merchandise goods, services, investment income, and unilateral transfers.

Current and Constant Dollars. Values expressed in *current* dollars reflect prices that were current in each year (or unit of time) of the period under study. Current dollar values thus may rise or fall in a particular year simply because of price changes. Values expressed in *constant* dollars reflect constant prices—those that prevailed in a single base year.

Customs, Insurance, and Freight (c.i.f.) Import Value. The value of imports plus freight, insurance, and other charges (excluding import duties) incurred in bringing the merchandise from the country of exportation to the first port of arrival at the country of importation.

Debt Service Ratio. Ratio of interest and principal payments due in a year to exports for the year.

Development Assistance. Economic aid that is extended bilaterally or multilaterally for the purpose of promoting development.

Development Assistance Committee (DAC). A specialized committee of the OECD that monitors development assistance levels and policies, as well as relations between developed and developing countries. All members of the OECD except Greece, Iceland, Ireland, Luxembourg, Portugal, Spain, and Turkey are members of the DAC.

Direct Investment Abroad. Equity ownership in a foreign firm or enterprise implying significant managerial control. According to the U.S. government, a private U.S. investment abroad is considered *direct* if a single U.S. resident, or an affiliated group of U.S. residents, owns "at least 10 per cent of the voting securities (or the equivalent) of a foreign business enterprise." If not, the investment is deemed *portfolio.*

Economic Support Fund (ESF). U.S. economic assistance to countries on the basis of special U.S. economic, political, or security needs and U.S. interests. The ESF used to be called Security Support Assistance.

Free Alongside Ship (f.a.s.) Export Value. Value of goods at the port of exportation, based on the transaction price, including inland freight, insurance, and other charges incurred in placing the merchandise alongside the carrier at the port of exportation.

Free On Board (f.o.b.) Export Value. Value of goods on the carrier at the port of exportation, based on the transaction price, including inland freight, insurance, and other charges incurred in placing the merchandise on the carrier at the port of exportation.

Foreign Exchange. Financial assets used in carrying out international economic transactions. The sources of foreign exchange that a country can draw upon to make international payments are known, collectively, as that nation's *international reserves*—foreign currency, gold, Special Drawing Rights (SDRs), or other assets which can be readily converted into foreign exchange.

General Agreement on Tariffs and Trade (GATT). The multilateral treaty, subscribed to by over 80 governments, that lays down agreed rules for international trade. As an institution, GATT functions as the principal body concerned with negotiating the reduction of trade barriers and with international trade relations.

Gross Domestic Product (GDP). The total market value of all final goods and services produced during a given period of time by all factors of production that earn income within a country. GDP includes income earned by foreigners within a country but excludes income earned abroad by that country's citizens and corporations.

Gross National Product (GNP). The total market value of all final goods and services produced in a particular country during a given period of time. GNP includes income earned abroad by that country's citizens and corporations but excludes income earned by foreigners in the country concerned.

International Monetary Fund (IMF). The international financial institution that oversees the management of international financial exchange and liquidity, facilitates agreement on changes in the international monetary system, allocates additional international reserves in the form of Special Drawing Rights, and provides loans to member countries for several purposes, but primarily to ameliorate the effects of temporary balance-of-payments deficits.

Labor Force. Includes civilian labor force, comprised of all civilians in the non-institutional population sixteen years old and over who seek employment, as well as the armed forces.

Long-Term Debt. Debt which does not reach maturity (is not fully due) before one year's time.

Multilateral Assistance. Economic assistance provided to developing countries through multilateral development banks and other international organizations.

Official Development Assistance (ODA). ODA is defined by DAC as "those flows to developing countries and multilateral institutions provided by official agencies . . . which meet the following test: a) it is administered with the promotion of economic development and welfare of developing countries as its main objective, and b) it is concessional in character and contains a grant element of at least 25 per cent." ODA consists of soft (low-interest) bilateral loans, bilateral grants, and multilateral flows in the form of grants, capital subscriptions, and concessional loans to multilateral agencies.

Offshore Banking Center. Major financial centers (financed almost entirely by foreign banks) which do most of their business outside the country where they are located. For instance, banks in Panama act as clearinghouses of debt for other developing countries. Therefore, although U.S. bank claims in Panama are large, Panama's debt is not.

ODA Commitments. Obligations to provide assistance to recipient countries under specified terms. Funds may be committed in one year but not disbursed until future years.

ODA Disbursements. The actual international transfer of financial resources associated with development assistance. Gross disbursements minus repayments on prior loans equals "net disbursements" or "net flows."

ODA Grants. Outright gifts to developing countries, in money or in kind, for which no repayment is required.

Organisation for Economic Co-Operation and Development (OECD). The organization of Western industrialized nations designed to promote economic growth and stability in member countries and to contribute to the development of the world economy. Member countries of the OECD are Australia, Austria, Belgium, Canada, Denmark, Finland, France, the Federal Republic of Germany, Greece, Iceland, Ireland, Italy, Japan, Luxembourg, the Netherlands, New Zealand, Norway, Portugal, Spain, Sweden, Switzerland, Turkey, the United Kingdom, and the United States.

Organization of Petroleum Exporting Countries (OPEC). An organization devoted to seeking agreement among producers regarding selling prices and other matters relating to oil exports. Includes Algeria, Ecuador, Gabon, Indonesia, Iran, Iraq, Kuwait, Libya, Nigeria, Qatar, Saudi Arabia, the United Arab Emirates, and Venezuela.

P.L. 480 (Food for Peace Program). Established in 1954 as the U.S. government's program of food assistance, and administered jointly by A.I.D. and the U.S. Department of Agriculture, the P.L. 480 program's objectives are the provision of humanitarian food aid, the furtherance of international economic development, the expansion of U.S. agricultural and commercial export markets, and the promotion of U.S. political interests.

Security Assistance. Economic or military aid that is extended for promoting U.S. strategic and political interests.

Short-Term Debt. Debt which reaches maturity (is fully due) within one year's time.

Special Drawing Rights (SDRs). International liquidity and reserves created and managed by the IMF, valued on the basis of a basket of currencies, and designed to replace gold and the U.S. dollar as the principal international reserve assets. Constituting claims on the IMF, SDRs may be exchanged for convertible currencies to settle international official transactions.

Terms of Trade. The ratio of export prices to import prices. If, for instance, a country's export prices rise relative to its import prices—a terms-of-trade improvement—this means that it can buy a greater quantity of imports for any given quantity of exports. Similarly, if export prices fall relative to import prices—a terms-of-trade deterioration—it means that a country can buy a lesser quantity of imports for any given quantity of exports.

World Bank Group. International financial institutions providing intermediate and long-term loans for economic development purposes. The World Bank Group consists of the International Bank for Reconstruction and Development (IBRD), which extends nonconcessional loans, the International Development Association (IDA), which extends concessional loans, and the International Finance Corporation (IFC), which extends loans for projects involving the private sector.

Survey of U.S.-Third World Interdependence

During the 1970s, economic relations between the United States and the developing countries exhibited growing interdependence. Trade, investment, and lending flows increased rapidly and profitably throughout that period. The global recession of 1980-83 badly shook up this network of interdependence. As is well known, tight monetary policy and high interest rates in the United States seriously affected the economies of developing countries. But the global recession also cost the United States heavily in terms of export sales, U.S. jobs in the export sector, income from overseas investment, and debt repayments to U.S. banks.

The near-term growth prospects of many developing countries remain poor. The continuing debt crisis, deteriorating U.S. export opportunities, and the predictable effects of declining U.S. official development assistance all threaten further damage not only to the developing countries but also to the United States.

A-1. U.S. Fiscal Policy: Federal Debt and Deficit, 1970-1989

In 1984, the U.S. federal debt relative to gross national product rose to 36 per cent —higher than at any point in the 1970s. With current federal government deficit spending at record levels, the federal debt is projected to rise to 50 per cent of GNP by the end of the 1980s.

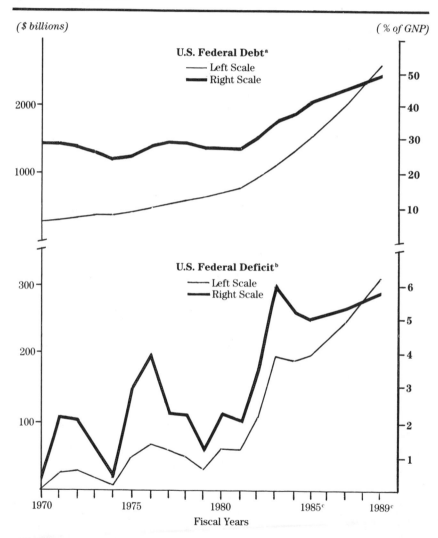

^aGross Federal Debt held by the public.
^bFederal government yearly budget deficit.
^cProjections.

Sources: *Economic Report of the President* (Washington, D.C.: U.S. Government Printing Office, February 1984), Tables B-1 and B-73, and Alice M. Rivlin, ed., *Economic Choices 1984* (Washington, D.C.: The Brookings Institution, 1984), Table 2-2.

A-2. Real U.S. Interest Rate[a]

As U.S. monetary policy became tighter in the late 1970s and early 1980s, the real interest rate rose sharply.

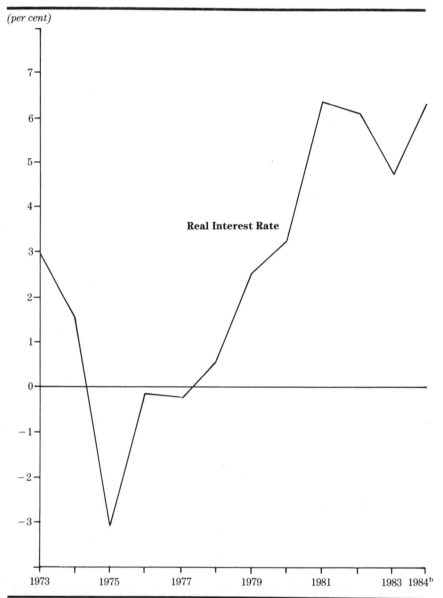

(per cent)

Real Interest Rate

[a]The "real" interest rate is estimated to equal the average U.S. federal funds rate deflated by the U.S. GNP deflator.
[b]1984 estimate is based on first three quarters.
  Source: IMF, *International Financial Statistics, Yearbook 1984;* and *International Financial Statistics,* November 1984.

A-3. Soaring Dollar, Plunging Trade Balance

With the value of the dollar rising by 47 per cent between 1980 and the third quarter of 1984, merchandise has become more costly to foreign purchasers while foreign goods are less expensive for American consumers. The result has been a rapidly deteriorating U.S. trade balance.

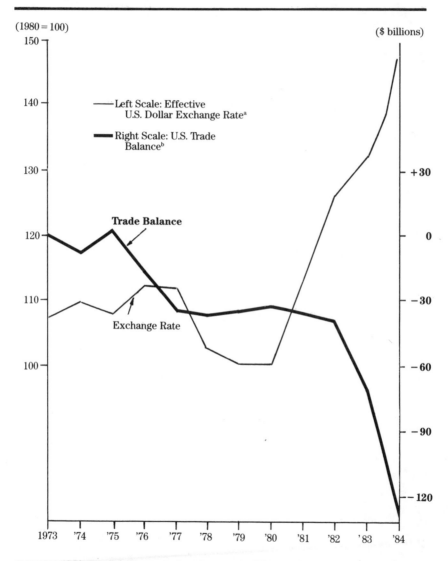

(1980 = 100)   ($ billions)

——Left Scale: Effective
    U.S. Dollar Exchange Rate[a]

▬ Right Scale: U.S. Trade
    Balance[b]

Trade Balance

Exchange Rate

[a]The value of the U.S. dollar in terms of a weighted average of 17 major currencies.
[b]Exports (free alongside ship) minus imports (customs, insurance, and freight) of merchandise.

Sources: IMF, *International Financial Statistics*, November 1984; U.S. Department of Commerce, *Highlights of U.S. Export and Import Trade*, December issues 1973-1983; and Department of Commerce projection for 1984.

A-4. Real Rates of Output Growth of Developing and Industrial Countries (percentages)

The effects of the global recession of 1980-83 and of the subsequent recovery have varied greatly by region: Although lowered by the recession, Asian developing-country growth rates have remained high, while Latin America's recovery has been extremely weak.

	1970-79[a]	1980	1981	1982	1983	1984[d]	1985[d]
Non-Oil Developing Countries	5.3	5.0	3.1	1.7	1.8	3.7	4.3
Latin America[b]	6.1	6.0	1.1	-1.2	-2.8	1.1	3.4
Africa[b]	3.1	3.0	1.7	1.2	0.8	3.2	3.6
Asia[b]	4.7	5.5	5.0	4.5	7.0	6.6	5.8
Oil-Exporting Developing Countries	6.7	-2.1	-4.1	-4.2	-0.8	3.8	4.6
Industrial Countries[c]	3.5	1.3	1.6	-0.2	2.6	4.9	3.4
United States	3.4	-0.3	2.5	-2.1	3.7	7.3	4.0

[a] Annual average.
[b] Excludes oil exporters in area. Asia includes China.
[c] OECD countries excluding Greece, Portugal, and Turkey.
[d] Projections.

Sources: IMF, *World Economic Outlook*, September 1984, Occasional Paper No. 32, Tables 1 and 2, and *International Financial Statistics, Yearbook 1984*, pp. 121-23.

A-5. The World Debt Crisis

Despite major debt renegotiations in 1983-84, the outstanding debt of developing countries continued to grow. The continuing debt crisis is a major reason for the fragility of Latin America's recovery in 1984.

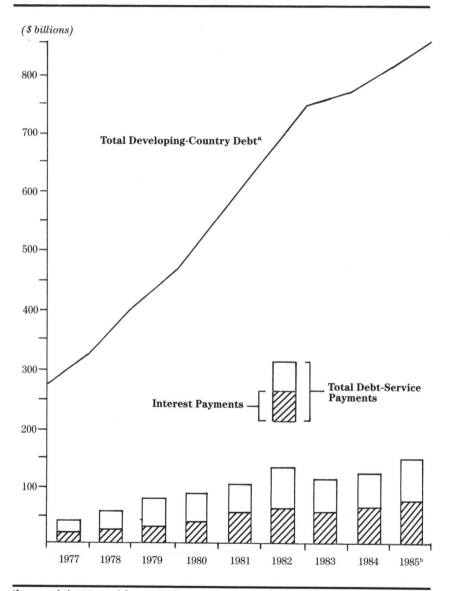

($ billions)

[a]Long- and short-term debt outstanding.
[b]IMF projection.
  Source: IMF, *World Economic Outlook, September 1984*, Occasional Paper 32, Tables 35 and 38.

A-6. Commodity Prices and Terms of Trade of Non-Oil Developing Countries

The slump in commodity prices is another factor darkening the prospects for recovery in developing countries. Even though commodity prices rose in the 1970s, developing-country terms of trade were declining. The slump in prices since May 1984 will bring even lower export earnings.

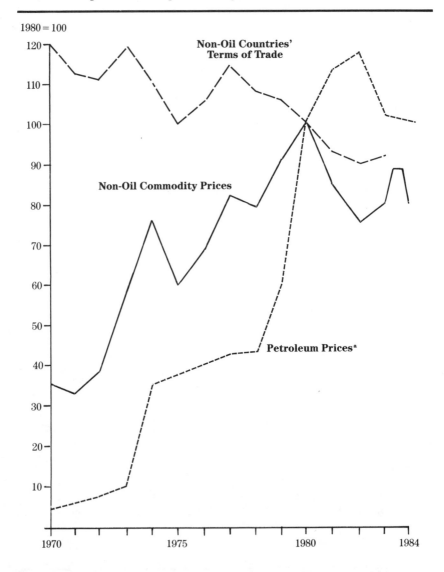

1980 = 100

Non-Oil Countries' Terms of Trade

Non-Oil Commodity Prices

Petroleum Prices[a]

[a]Based on the dollar price of Saudi Arabian petroleum at Ras Tanura.
Source: IMF, *International Financial Statistics, Yearbook 1984,* and *International Financial Statistics,* November 1984.

A-7. Global Current Account Balances

Since 1981, through their austerity and export promotion programs, the non-oil developing countries have made huge strides toward reducing their current-account deficits—despite their heavy debt-service burdens and declining commodity prices.

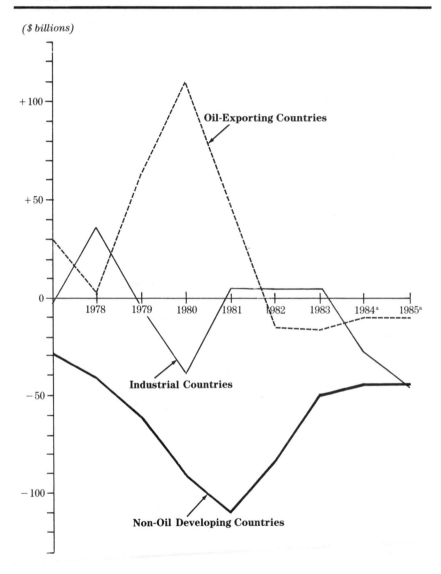

($ billions)

Oil-Exporting Countries

Industrial Countries

Non-Oil Developing Countries

[a]IMF estimates for 1984 and 1985.
Source: IMF, *World Economic Outlook, September 1984*, Occasional Paper 32, Table 17.

A-8. The U.S. Current Account with Developing Countries

In the past, the United States has been able to counter-balance its trade deficit with developing countries because of its surplus in the trade of services and its receipts of income from overseas investment and debt service. Since 1981, however, the global recession and debt crisis have diminished this income.

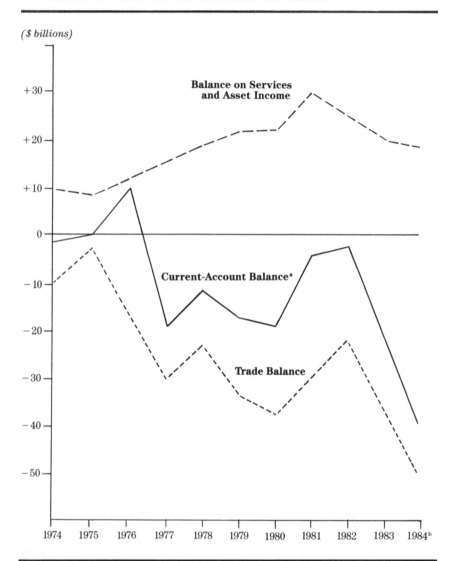

($ billions)

[a]Sum of balances on trade, services and asset income, and unilateral transfers.
[b]Estimate based on first half of 1984.
  Source: U.S. Department of Commerce, *Survey of Current Business,* March editions, 1975-1984.

A-9. U.S. Trade with Developing Countries,[a] 1977-1983

*During the U.S. recession, U.S. imports from developing countries fell more than exports, **improving** the balance of trade. Likewise, as the U.S. recovery precedes that of developing countries, U.S. demand for imports is outpacing foreign demand for U.S. exports, **worsening** the trade balance.*

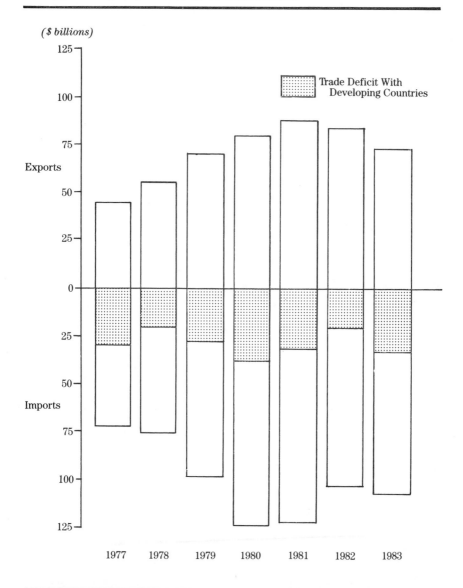

($ billions)

Trade Deficit With
Developing Countries

Exports

Imports

1977　1978　1979　1980　1981　1982　1983

[a]Portugal and South Africa are excluded.
　Source: U.S. Department of Commerce, *Highlights of U.S. Export and Import Trade*, December issues 1978-1983, Tables E-3 and I-6.

A-10. Accumulated U.S. Direct Investment in Developing Countries, 1970-1983

Declining investment income in developing countries during the global recession led to shifts in U.S. investment—mostly away from Latin America and toward Asia. Yet seven of the top ten recipients of U.S. investment are in the Western Hemisphere.

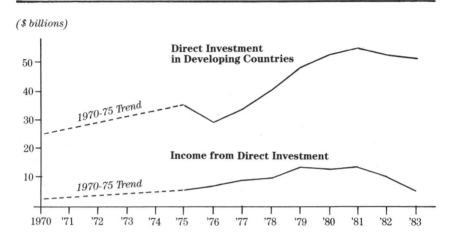

($ billions)

Accumulated U.S. Direct Investment

	1970	1975	1980	1981	1982	1983
			($ billions)			
Total, All Developing Countries	25.7	34.9	52.7	56.1	53.2	51.0
			(percentages)			
Latin America	57.2	63.6	72.7	69.3	62.0	57.8
Asia	n.a.	16.3	15.9	19.6	23.1	26.1
Africa	n.a.	6.9	7.0	7.7	9.6	10.2
Middle East	n.a.	12.9	4.4	3.6	5.1	5.9

Ten Largest Recipients, as of 1983

	All Industries *($ billions)*	Key Sectors *(% share of country total)*
Bermuda	11.5	Finance,[a] 93%
Brazil	9.0	Manufacturing, 68%
Mexico	5.0	Manufacturing, 74%
Panama	4.5	Finance,[a] 47%
Bahamas	4.1	Banking & Finance,[a] 71%
Hong Kong	3.3	Trade, 30%; Banking & Finance,[a] 30%
Argentina	3.1	Manufacturing, 55%
Indonesia	3.0	Petroleum, 87%
Peru	2.3	(not available)
Singapore	2.0	Manufacturing, 35%
Total	47.8	Finance,[a] 33%

[a]Includes finance, insurance, and real estate.

Source: U.S. Department of Commerce, *Survey of Current Business,* various August issues 1971-1984.

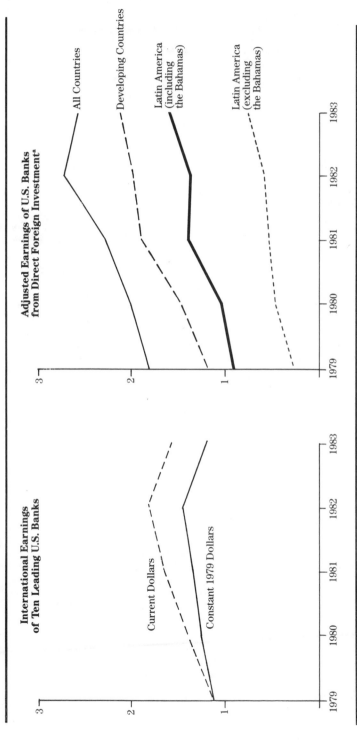

A-11. International Earnings of U.S. Commercial Banks[a] ($ billions)

International Earnings of Ten Leading U.S. Banks

Current Dollars

Constant 1979 Dollars

1979 1980 1981 1982 1983

Adjusted Earnings of U.S. Banks from Direct Foreign Investment[a]

All Countries

Developing Countries

Latin America (including the Bahamas)

Latin America (excluding the Bahamas)

3

2

1

1979 1980 1981 1982 1983

[a] Adjusted earnings from direct investment constitutes slightly more than half of U.S. bank income from overseas. The other portion is earnings from direct lending.

Sources: Salomon Brothers, Inc., *A Review of Bank Performance: 1984 Edition* (New York: 1984), p. 66, and U.S. Department of Commerce, *Survey of Current Business*, August issues 1980-84.

A-12. U.S. Export Reliance: U.S. Jobs Linked to U.S. Production for Export, by State, 1981

The United States was not immune to the problems of other countries when the global recession began. More than 8 per cent of total U.S. output—produced by 7.4 million U.S. workers—was exported in 1981. Heavily populated states were the most export-reliant and therefore the most seriously affected states.

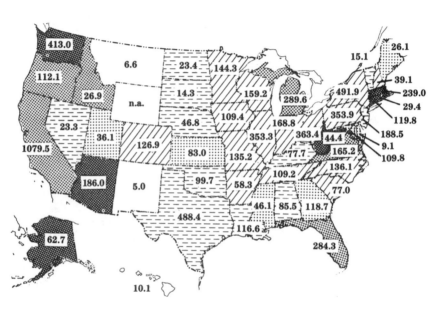

KEY
- Numbers marked on states indicate thousands of export-generated U.S. jobs.
- Shading of each state indicates production for export as a percentage of total production.

☐ 0-3.9%	▨ 7-8.9%
▥ 4-5.9	▩ 9-9.9
▤ 6-6.9	▦ 10 and over

Sources: U.S. Department of Commerce, *Michigan State Exports* (1984) Table 3; and *1981 Annual Survey of Manufactures: Origin of Exports of Manufactured Products* (1983), Table 2a.

The Debt Crisis

The oil price rises of the 1970s resulted in massive inflows of petro-dollar deposits to industrial-country banks and in greatly increased demand for credit by oil-importing developing countries. Consequently, commercial bank lending to non-oil developing countries grew rapidly. The global recession of the early 1980s caught both the banks and the borrowing countries overextended. Recent debt renegotiations have shored up the international financial system, but the weak growth prospects of many debtor countries jeopardize future debt repayments.

B-1. Foreign Loans of U.S. Commercial Banks[a]

In the first half of 1984, net lending became negative as repayments outpaced new loans.

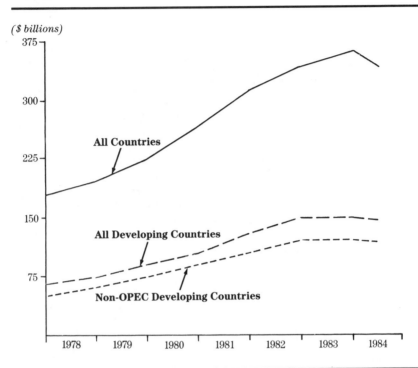

($ billions)

	December 1977	December 1980	June 1984
		($ billions)	
All Countries	**174.4**	**262.8**	**349.9**
Non-OPEC Developing Countries[b]	**52.8**	**88.4**	**121.3**
Latin America[b]	36.0	56.1	77.7
Mexico	10.9	15.7	25.8
Brazil	11.7	16.3	24.1
Argentina	2.4	7.2	8.7
Asia[b]	13.9	27.7	39.7
Korea, Rep.	3.3	7.6	12.1
Philippines	2.0	4.4	5.3
Africa[b]	2.9	4.6	4.0
Egypt	0.4	0.8	1.2
Morocco	0.5	0.7	0.8
OPEC Countries	**14.2**	**20.3**	**23.8**
Venezuela	5.2	9.3	11.0
Indonesia	1.9	1.8	3.2

[a]Includes adjustments for guarantees and indirect borrowings.
[b]Includes offshore banking centers; excludes Eastern European countries.
    Source: Federal Financial Institutions Examination Council, *Country Lending Exposure Survey*, December issues, 1978-83, and June 1984 issue (Washington, D.C.).

B-2. Major Third World Debtor Countries

	Total Debt ($ billions)			Debt/GNP (percentages)			Debt/Exports (percentages)			GNP/Person 1983[b] ($)	Debt/Person 1983 ($)	Growth of Debt 1973-1983[a] (%)
	1973	1980	1983	1973	1980	1983[b]	1973	1980	1983			
Total, nine countries	**52.5**	**249.8**	**372.0**	**21.4**	**32.0**	**40**	**177**	**170**	**261**	**1,640**	**650**	**21.6**
Brazil	13.8	66.1	97.0	17.9	25.9	35	223	328	443	2,220	770	21.5
Mexico	8.6	53.8	83.0	17.3	39.1	50	380	346	392	2,200	1,100	25.4
Argentina	6.4	27.2	42.0	16.1	37.9	55	195	339	531	2,630	1,440	20.7
Korea, Rep.	4.6	26.4	42.0	34.7	46.4	49	143	151	176	2,140	1,040	24.8
Venezuela	4.6	27.5	33.0	25.1	47.1	45	94	143	204	4,300	1,940	21.8
Indonesia	5.7	17.0	23.0	35.7	25.6	24	178	78	109	620	150	15.0
Chile	3.7	11.1	18.0	50.3	43.7	66	301	237	469	2,330	1,540	17.1
Algeria	2.9	15.1	17.0	34.8	41.2	34	154	115	139	2,400	810	19.3
Nigeria	2.2	5.6	17.0	14.6	7.6	23	64	21	119	830	190	22.7

[a] Annual average.
[b] Estimates.

Sources: Albert Fishlow, "The Debt Crisis: Round Two Ahead?," in Richard E. Feinberg and Valeriana Kallab, eds., *Adjustment Crisis in the Third World* (New Brunswick, N.J.: Transaction Books, for the Overseas Development Council, 1984), pp. 34–35; IMF, *Direction of Trade Statistics Yearbook* (1984); Population Reference Bureau, "1984 World Population Data Sheet," Washington, D.C., April 1984; and World Bank, *World Bank Atlas*, 1983 and 1975 editions.

B-3. Debt of Non-Oil Developing Countries[a]

	1977	1978	1979	1980	1981	1982	1983	1984[b]	1985[b]
Debt					($ billions)				
Non-Oil Developing Countries	288.0	342.9	403.6	484.6	572.4	649.7	685.5	728.9	764.6
Africa[c]	31.0	37.1	45.1	50.8	56.3	62.7	66.2	69.3	71.8
Asia	69.8	79.5	93.6	115.8	133.9	154.0	167.7	185.5	200.0
Europe	37.9	47.0	54.7	66.3	70.3	72.1	75.0	77.6	79.5
Latin America	109.5	132.5	158.1	193.4	246.7	287.5	299.1	315.3	327.6
Middle East	21.9	30.8	36.2	41.5	46.2	50.8	55.6	58.7	62.9
Debt/Export Ratio[d]					(percentages)				
Non-Oil Developing Countries	129.5	131.0	119.5	113.1	125.0	148.3	154.4	147.4	139.8
Africa[c]	136.4	151.6	149.2	141.2	170.9	204.0	220.7	212.0	201.4
Asia	81.9	76.1	68.9	68.1	70.4	80.6	83.1	81.0	78.4
Europe	115.7	123.7	115.2	116.1	109.5	119.5	127.2	119.9	113.1
Latin America	203.9	217.8	198.8	187.9	220.3	283.2	300.0	285.9	264.4
Middle East	138.9	162.2	149.4	124.4	133.3	149.8	173.2	165.5	163.4
Debt Service Ratio[e]									
Non-Oil Developing Countries	16.1	19.8	19.7	18.1	21.4	25.0	22.3	21.7	22.7
Africa[c]	11.9	15.4	15.5	16.5	18.7	22.2	22.6	24.9	27.0
Asia	7.6	9.6	8.3	8.2	9.5	11.2	10.0	9.9	10.1
Europe	14.9	16.8	18.9	18.8	20.1	22.1	21.7	21.4	23.3
Latin America	32.0	41.7	42.2	35.7	44.6	55.1	47.9	44.6	46.7
Middle East	14.1	14.5	16.9	16.9	20.1	22.9	22.9	23.1	25.5

[a] Long- and short-term debt.
[b] Estimates.
[c] Excludes South Africa.
[d] Debt as a percentage of exports.
[e] Repayments of principal and interest on debt as a percentage of exports.
Source: IMF, *World Economic Outlook*, September 1984, Tables 35, 36, and 38.

B-4. Net New Lending by Banks Worldwide[a]

Not only did net lending decline in 1981-83, but non-OPEC developing countries received a decreasing share of the money that was loaned.

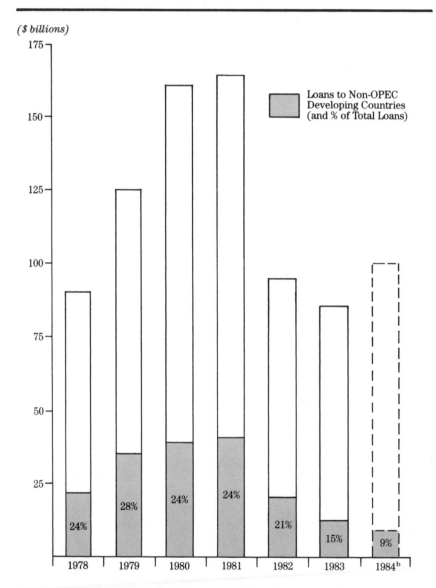

(*$ billions*)

Loans to Non-OPEC Developing Countries (and % of Total Loans)

[a]Encompasses all banks reporting to the Bank for International Settlements.
[b]Projection based on annualized data for January-June.

Sources: Bank for International Settlements (Basel, Switzerland), *Fifty-Second Annual Report,* 1982, p. 122, *Fifty-Fourth Annual Report,* 1984, p. 122, and "International Banking Developments, Second Quarter 1984," November 8, 1984.

B-5. Per Capita Debt of the Non-Oil Developing Countries[a]

Latin America has the heaviest per capita debt burden. Yet Africa's accumulated debt in relation to GDP is heavier, amounting to a larger proportion of Africa's income.

	Debt/Person			GDP/ Person	Debt/ GDP
	1973[b]	1980	1983	1983[c]	1983
	($)	($)		($)	(%)
Non-Oil Developing Countries	79	252	322	877	36.7
Latin America	178	580	804	1,467	54.8
Middle East	171	519	685	1,354	50.6
Europe	155	560	594	1,732	34.3
Africa	67	181	207	347	59.7
Asia	37	106	139	650	21.4

[a] Debt includes both long- and short-term debt. Non-Oil Developing Countries are those defined as such by the IMF.
[b] For 1973, regional figures are estimates of long-term and short-term debt based upon actual figures for long-term debt.
[c] Computed from debt/GDP ratios in IMF, *World Economic Outlook*.
   Sources: For debt figures, IMF, *World Economic Outlook*, 1983 and 1984; for population figures, *World Bank Atlas*, 1975 and 1983, and Population Reference Bureau, "1983 World Population Data Sheet," Washington, D.C., April 1984.

B-6. Average Effective Interest Rates and Spreads Charged to Non-Oil Developing Countries [a]

Although world market interest rates have fallen considerably since their recent high in 1981, the rate charged developing countries by commercial banks has not fallen as quickly. As a result, the effective interest rate charged non-oil developing countries (including concessional lending) has fallen less than one percentage point.

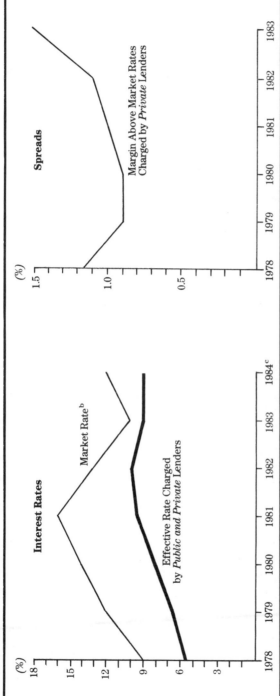

[a]The average effective interest rate is the ratio of the total actual payments of interest divided by the year-end debt outstanding. As such, all delays of interest payments due to renegotiation effectively lower the interest rate for the debtor.

[b]Ninety-day London Interbank Offered Rate.

[c]Estimates for 1984.

Sources: IMF, *International Financial Statistics Yearbook, 1984* and *International Financial Statistics*, November 1984; IMF, *World Economic Outlook*, September 1984, Occasional Paper 32, Tables 35 and 38; and IMF, *International Capital Markets: Developments and Prospects, 1984*, August 1984, Occasional Paper 31, Chart 2.

U.S. and World Trade with Developing Countries

In the early 1980s, world trade was buffeted by three interrelated events: The global recession compressed the demand for goods and therefore drove down trade levels. Protectionism intensified worldwide as labor and business interests in import-competing industries increased pressures on their governments for protection from foreign competition. The debt crisis forced debtor countries to cut their imports severely in order to meet their debt-service obligations. These three factors made trade contraction much sharper than the decline of income during the recession.

180

C-1. The Real Value of U.S. Exports ᵃ

The global recession adversely affected U.S. exports, especially those to developing countries. While the absolute drop in the real (adjusted for inflation) value of U.S. exports to developing countries between 1980 and 1983 was smaller than that of U.S. exports to other countries, this fall represented a larger proportion of exports to developing countries (24 per cent) than of exports to other countries (17 per cent).

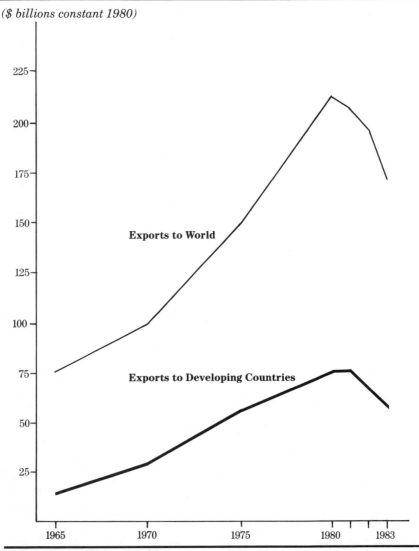

($ billions constant 1980)

Exports to World

Exports to Developing Countries

ᵃDeflated by the U.S. export deflator.
Sources: United Nations, *Monthly Bulletin of Statistics* (July 1981 and June 1984), Special Table B; and UNCTAD, *Handbook of International Trade and Development Statistics 1983,* Table 3.12B.

C-2. The Real Value of World Exports

The real value of world trade fell 25 per cent between 1980 and 1983.

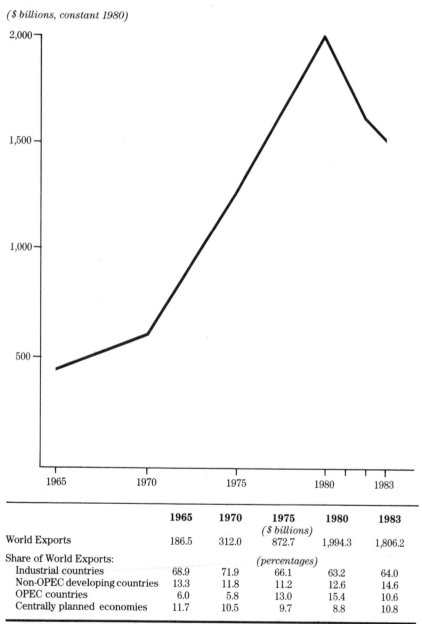

($ billions, constant 1980)

	1965	**1970**	**1975**	**1980**	**1983**
			($ billions)		
World Exports	186.5	312.0	872.7	1,994.3	1,806.2
Share of World Exports:			*(percentages)*		
Industrial countries	68.9	71.9	66.1	63.2	64.0
Non-OPEC developing countries	13.3	11.8	11.2	12.6	14.6
OPEC countries	6.0	5.8	13.0	15.4	10.6
Centrally planned economies	11.7	10.5	9.7	8.8	10.8

Sources: U.N., *Monthly Bulletin of Statistics* (July 1981 and June 1984), Special Table B, and UNCTAD, *Handbook of International Trade and Development Statistics 1983*, Table 3.2B.

C-3. Ten Largest Developing-Country Markets for U.S. Exports, 1983

Developing countries purchased 36.1 per cent of U.S. exports in 1983. Three-fifths of those exports went to ten developing countries.

	U.S. Exports ($ billions)	Share of U.S. Exports to All Developing Countries (percentages)
Mexico	9.1	12.6
Saudi Arabia	7.9	10.9
Korea, Rep.	5.9	8.1
Taiwan	4.7	6.5
Singapore	3.8	5.2
Egypt	2.8	3.9
Venezuela	2.8	3.9
Hong Kong	2.6	3.6
Brazil	2.6	3.6
China	2.2	3.0
Total, Ten Developing Countries	44.4	61.3

Total, All Developing Countries		
Value ($ billions)	$ 72.4	
Percentage of total U.S. exports	*36.1%*	
Total, Developed Countries		
Value ($ billions)	$122.8	
Percentage of total U.S. exports	*61.2%*	
Total U.S. Exports		
($ billions)	$200.5	

Source: U.S. Department of Commerce, *Highlights of U.S. Export and Import Trade*, December 1983, Tables 3 and E-3.

C-4. Twenty Largest U.S. Trading Partners, 1983

Ten of the twenty largest U.S. trade partners in 1983 were developing countries.

	Total Transactions	U.S. Exports	U.S. Imports
		($ billions)	
Canada	90.7	38.2	52.5
Japan	65.5	21.9	43.6
Mexico	**26.1**	**9.1**	**17.0**
United Kingdom	23.5	10.6	12.9
Germany, Fed. Rep.	21.9	8.7	13.2
Taiwan	**16.8**	**4.7**	**12.1**
Korea, Rep.	**13.6**	**5.9**	**7.7**
France	12.3	6.0	6.3
Saudi Arabia	**11.7**	**7.9**	**3.8**
Netherlands	10.9	7.8	3.1
Italy	9.7	3.9	5.8
Hong Kong	**9.4**	**2.6**	**6.8**
Venezuela	**8.0**	**2.8**	**5.2**
Brazil	**8.0**	**2.6**	**5.4**
Belgium-Luxembourg	7.5	5.0	2.5
Indonesia	**7.2**	**1.5**	**5.7**
Singapore	**6.8**	**3.8**	**3.0**
Australia	**6.4**	**4.0**	**2.4**
Switzerland	5.6	3.0	2.6
Nigeria	**4.8**	**0.9**	**3.9**
Total, Twenty Countries	366.4	150.9	215.5
Total, Ten Developing Countries	112.4	41.8	70.6
TOTAL U.S. TRADE	470.4	200.5	269.9
	(percentages)		
Ten Developing Countries, as a percentage of total U.S. trade	23.9	20.8	26.2

Note: Developing countries in bold type. Export figures are f.a.s. (free alongside ship) transaction values; import figures are c.i.f. (customs, insurance, and freight).

Sources: U.S. Department of Commerce, *Highlights of U.S. Export and Import Trade*, December 1983, Tables E-3 and I-6.

184

C-5. U.S. Trade, 1983 (percentages)

Developing countries buy more U.S. goods than Japan and the European Common Market combined. They supply an even greater portion of U.S. imports.

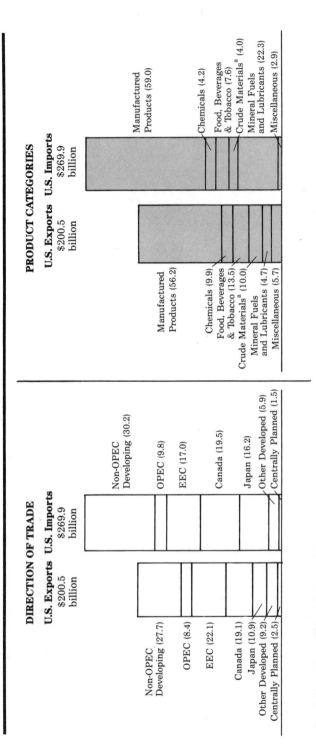

DIRECTION OF TRADE

U.S. Exports U.S. Imports
$200.5 $269.9
billion   billion

Non-OPEC Developing (27.7) / (30.2)
OPEC (8.4) / (9.8)
EEC (22.1) / (17.0)
Canada (19.1) / (19.5)
Japan (10.9) / (16.2)
Other Developed (9.2) / (5.9)
Centrally Planned (2.5) / (1.5)

PRODUCT CATEGORIES

U.S. Exports U.S. Imports
$200.5 $269.9
billion   billion

Manufactured Products (56.2) / (59.0)
Chemicals (9.9) / (4.2)
Food, Beverages & Tobacco (13.5) / (7.6)
Crude Materials[a] (10.0) / (4.0)
Mineral Fuels and Lubricants (4.7) / (22.3)
Miscellaneous (5.7) / (2.9)

[a]Includes animal and vegetable oils and fats and inedible crude materials (except fuels).

Note: Export figures are f.a.s. (free alongside ship) and import figures are c.i.f. (customs, insurance, and freight). Figures do not sum to 100 per cent due to rounding.

Source: U.S. Department of Commerce, *Highlights of U.S. Export and Import Trade* (December 1983), Tables E-2, E-3, I-3, and I-6.

C-6. U.S. Export and Import Trade with Developing Countries

The developing countries are supplying the United States with a rising proportion of its imports of industrial goods.

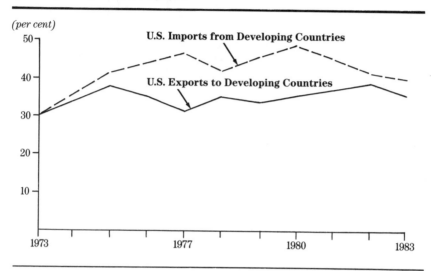

	Total U.S. Trade			Developing Countries' Share[a] of Total U.S. Trade		
	1975	1981	1983	1975	1981	1983
	($ billions)			*(percentages)*		
EXPORTS[b]						
Food, Feeds, and Beverages	19.1	37.9	30.9	35.0	37.3	41.6
Fuels	4.8	10.7	9.9	15.3	19.5	28.9
Industrial Supplies	25.4	57.0	46.8	38.6	37.2	34.9
Capital Goods	35.4	80.2	67.2	42.7	44.8	40.6
Autos	10.1	18.0	16.8	27.4	33.7	18.8
Consumer Goods	6.5	15.8	13.4	35.6	44.1	38.6
Other	6.4	14.1	15.4	53.3	42.8	46.9
Total	**107.7**	**233.7**	**200.5**	**37.9**	**39.5**	**37.4**
IMPORTS[c]						
Foods, Feeds, and Beverages	10.5	19.7	19.6	58.8	56.5	53.2
Fuels	28.4	85.1	61.0	79.5	79.7	72.6
Industrial Supplies	24.1	55.6	50.9	24.1	25.4	26.4
Capital Goods	10.1	35.5	42.1	18.6	24.7	30.5
Autos	12.8	31.0	42.2	2.0	3.3	5.1
Consumer Goods	14.7	40.6	47.6	42.8	51.4	53.6
Other	2.8	5.8	6.4	23.6	24.4	24.8
Total	**103.4**	**273.4**	**269.9**	**42.2**	**45.8**	**40.9**

[a]Israel is included; Oceania, Turkey, Portugal, and all centrally planned economies are omitted from developing countries' share.
[b]Exports are f.a.s. (free alongside ship) values.
[c]Imports are c.i.f. (customs, insurance, and freight) values.

Sources: U.S. Department of Commerce, *Highlights of U.S. Export and Import Trade* (December 1975), Tables E-7 and I-8C; (December 1981), Tables E-7 and I-13; and (December 1983), Table E-6. Unpublished U.S. Department of Commerce import data for 1983.

C-7. U.S. Trade with Developing Countries,[a] by Region

In 1983, Asia surpassed Latin America as the most important Third World region for U.S. trade.

	1975			1981			1983			Growth Rates[b]			
										1975-1981		1981-1983	
	U.S Imports	U.S. Exports	Trade Balance	U.S Imports	U.S. Exports	Trade Balance	U.S Imports	U.S. Exports	Trade Balance	U.S. Imports	U.S. Exports	U.S. Imports	U.S. Exports
	($ millions)			($ millions)			($ millions)			(percentages)		(percentages)	
Asia	11,290	10,095	-1,195	36,248	23,448	-12,800	43,751	25,929	-17,822	21.5	15.1	9.9	5.2
Latin America	17,065	17,114	49	40,805	42,102	1,297	43,581	25,726	-17,855	15.6	16.2	3.3	-21.8
Africa	8,925	4,949	-3,976	28,127	11,097	-17,030	15,206	8,768	-6,438	21.1	14.4	-26.5	-11.1
Near East[c]	5,779	6,743	964	18,300	12,443	-5,857	6,192	11,779	5,587	21.2	10.8	-41.8	-2.7
Europe[d]	613	1,405	792	1,026	2,692	1,666	1,097	2,715	1,618	9.0	11.4	3.4	0.4
Oceania	135	112	-23	191	272	81	104	252	148	6.0	15.9	-26.2	-3.7
Total	43,807	40,418	-3,389	124,697	92,054	-32,643	109,931	75,169	-34,762	19.0	14.7	-6.1	-9.6

[a] Excludes centrally planned economies.
[b] Average annual growth rates.
[c] Excludes Israel.
[d] Includes Portugal and Turkey.
Note: Export figures are f.a.s. (free alongside ship) transaction values; import figures are c.i.f. (customs, insurance, and freight).
Sources: U.S. Department of Commerce, *Highlights of U.S. Export and Import Trade*, December 1975, Tables E-3 and I-4B; December 1981 and 1983, Tables E-3 and I-6.

C-8. U.S. Energy Consumption and Imports of Crude Oil and Petroleum Products

U.S. dependence on Arab sources of oil shrank from 36.9 per cent of imports in 1980 to 12.5 per cent in 1983. Non-OPEC sources such as Mexico, Canada, and the United Kingdom have become major suppliers (34.8 per cent of 1983 imports).

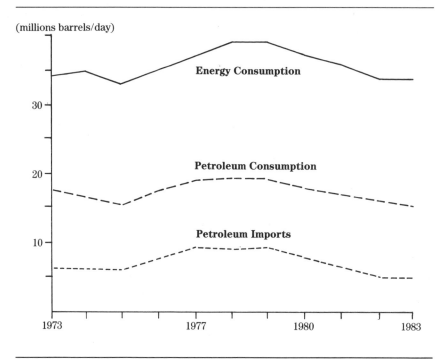

(millions barrels/day)

	1973	1977	1978	1979	1980	1981	1982	1983
Total U.S. Imports of Crude Oil and Petroleum Products (mb/d)	6.3	8.8	8.4	8.5	6.9	6.0	5.1	5.1
Major Suppliers	*(percentage share of U.S. imports)*							
Mexico*	0.3	2.0	3.8	5.2	7.7	8.7	13.4	16.4
Canada*	21.2	5.9	5.6	6.4	6.6	7.5	9.4	10.8
Venezuela	18.1	7.8	7.7	8.2	7.0	6.8	8.1	8.4
United Kingdom*	0.2	1.4	2.2	2.4	2.5	6.3	8.9	7.6
Indonesia	3.4	6.1	6.9	5.0	5.0	6.1	4.9	6.7
Saudi Arabia	7.8	15.7	13.7	16.0	18.3	18.8	10.8	6.7
Nigeria	7.3	13.0	11.0	12.8	12.4	10.3	10.1	6.0
OPEC[a]	47.8	70.3	68.8	66.7	62.2	55.4	42.0	36.9
OAPEC[b]	14.6	36.1	35.4	36.1	36.9	30.8	16.7	12.5

[a]Organization of Petroleum Exporting Countries.
[b]Organization of Arab Petroleum Exporting Countries.
*Not members of OPEC.

Sources: ODC figure and table based on U.S. Energy Information Administration, *Petroleum Supply Annual 1983* (June 1984), Vol. I, pp. x, 2-3, 8-9; and Central Intelligence Agency, *Handbook of Economic Statistics* (Washington, D.C.: 1983), p. 115.

C-9. U.S. Imports and Reserves of Selected Metals and Minerals, 1983

Developing countries remain key suppliers of important strategic metals and minerals.

Metal/Mineral	U.S. Reliance on Imports in 1983 (%)	Principal Suppliers, 1979-1982, (share of total U.S. imports)	Developing Countries' Share of U.S. Market in 1982 (%)	U.S. Reserve Base[b] (% of world reserve base)
Strontium	100	Mexico, 99%	99	11
Columbium	100	Brazil, 75%; Canada, 6%; Thailand, 6%	42	*
Graphite	100[a]	Mexico, 63%; China, 8%; Brazil, 7%	70	1
Manganese ore	99	South Africa, 33%; Gabon, 26%; Australia, 20%; Brazil, 12%	71	*
Bauxite	96	Bauxite—Jamaica, 39%; Guinea, 32%; Suriname, 10% Alumina—Australia, 78%; Jamaica, 13%; Suriname, 7%	14	*
Cobalt	96	Zaire, 37%; Zambia, 13%; Canada, 8%; Belgium-Luxembourg, 8%	59	12
Platinum	84	South Africa, 56%; U.S.S.R., 16%; United Kingdom, 11%	66	1
Chromium	77	Chromite—South Africa, 48%; U.S.S.R., 17%; Philippines, 13% Ferrochromium—South Africa, 44%; Yugoslavia, 9%; Zimbabwe, 9%	91	1
Nickel	77	Canada, 41%; Australia, 11%; Norway, 10%; Botswana, 10%	23	3

Tin	72	Malaysia, 31%; Thailand, 25%; Bolivia, 16%; Indonesia, 14%	98	1
Cadmium	69	Canada, 26%; Australia, 19%; Mexico, 9%; Korea, 8%	31	19
Zinc	66	Ore Concentrates—Canada, 56%; Peru, 18%; Mexico, 10% Metals—Canada, 54%; Spain, 6%; Australia, 6%; Peru, 5%		18
Silver	61	Canada, 34%; Mexico, 23%; Peru, 21%; United Kingdom, 8%	24	18
Antimony	52	Metals—Bolivia, 48%; China, 31%; Belgium-Luxembourg, 8%; Mexico, 6% Ores & Concentrates—Bolivia, 40%; Mexico, 20%; Canada, 16%; South Africa, 7%	46	
Vanadium	52	South Africa, 54%; Canada, 10%; Finland, 7%	64	3
Tungsten	39	Canada, 20%; Bolivia, 18%; China, 17%	68	13
Iron ore	37	Canada, 67%; Venezuela, 15%; Brazil, 8%; Liberia, 8%	54	5
Copper	17	Chile, 34%; Canada, 25%; Peru, 10%; Zambia, 7%	14	6
			75	18

* Negligible or less than 0.5 per cent.
a 1981 figure.
b Reserve base refers to resources demonstrated to exist.
Source: U.S. Department of the Interior, Bureau of Mines, *Mineral Commodity Summaries 1984* and *Minerals Yearbook* (1982), Vol. I.

C-10. Volume of World Trade, Annual Changes (percentages)

Recession and debt-induced austerity measures in non-oil developing countries in 1982-83 caused a severe contraction in the volume of their trade.

	1973-1979[a] (%)	1980	1981	1982	1983	1984[b]	1985[b]
				(percentages)			
World Trade Volume	4.7	2.0	1.0	−2.5	2.0	8.5	5.5
Exports by:							
Industrial Countries	5.1	3.9	3.3	−2.3	2.6	8.6	5.1
Oil-Exporting Developing Countries	0.3	−12.2	−15.2	−18.5	−7.5	6.0	5.2
Non-Oil Developing Countries	5.0	9.0	7.7	1.7	5.8	9.1	6.2
Imports by:							
Industrial Countries	3.9	−1.5	−2.2	−0.6	4.4	11.9	6.5
Oil-Exporting Developing Countries	16.6	12.4	21.3	5.9	−10.9	−2.7	1.7
Non-Oil Developing Countries	5.6	7.3	3.1	−8.2	−1.8	6.4	5.7

[a] Annual average.
[b] IMF projection.
Source: IMF, *World Economic Outlook*, May 1983, Table 8, and September 1984, Table 9.

C-11. Developed-Country Imports from Developing Countries (as a percentage of total imports of commodity)

Increasingly, developing countries are supplying manufactured products to industrialized countries, especially to the United States and Japan.

	Developed Countries			United States			European Economic Community			Japan		
	1970	1980	1982	1970	1980	1982	1970	1980	1982	1970	1980	1982
Primary Products	**40.0**	**55.2**	**48.8**	**54.0**	**78.7**	**66.5**	**35.9**	**42.5**	**37.1**	**48.4**	**72.5**	**70.9**
Foods, Beverages, and Tobacco	32.7	27.3	26.7	56.4	57.4	53.1	26.0	21.1	19.7	34.1	31.1	35.0
Crude Materials (excluding Fuels), Oils, and Fats	28.5	26.3	24.8	37.2	34.2	33.2	24.5	21.7	19.9	38.6	39.9	38.9
Mineral Fuels and Materials	64.1	72.2	62.9	66.9	88.1	74.8	65.7	59.4	50.3	73.6	90.0	86.5
Manufactured Products	**6.4**	**8.9**	**10.5**	**12.7**	**20.9**	**23.1**	**5.5**	**6.1**	**6.3**	**18.7**	**29.3**	**31.3**
Chemicals	3.6	4.8	5.5	11.8	12.4	14.4	2.5	2.4	2.5	8.0	25.7	24.8
Machinery and Transport Exports	1.3	4.5	5.8	4.5	12.4	14.0	0.6	2.5	3.4	2.4	14.1	14.6
Other Manufactured Goods	11.6	14.2	17.0	19.9	31.7	35.5	9.7	10.1	10.4	36.0	39.2	44.4
Miscellaneous	**3.7**	**15.6**	**18.2**	**12.1**	**29.8**	**38.4**	**2.3**	**13.6**	**11.4**	**8.8**	**35.1**	**61.3**
Total Imports	**18.1**	**29.2**	**26.6**	**25.9**	**48.4**	**39.8**	**16.8**	**21.3**	**19.2**	**38.5**	**62.7**	**61.3**

Source: United Nations, *Monthly Bulletin of Statistics*, May 1984, Special Table C.

C-12. Developing-Country Trade with Other Developing Countries, 1965-1983

Trade among developing countries, though still small as a percentage of world trade (7.9 per cent in 1983), became much more significant for those countries during the global recession, when demand for goods dropped in the industrial countries.

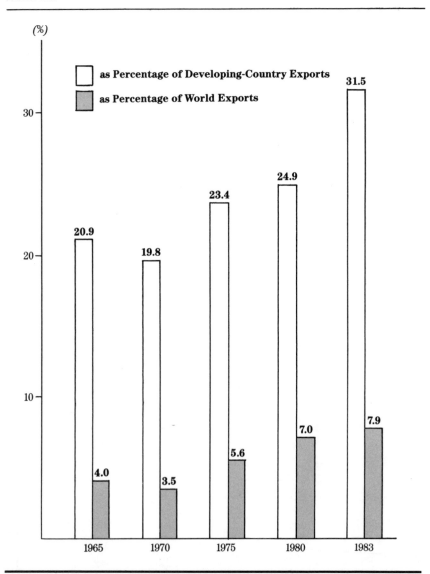

Sources: United Nations, *Monthly Bulletin of Statistics* (July 1981 and June 1984), Special Table B, and UNCTAD, *Handbook of International Trade and Development Statistics 1983*, Tables 3.2B and 3.4A.

C-13. Trade of Centrally Planned Economies

During the recession, the centrally planned economies augmented their trade with developing countries while cutting back trade with Western industrialized countries, though the majority of their trade is with other centrally planned economies.

Exports to:	1970	1980	1983
		($ billions)	
World	32.8	175.1	194.4
		(percentages)	
Centrally planned economies	60.6	48.8	49.0
Industrial countries	23.6	32.2	30.3
Developing countries	15.6	18.1	20.4
(Non-OPEC developing countries)	(13.2)	(14.5)	(16.3)

Imports from:		*($ billions)*	
World	32.3	167.2	169.8
		(percentages)	
Centrally planned economies	61.6	51.1	56.2
Industrial countries	27.7	36.6	30.1
Developing countries	10.7	12.3	13.7
(Non-OPEC developing countries)	(9.7)	(9.9)	(11.5)

Source: United Nations, *Monthly Bulletin of Statistics*, June 1984, Special Table B.

194

C-14. Manufactured Exports of Newly Industrialized Developing Countries[a]

Over the period 1966-1980, eight newly industrialized countries (NICs) increased their share of developing-country manufactured exports from 65 to 74 per cent. The decline in the share of manufactured exports of other developing countries suggests that the success of those NICs has not been widely achieved elsewhere.

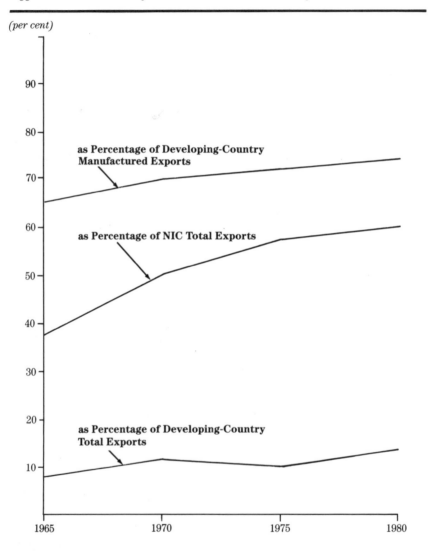

(per cent)

as Percentage of Developing-Country Manufactured Exports

as Percentage of NIC Total Exports

as Percentage of Developing-Country Total Exports

[a]Brazil, Hong Kong, Republic of Korea, Mexico, Portugal, Singapore, Taiwan, and Yugoslavia.
   Sources: United Nations, *Monthly Bulletin of Statistics*, July 1981 and June 1984, Special Table B, and May 1984, Special Table D; UNCTAD, *Handbook of International Trade and Development Statistics 1983*, Tables 3.2B and 4.1; and Republic of China, *Statistical Yearbook of the Republic of China, 1983*.

C-15. Major Primary Commodity Exports of Developing Countries, 1979-1981

Primary commodities remain an important source of income for many developing countries.

Commodity	Developing-Country Exports 1979-1981 Average		Major Suppliers 1979-1981
	($ billions)	(% of world exports)	(% of world exports of commodity)
Petroleum	253.0	83.4	Saudi Arabia, 28.3; Nigeria, 6.7; Iraq, 6.4; Libya, 5.8
Coffee	10.2	91.9	Brazil, 17.9; Colombia, 17.6; Ivory Coast, 5.8; El Salvador, 5.2
Copper	5.8	60.7	Chile, 19.9; Zambia, 12.0; Zaire, 7.3; Peru, 6.8
Timber	5.7	30.1	Malaysia, 9.2; Indonesia, 7.8; Ivory Coast, 1.7; Philippines, 1.7
Sugar	4.6	35.3	Brazil, 7.0; Philippines, 3.6; Dominican Rep., 2.6; Thailand, 2.1
Rubber	3.9	98.4	Malaysia, 49.1; Indonesia, 25.0; Thailand, 14.5; Sri Lanka, 3.9
Cotton	3.2	43.3	Egypt, 5.8; Mexico, 4.4; Pakistan, 4.2; Turkey, 4.1
Iron Ore	3.1	45.1	Brazil, 22.4; India, 4.9; Liberia, 4.3
Bauxite	2.8	26.9	Jamaica, 6.9; Suriname, 3.2; Guinea, 2.9; Venezuela, 2.8
Cocoa	2.7	94.0	Ivory Coast, 23.4; Ghana, 20.5; Nigeria, 15.0; Brazil, 12.0
Tin	2.5	79.2	Malaysia, 33.4; Thailand, 15.2; Indonesia, 13.9; Bolivia, 11.6
Rice	2.4	47.9	Thailand, 19.6; Pakistan, 8.9; India, 5.0; Burma, 3.7
Tobacco	1.7	42.3	Brazil, 7.9; Turkey, 6.7; Zimbabwe, 5.1; India, 4.2
Maize	1.7	15.4	Argentina, 6.9; Thailand, 3.0
Palm Oil	1.4	77.8	Malaysia, 63.2; Indonesia, 10.2; Ivory Coast, 2.0
Tea	1.4	73.4	India, 26.7; Sri Lanka, 18.7; Kenya, 8.6; Indonesia, 5.2
Beef	1.4	16.3	Argentina, 7.1; Uruguay, 1.8
Phosphate Rock	1.3	62.8	Morocco, 34.4; Jordan, 6.9; Togo, 5.4; Senegal, 2.8
Bananas	1.2	92.5	Costa Rica, 17.3; Honduras, 17.0; Ecuador, 16.8; Philippines, 8.8

Source: World Bank, *Commodity Trade and Price Trends*, 1983-84 Edition, Tables 10 and 11.

C-16. Developing-Country Arms Exports, as Percentages of World Arms Exports

After many years of buying military weapons, some developing countries have turned to manufacturing arms in recent years. They have found the arms industry to be one of the most dynamic, recession-proof export industries (with 12.5 per cent growth in real terms between 1980 and 1982).

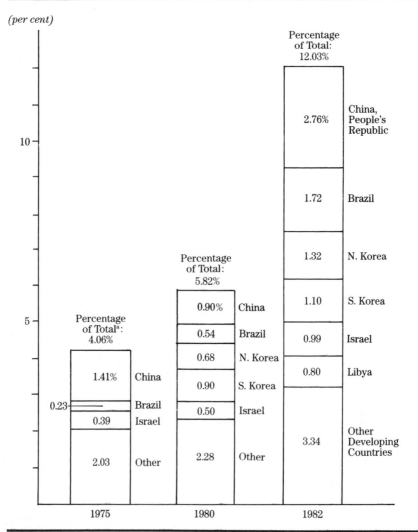

(per cent)

^aIncludes shares of North Korea, South Korea, and Libya (0.08, 0.84, and 0.04 per cent, respectively).

Note: World arms exports (in constant 1981 dollars) were $19.8 billion in 1975, $30.4 billion in 1980, and $34.2 billion in 1982.

Source: U.S. Arms Control and Disarmament Agency, *World Military Expenditures and Arms Transfers, 1972-1982* (Washington, D.C.: 1984), Table II.

C-17. U.S. Arms Exports

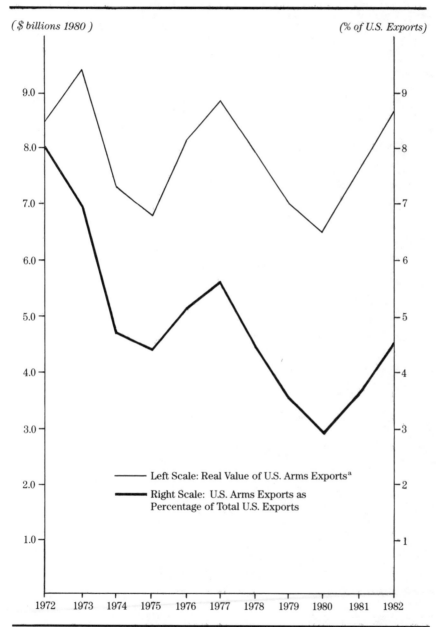

($ billions 1980)   *(% of U.S. Exports)*

—— Left Scale: Real Value of U.S. Arms Exports[a]

—— Right Scale: U.S. Arms Exports as
Percentage of Total U.S. Exports

[a]Deflated by the U.S. export deflator.

Note: In 1978-1982, 44 per cent of U.S. arms exports went to developing countries.

Source: U.S. Arms Control and Disarmament Agency, *World Military Expenditures and Arms Transfers 1972-1982* (Washington, D.C.: 1984), Tables II and III.

Development Assistance

The downturn in private investment and lending since 1981 makes it even more important that official development aid levels be augmented to help fill the financing gap. Trade and finance are critical to developing countries, but only development assistance—with its central purpose of promoting development objectives—aims specifically at alleviating the worst aspects of poverty for individuals.

In relation to GNP as well as average expenditures per person, U.S. official development assistance (ODA) falls below levels provided by most other industrial countries—despite the fact that the United States remains the world's largest donor in absolute terms. Four industrial countries have attained the U.N. goal of raising net ODA to 0.7 per cent of GNP; at its level of 0.24 percent, the United States ranks fifteenth among the developed countries.

D-1. Net Official Development Assistance, by Donor Groups, 1970-1983

U.S. net ODA has not been above 0.30 per cent of GNP for twelve years. During that period, net ODA from other DAC countries has risen from 0.38 per cent to 0.45 per cent of GNP. After the 1973 oil price rise, the net ODA of OPEC countries rose sharply, but it has currently stabilized at about 1.05 per cent.

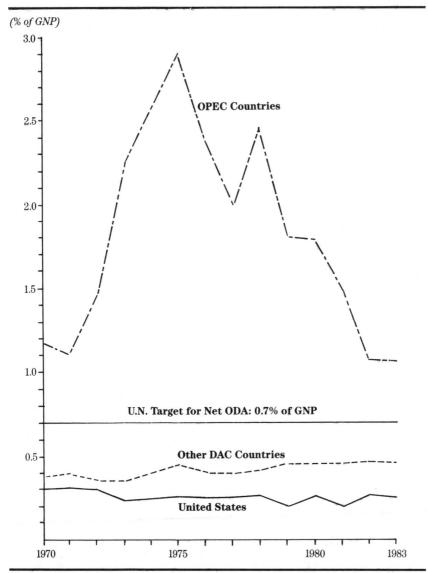

(% of GNP)

OPEC Countries

U.N. Target for Net ODA: 0.7% of GNP

Other DAC Countries

United States

Sources: OECD (DAC), *Development Co-operation, 1984 Review* (Paris: 1984), Table II.B.4; *1982 Review,* Table II.F.2; *1981 Review, 1977 Review,* and *1975 Review,* Tables A.16 and A.17; and *1973 Review,* Table III.8.

D-2. Net Flow of Resources from the United States to Developing Countries and Multilateral Institutions

In 1983 there was a significant fall in the level of U.S. business resource flows to developing countries. However, in the face of the worsening global recession, U.S. private voluntary agencies channeled a record level of resources to needy nations.

	1972-1974 (Average)	1980	1981	1982	1983
			($ millions)		
Official Flows	3,933	8,250	6,698	9,780	8,048
Official development assistance (ODA)	3,429	7,138	5,782	8,202	7,992
Bilateral	2,546	4,366	4,317	4,861	5,493
Grants[a]	1,589	2,975	3,164	3,791	4,470
Loans[b]	957	1,391	1,153	1,070	1,023
Contributions to multilateral institutions	883	2,772	1,465	3,341	2,499
Grants	319	897	806	854	833
Capital subscription payments	564	1,844	634	2,473	1,650
Concessional loans	—	31	25	14	16
Other official flows[c]	504	1,112	916	1,578	56
Private Flows	1,474	4,301	18,658	19,099	13,580
Direct and portfolio investment[d]	1,124	3,400	17,725	18,794	11,939
Private export credits	350	901	933	305	1,641
Grants by Private Voluntary Agencies	770	1,301	1,018	1,280	1,320
Total	6,176	13,852	26,374	30,159	22,948
Total *(as % of GNP)*	0.48	0.53	0.90	0.99	0.69
ODA *(as % of GNP)*	0.26	0.27	0.20	0.27	0.24

[a] Technical assistance, food aid, and other grants.
[b] New development lending, food-aid loans, debt reorganization, and equities and other bilateral assets.
[c] Official export credits (including official funds in support of private export credits), debt relief, equities and other bilateral assets, and contributions to multilateral institutions on terms not concessional enough to qualify as ODA.
[d] Includes bilateral and multilateral portfolio investment.
Note: Figures include capital subscriptions to multilateral organizations made in the form of notes payable on demand. After 1975, such subscriptions are reported in the year in which they are issued rather than the year in which they are cashed.
Source: OECD (DAC), *Development Co-operation, 1984 Review* (Paris: 1984), Table II.I.8.

D-3. Net Flow of Resources from the DAC Countries to Developing Countries and Multilateral Institutions

	1972-1974 (Average)	1980	1981	1982	1983
			($ millions)		
Official Flows	**12,626**	**32,537**	**32,147**	**35,149**	**32,499**
Official development assistance (ODA)	9,970	27,267	25,540	27,731	27,458
Bilateral	7,320	18,110	18,195	18,433	18,534
Grants[a]	4,718	14,125	13,180	13,411	14,132
Loans[b]	2,602	3,985	5,015	5,022	4,403
Contributions to multilateral institutions	2,650	9,157	7,345	9,297	8,930
Grants	1,167	4,160	4,024	4,124	3,961
Capital subscription payments	1,418	4,959	3,289	5,175	4,965
Concessional loans	66	38	32	4	4
Other official flows[c]	2,655	5,270	6,606	7,414	5,034
Private Flows	**7,866**	**40,403**	**57,235**	**46,425**	**34,300**
Direct and portfolio investment[d]	6,660	28,914	46,686	39,097	29,104
Private export credits	1,206	11,489	10,549	7,328	5,196
Grants by Private Voluntary Agencies	**1,206**	**2,386**	**2,005**	**2,317**	**2,344**
Total	**21,697**	**75,326**	**91,387**	**83,886**	**69,131**
Total (*as % of GNP*)	0.71	1.04	1.25	1.15	0.92
ODA (*as % of GNP*)	0.33	0.38	0.35	0.38	0.36

[a] Technical assistance, food aid, and other grants.

[b] New development lending, food-aid loans, debt reorganization, and equities and other bilateral assets.

[c] Official export credits (including official funds in support of private export credits), debt relief, equities and other bilateral assets, and contributions to multilateral institutions on terms not concessional enough to qualify as ODA.

[d] Includes bilateral and multilateral portfolio investment.

Note: Figures include capital subscriptions to multilateral organizations made in the form of notes payable on demand. After 1975, such subscriptions are reported in the year in which they are issued rather than the year in which they are cashed.

Source: OECD (DAC), *Development Co-operation, 1984 Review* (Paris: 1984), Table III.8.

D-4. Net ODA Flows to Developing Countries and Multilateral Institutions

	Amount (constant 1982 $ millions)				As Share of Total (percentages)				As Share of GNP (percentages)			
	1970	1975	1980	1983	1970	1975	1980	1983	1970	1975	1980	1983
United States	7,022	6,788	8,252	7,670	32.8	20.9	21.8	21.1	0.32	0.27	0.27	0.24
Other DAC Countries	10,718	14,048	17,706	19,880	50.1	43.2	46.7	54.8	0.35	0.43	0.47	0.45
Other OECD Countries	—	—	189	118	—	—	0.5	0.3	—	—	0.09	0.06
OPEC Countries	1,039	9,396	9,038	5,504	4.9	28.9	23.8	15.2	1.18	2.92	1.80	1.05
Centrally Planned Economies of Eastern Europe[a]	2,614	2,274	2,506	2,954	12.2	7.0	6.6	8.1	0.16	0.14	0.17	0.17
Other Donors	—	—	229	203	—	—	0.6	0.6	—	—	n.a.	n.a.
Total	21,393	32,506	37,920	36,329	100.0	100.0	100.0	100.0	n.a.	n.a.	n.a.	n.a.

[a] U.S.S.R. and Eastern Europe.

Note: Figures may not sum due to rounding.

Source: OECD (DAC), Development Co-operation, 1984 Review (Paris: 1984), Tables II.B.2 and II.B.4.

D-5. Composition of Industrial-Country (DAC) Transfers[a] to Developing Countries (percentages and $ billions)

Although Official Development Assistance (ODA) in 1983 was a greater portion of total real resource flows to developing countries than in 1981, this was due not to a rise in ODA but to the fall in total flows. In fact, ODA fell slightly. The major reason for the decline in real resource flows was the rapid contraction of private investment, lending, and export credits.

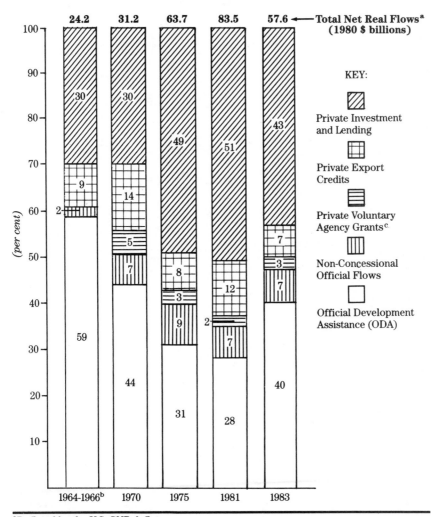

KEY:

Private Investment and Lending

Private Export Credits

Private Voluntary Agency Grants[c]

Non-Concessional Official Flows

Official Development Assistance (ODA)

[a]Deflated by the U.S. GNP deflator.
[b]Average.
[c]Data on private voluntary grants are not available for 1964-1966 average.
  Source: OECD (DAC), *Development Co-operation, 1984 Review* (Paris: 1984), Table II.A.1 and *1975 Review*, Table 17.

D-6. Real Net Flows of ODA and Private Voluntary Assistance, by DAC Country, 1970 and 1983 (in 1983 dollars)

| | Private Voluntary Assistance | | | | Official Development Assistance | | | |
| | Total Contribution ($ millions) | | Average Contribution Per Capita ($) | | Total Contribution ($ millions) | | Contribution as Share of GNP (percentages) | |
	1970	1983	1970	1983	1970	1983	1970	1983
Norway	10	43	2.58	10.41	95	584	.32	1.06
Netherlands	14	107	1.07	7.45	510	1,195	.61	.91
Sweden	65	61	8.08	7.32	304	754	.38	.86
France	16	36	.32	.66	2,522	3,815	.66	.74
(excluding DOM/TOM)a	n.a.	n.a.	n.a.	n.a.	1,613	2,430	.42	.47
Denmark	8	13	1.62	2.54	154	395	.38	.73
Belgium	38	30	3.94	3.04	311	480	.46	.59
Germany	202	370	3.33	6.02	1,155	3,176	.39	.49
Australia	41	32	3.28	2.08	526	753	.59	.49
Canada	134	132	6.28	5.30	899	1,429	.42	.45
United Kingdom	87	83	1.57	1.47	1,161	1,605	.37	.35
Finland	2	16	.43	3.29	18	153	.06	.33
Japan	8	30	.08	.25	1,190	3,761	.23	.33
Switzerland	28	48	4.47	7.38	78	320	.15	.32
New Zealand	4	7	1.42	2.19	36	61	.23	.28
United States	1,553	1,320	7.58	5.63	7,922	7,992	.31	.24
Italy	13	3	.24	.05	382	827	.16	.24
Austria	28	12	3.77	1.59	28	158	.07	.23
DAC Total	2,251	2,344	3.61	3.41	17,241	27,458	.34	.36

* Less than .005 per cent of GNP.

a French Overseas Departments and Territories.

Note: Countries are ranked according to 1983 ODA as a percentage of GNP.

Sources: OECD (DAC), *Development Co-operation, 1984 Review* (Paris: 1984), Tables II.B.4, II.I.2, II.I.10-11, and *1975 Review*, Tables 11-17 and 46.

D-7. Multilateral-Bilateral Mix of ODA from the United States and DAC Countries ($ billions and percentages)

	1972-1974[a]	1980	1981	1982	1983	1981-1983[a]
United States:						
Official Development Assistance *($ billions)*	3.4	7.1	5.8	8.2	8.0	7.3
Contributions to Multilateral Institutions *(as % of ODA)*	25.8%	38.8%	25.3%	40.7%	31.3%	32.2%
Other DAC Countries:						
Official Development Assistance *($ billions)*	6.5	20.1	19.8	19.5	19.7	19.7
Contributions to Multilateral Institutions *(as % of ODA)*	27.0%	31.7%	29.8%	31.5%	33.7%	31.3%

[a] Average.
Source: OECD (DAC), *Development Co-operation, 1984 Review* (Paris: 1984), Table II.I.8.

D-8. Recipients of U.S. and DAC Bilateral ODA, by Income Group and Region, 1982

In 1982, bilateral ODA flows from the United States and DAC countries exhibited regional biases toward areas of geopolitical interest. The United States concentrated its bilateral ODA on lower middle-income countries in the Caribbean Basin and on Israel, while other DAC (mostly European) countries concentrated theirs on African countries. In per capita terms, low-income countries received the least amount of aid both from DAC countries as a whole and from the United States.

	Number of Countries in Category	United States			DAC Countries[a]		
		Number of Countries Receiving ODA	Total ODA ($ millions)	ODA Per Capita[b] ($)	Number of Countries Receiving ODA	Total ODA ($ millions)	ODA Per Capita[b] ($)
Low-Income Countries	**40**	**31**	**723.0**	**.32**	**36**	**5,673.9**	**2.50**
Africa	27	23	272.0	1.28	24	2,680.3	12.63
Asia	12	7	408.0	.20	11	2,915.0	1.42
Latin America	1	1	43.0	7.05	1	78.7	12.90
Lower Middle-Income Countries	**40**	**25**	**1,747.0**	**3.37**	**30**	**5,168.7**	**9.98**
Africa	16	15	1,285.0	5.82	16	3,003.8	13.60
Asia	7	4	181.0	0.69	5	1,394.5	5.32
Latin America	11	5	280.0	9.92	6	455.4	16.13
Oceania	5	1	1.0	.26	3	315.0	80.77
Europe	1	0	0	0	0	0	0
Upper Middle-Income Countries	**39**	**31**	**663.0**	**1.12**	**34**	**2,478.8**	**3.71**
Africa	7	5	15.0	.25	5	503.7	8.31
Asia	10	7	49.0	.30	8	314.3	1.91
Latin America	18	15	243.0	.76	17	1,085.9	3.41
Oceania	1	1	2.0	2.86	1	30.0	15.00
Europe	3	3	354.0	4.41	3	544.9	6.79

	Number of Countries in Category	United States — Number of Countries Receiving ODA	United States — Total ODA ($ millions)	United States — ODA Per Capita[b] ($)	DAC Countries — Number of Countries Receiving ODA	DAC Countries — Total ODA ($ millions)	DAC Countries — ODA Per Capita[b] ($)
High-Income Countries	**23**	**2**	**779.0**	**10.97**	**8**	**948.7**	**13.36**
Africa	3	1	1.0	.23	1	58.0	13.18
Asia[c]	9	1	778.0	35.05	3	875.2	39.42
Latin America	6	0	0	0	3	1.5	0.07
Oceania	2	0	0	0	0	0	0
Europe	3	0	0	0	1	14.0	23.33
Total	142	89	3,912.0	1.12	108	14,270.1	4.10

[a] Including the United States.
[b] Calculated using the total number of countries in the category, not just those that received ODA.
[c] For the purposes of this table, Israel is included as a developing country.
Note: Countries are classified by income group in the same manner as in Annex E-1.
Source: OECD, *Geographical Distribution of Financial Flows to Developing Countries, 1979/1982* (Paris: 1984).

D-9. Net Flow of Resources[a] from Multilateral Institutions to Developing Countries ($ millions)

	Concessional				Total			
	1970	1976	1980	1983	1970	1976	1980	1983
World Bank Group	**163**	**1,326**	**1,650**	**2,383**	**739**	**3,243**	**5,111**	**7,666**
International Development Association	163	1,310	1,543	2,336	163	1,310	1,543	2,336
International Finance Corporation	—	—	—	47	68	193	295	166
World Bank	—	16	107	47	508	1,740	3,273	5,164
IMF Trust Fund	**—**	**—**	**1,636**	**—**	**—**	**—**	**1,636**	**—**
United Nations	**498**	**1,252**	**2,487**	**2,739**	**498**	**1,252**	**2,487**	**2,739**
International Fund for Agricultural Development	**—**	**—**	**45**	**144**	**—**	**—**	**45**	**144**
Regional Banks	**225**	**369**	**614**	**775**	**326**	**936**	**1,619**	**2,435**
Inter-American Development Bank	224	282	326	364	308	567	893	1,321
Asian Development Bank	1	62	149	222	16	294	477	771
African Development Bank and Fund	—	11	96	158	2	55	193	303
Caribbean Development Bank	—	14	43	31	—	20	56	40
European Community	**210**	**501**	**1,013**	**1,215**	**221**	**559**	**1,270**	**1,417**
Arab/OPEC Funds	**—**	**419**	**286**	**311**	**—**	**554**	**414**	**391**
Total	**1,096**	**3,867**	**7,731**	**7,567**	**1,784**	**6,544**	**12,581**	**14,792**

[a] Net disbursements.
Source: OECD (DAC), *Development Co-operation, 1984 Review* (Paris: 1984), Table II.C.1, and *1982 Review*, Table II.C.2.

D-10. Selected U.S. Personal Consumption Expenditures and Net ODA, 1983 ($ billions)

Total U.S. GNP, 1983 = $3,304.8 billion

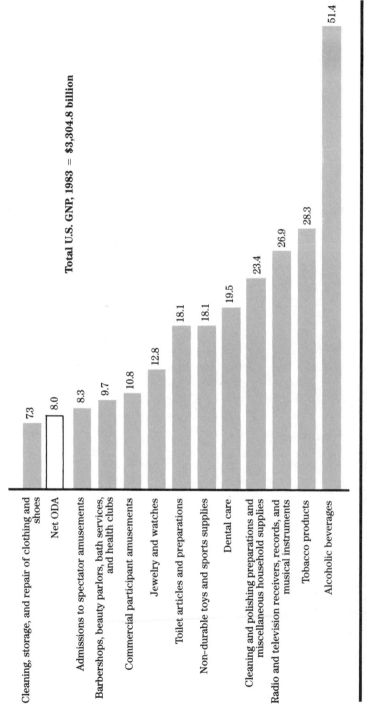

Category	$ billions
Cleaning, storage, and repair of clothing and shoes	7.3
Net ODA	8.0
Admissions to spectator amusements	8.3
Barbershops, beauty parlors, bath services, and health clubs	9.7
Commercial participant amusements	10.8
Jewelry and watches	12.8
Toilet articles and preparations	18.1
Non-durable toys and sports supplies	18.1
Dental care	19.5
Cleaning and polishing preparations and miscellaneous household supplies	23.4
Radio and television receivers, records, and musical instruments	26.9
Tobacco products	28.3
Alcoholic beverages	51.4

Sources: U.S. Department of Commerce, *Survey of Current Business* (July 1984), pp. 37-38, and OECD (DAC), *Development Co-operation, 1984 Review* (Paris: 1984), Table III.I.8.

D-11. Twenty Major Recipients of U.S. Military Assistance, FY1983

	Per Cent of U.S. Total (%)	Amount ($ millions)
Israel	30.4	1,700.0
Egypt	23.7	1,326.9
Turkey	7.2	402.8
Spain	7.2	402.5
Greece	5.0	281.3
Pakistan	4.7	260.8
Korea, Rep.	3.3	186.7
Portugal	2.0	111.2
Tunisia	1.8	102.0
Lebanon	1.8	101.7
Morocco	1.8	101.3
Thailand	1.7	96.2
El Salvador	1.5	81.3
Jordan	0.9	52.8
Philippines	0.9	51.4
Honduras	0.9	48.3
Sudan	0.8	44.3
Somalia	0.5	30.6
Oman	0.5	30.1
Indonesia	0.5	27.4
Total (20 countries)	97.2	5,439.5
Total (all countries)		5,599.0

Source: A.I.D., *U.S. Overseas Loans and Grants, 1945-1983.*

Indicators of Poverty and Development

In infant mortality, life expectancy, literacy, caloric intake, income, population per doctor or teacher, and other indicators of poverty and development, the gulf between living conditions in rich and poor countries is enormous.

Abject poverty is known to be widespread among the majority of the developing world's people, but data on its specific economic and physical manifestations remains very inadequate in most countries. Much of the available data on the physical quality of life predates the global recession. Very few comparable national income distribution studies have been conducted in the last decade. The level of unemployment and underemployment in developing countries is known to be vast, but it is very inadequately reflected in national statistics. Nor are there firm figures on deaths due to the current famine in Africa. And while it is certain that developing countries have suffered from the recent and continuing recession, there still are no reliable estimates of the extent of its impact on the poor.

E-1. Economic and Social Indicators of Development

	Population mid-1984 (mil.)	Physical Quality of Life Index (PQLI)[a] 1981	Per Capita GNP 1982 ($)	Per Capita GNP (Real) Growth Rate 1960-1982 (%)	Share of Labor Force in Industry 1980 (%)
WORLD (171)	4,718.1	69	2,842	3.2	23.0
DEVELOPING COUNTRIES (141)	3,602.6	61	787	3.1	17.5
DEVELOPED COUNTRIES (30)	1,115.5	96	9,477	3.4	39.9
AFRICA (53)	530.6	46	801	1.8	16.0
ASIA (40)	2,692.6	63	959	3.5	17.7
LATIN AMERICA (36)	393.8	77	2,062	3.3	23.7
OCEANIA (10)	23.8	88	8,618	2.2	29.0
EUROPE (30)	815.9	93	7,343	3.4	40.6
NORTH AMERICA (2)	261.4	97	12,983	2.3	31.7
Low-Income (40) (p/c GNP <$420)	2,365.2	58	276	2.9	15.5
Low-Income (39) (excluding China)	1,330.7	46	250	1.2	12.7
Lower Middle-Income (40) (p/c GNP $420 - $1,069)	548.9	57	714	3.3	16.4
Upper Middle-Income (39) (p/c GNP $1,070 - $3,699)	620.1	74	2,058	3.6	24.7
High-Income (52) (p/c GNP >$3,699)	1,183.9	95	9,364	3.4	39.3
AFRICA (53)					
Low-Income (27)	226.4	42	246	0.5	9.9
Benin	3.9	38	310	0.6	16.0
Burkina Faso (Upper Volta)	6.7	20	210	1.1	13.0
Burundi	4.7	35	280	2.5	5.0
Cape Verde	0.3	59	350	n.a.	14.0
Central African Republic	2.6	33	310	0.6	4.0
Chad	5.0	27	80	−2.8	7.0
Comoros	0.5	37	340	0.9	n.a.
Equatorial Guinea	0.3	33	417[g]	n.a.	n.a.
Ethiopia	32.0	31	140	1.4	7.0
Gambia	0.7	16	360	2.5	9.0
Ghana	14.3	48	360	−1.3	20.0
Guinea	5.6	25	310	1.5	11.0
Guinea-Bissau	0.8	27	170	−1.7	n.a.
Kenya	19.4	56	390	0.9	10.0

Population Growth Rate[b] (%)	Life Expectancy at Birth[c] (years)	Infant Mortality per 1,000 Live Births[d]	Literacy[e] (%)	Per Capita Public Education Spending 1980 ($)	Per Capita Military Spending 1980 ($)	Total Exports, f.o.b. 1983 ($ mil.)	Total Imports, c.i.f. 1983 ($ mil.)	U.S. Bilateral Economic Aid[f] FY 1983 ($ mil.)
1.7	62	74	66	128	119	1,750,853	1,803,857	5,203.5
2.1	59	92	56	31	33	503,591	488,551	4,368.5
0.6	74	15	99	440	398	1,247,262	1,315,306	835.0
2.9	51	116	39	38	27	87,389	87,494	1,868.0
1.8	60	89	57	44	38	456,122	440,817	1,926.6
2.3	65	63	79	74	25	100,636	79,726	1,036.3
1.2	70	26	88	472	192	27,294	26,709	1.6
0.7	72	25	96	328	337	802,132	835,976	371.0
0.7	75	11	99	591	590	277,280	333,135	0.0
1.9	58	99	51	11	16	45,869	61,040	1,171.6
2.3	52	121	37	7	7	23,736	39,727	1,171.6
2.5	55	94	55	27	27	70,888	83,399	2,182.7
2.4	64	69	73	83	58	221,341	213,248	982.5
0.7	74	17	97	430	401	1,412,755	1,446,170	866.7
2.9	49	122	37	10	10	7,730	10,634	344.2
3.0	50	152	28	13	6	85	523	1.6
2.6	44	208	9	6	6	99	249	8.8
2.6	45	120	25	6	8	77	205	7.5
2.7	61	80	37	n.a.	n.a.	2	83	4.9
2.0	43	146	33	12	6	120	118	1.5
2.1	43	146	15	3	5	185	144	5.3
2.9	47	92	15	n.a.	n.a.	17[g]	33[g]	0.4
2.4	47	142	20	n.a.	24	30	24	1.1
2.4	53	145	15	3	15	422	850	2.8
2.1	36	196	20	14	0	46	108	5.1
3.2	55	101	30	8	4	895	719	7.3
2.6	43	163	20	13	2	390	279	7.0
2.0	42	147	19	n.a.	n.a.	12	59	2.6
4.0	56	85	47	25	18	1,168	1,519	81.5

	Popu-lation mid-1984 (mil.)	Physical Quality of Life Index (PQLI)[a] 1981	Per Capita GNP 1982 ($)	Per Capita GNP (Real) Growth Rate 1960-1982 (%)	Share of Labor Force in Industry 1980 (%)
Madagascar	9.8	51	320	−0.5	4.0
˙ Malawi	6.4	29	210	2.6	5.0
˙ Mali	7.6	27	180	1.6	11.7
Mozambique	13.4	40	150[g]	n.a.	18.0
˙ Niger	6.3	27	310	−1.5	3.0
˙ Rwanda	5.8	45	260	1.7	2.0
˙ Sao Tome & Principe	0.1	n.a.	370	1.2	n.a.
˙ Sierra Leone	3.9	26	390	0.9	19.0
˙ Somalia	5.7	17	290	−0.1	8.0
˙ Tanzania	21.2	61	280	1.9	6.0
˙ Togo	2.9	37	340	2.3	15.0
˙ Uganda	14.3	49	230	−1.1	6.0
Zaire	32.2	51	190	−0.3	13.0
Lower Middle-Income (16)	**235.0**	**45**	**772**	**2.6**	**18.5**
Angola	7.8	27	940[h]	n.a.	16.0
˙ Botswana	1.0	48	900	6.8	7.7
Cameroon	9.4	47	890	2.6	7.0
˙ Djibouti	0.3	n.a.	840[h]	n.a.	n.a.
Egypt	47.0	57	690	3.6	30.0
Ivory Coast	9.2	40	950	2.1	4.0
˙ Lesotho	1.5	52	510	6.5	4.0
Liberia	2.2	41	490	0.9	14.0
Mauritania	1.8	30	470	1.4	8.0[j]
Morocco	23.6	49	870	2.6	21.0
†Nigeria	88.1	41	860	3.3	19.0
Senegal	6.5	30	490	0.0	10.0
˙ Sudan	21.1	39	440	−0.4	10.0
Swaziland	0.6	55	940	4.2	9.0
Zambia	6.6	48	640	−0.1	11.0
Zimbabwe	8.3	64	850	1.5	15.0
Upper Middle-Income (7)	**64.0**	**61**	**2,348**	**2.8**	**27.8**
†Algeria	21.4	50	2,350	3.2	25.0
Congo	1.7	57	1,180	2.7	26.0
Mauritius	1.0	81	1,240	2.1	24.0
Namibia	1.1	50	1,960[k]	n.a.	n.a.
Seychelles	0.1	74	1,960[h]	n.a.	n.a.
South Africa	31.7	68	2,670	2.1	29.0
Tunisia	7.0	65	1,390	4.7	32.0
High-Income (3)	**5.2**	**55**	**7,210**	**4.2**	**24.4**
†Gabon	1.0	35	4,000	4.4	11.0
†Libya	3.7	57	8,510	4.1	28.0
Reunion	0.5	82	4,010[m]	n.a.	n.a.

Popu-lation Growth Rate[b] (%)	Life Expec-tancy at Birth[c] (years)	Infant Mortality per 1,000 Live Births[d]	Liter-acy[e] (%)	Per Capita Public Education Spending 1980 ($)	Per Capita Military Spending 1980 ($)	Total Exports, f.o.b. 1983 ($ mil.)	Total Imports, c.i.f. 1983 ($ mil.)	U.S. Bi-lateral Economic Aid[f] FY 1983 ($ mil.)
2.8	47	69	50	14	11	360	516	9.0
3.2	44	169	25	5	9	220	289	8.1
2.4	45	152	10	9	6	106	343	15.4
2.8	47	113	33	2	13	260	656	9.7
2.9	45	143	10	14	3	311	361	24.1
3.1	46	106	50	6	4	87	206	8.6
2.9	n.a.	69	50	n.a.	n.a.	9[g]	20[g]	0.2
2.6	47	205	15	12	4	202	137	8.7
2.6	39	145	6	5	20	163	422	69.7
2.7	52	101	79	15	13	457	795	7.9
2.9	48	107	18	24	9	242	566	7.7
3.1	48	96	52	8	10	354	321	7.8
2.9	50	110	55	12	7	1,411	1,089	29.9
3.0	**51**	**115**	**36**	**36**	**33**	**31,259**	**38,154**	**1,494.2**
2.5	42	152	20	26	0	1,859	768	1.1
3.4	51	82	35	68	37	456[i]	580[i]	13.3
2.6	50	107	41	26	10	1,037	1,250	21.8
2.6	50	n.a.	20	n.a.	n.a.	40	292	3.4
2.7	57	80	44	25	44	4,531	13,273	1,005.1
2.9	47	125	35	104	16	2,421	1,878	0.0
2.9	52	113	52	13	0	102[i]	420[i]	21.0
3.0	53	152	25	33	14	841	2,170	62.8
2.8	44	141	17	21	20	246	498	12.5
2.9	57	104	28	53	53	2,058	3,715	53.9
3.2	49	133	34	39	30	14,272	8,583	0.0
3.0	44	145	21	19	11	585	984	33.1
3.0	47	122	32	20	11	684	1,695	166.3
3.2	53	133	65	57	22	306[i]	501[i]	8.0
3.2	51	104	44	28	89	866	539	27.9
3.5	55	72	69	31	63	955	1,008	64.0
2.8	**60**	**101**	**54**	**121**	**59**	**34,609**	**29,699**	**28.1**
3.3	56	115	35	171	37	12,197	10,434	0.0
2.6	60	127	50	70	39	1,053	650	1.0
1.6	66	34	79	62	6	366	440	6.1
2.9	52	119	50	n.a.	0	283[i]	543[i]	0.0
1.6	65	19	58	n.a.	n.a.	20	71	2.4
2.5	63	94	65	103	81	18,881	14,392	0.0
2.6	61	88	62	73	52	1,809	3,169	18.6
2.8	**56**	**92**	**45**	**342**	**151**	**13,791**	**9,007**	**1.5**
1.5	49	115	12	131	93	1,753	844	1.5
3.3	57	97	50	399	167	11,955	7,441	0.0
1.7	65	14	77	n.a.	n.a.	83	722	0.0

	Population mid-1984 (mil.)	Physical Quality of Life Index (PQLI)[a] 1981	Per Capita GNP 1982 ($)	Per Capita GNP (Real) Growth Rate 1960-1982 (%)	Share of Labor Force in Industry 1980 (%)
ASIA (40)					
Low-Income (12)	**2,133.3**	**60**	**280**	**3.2**	**16.2**
Afghanistan	14.4	17	220[n]	n.a.	8.0
Bangladesh	99.6	37	140	0.3	n.a.
Bhutan	1.4	25	120[m]	n.a.	n.a.
Burma	38.9	59	190	1.3	9.8
China, People's Republic	1,034.5	75	310	5.0	18.7[l]
India	746.4	46	260	1.3	13.2
Kampuchea	6.1	33	120[n]	n.a.	6.0
Laos	3.7	39	80[k]	n.a.	n.a.
Nepal	16.6	30	170	−0.1	2.0
Pakistan	97.3	39	380	2.8	20.0
Sri Lanka	16.1	85	320	2.6	14.0
Vietnam	58.3	75	190[j]	n.a.	n.a.
Lower Middle-Income (7)	**277.9**	**65**	**665**	**4.0**	**14.2**
†Indonesia	161.6	58	580	4.2	15.0
Maldives	0.2	57	440[n]	n.a.	n.a.
Mongolia	1.9	77	780[o]	n.a.	n.a.
Philippines	54.5	75	820	2.8	17.0
Thailand	51.7	79	790	4.5	9.0
Yemen, Arab Republic	5.9	28	500	5.1	11.0
Yemen, People's Dem. Republic	2.1	38	470	6.4	15.0
Upper Middle-Income (10)	**133.6**	**70**	**1,992**	**4.8**	**28.6**
†Iran	43.8	57	1,940[q]	n.a.	34.0
†Iraq	15.0	51	3,020[q]	n.a.	26.0
Jordan	3.5	71	1,690	6.9	20.0
Korea, Dem. People's Republic	19.6	84	1,130[o]	n.a.	n.a.
Korea, Republic	4.2	86	1,910	6.6	29.0
Lebanon	2.6	77	1,850[s]	4.9	27.0
Macao	0.3	n.a.	2,500[m]	n.a.	n.a.
Malaysia	15.3	73	1,860	4.3	16.0
Syria	10.1	71	1,680	4.0	31.0
Taiwan	19.2	92	2,540[t]	n.a.	n.a.
High-Income (11)	**147.8**	**93**	**10,377**	**6.0**	**37.7**
Bahrain	0.4	80	9,280	n.a.	38.6[o]
Brunei	0.2	78	17,790[m]	n.a.	n.a.
• Hong Kong	5.4	95	5,340	7.0	57.0
• Israel	4.2	92	5,090	3.2	36.0
• Japan	119.9	99	10,080	6.1	39.0
†Kuwait	1.6	78	19,870	−0.1	34.0
Oman	1.0	37	6,090	7.4	n.a.
†Qatar	0.3	53	21.880	n.a.	n.a.
†Saudi Arabia	10.8	45	16,000	7.5	14.0
Singapore	2.5	89	5,910	7.4	39.0
†United Arab Emirates	1.5	69	23,770	−0.7	n.a.
• U.S.S.R.	(See Europe)				

Population Growth Rate[b] (%)	Life Expectancy at Birth[c] (years)	Infant Mortality per 1,000 Live Births[d]	Literacy[e] (%)	Per Capita Public Education Spending 1980 ($)	Per Capita Military Spending 1980 ($)	Total Exports, f.o.b. 1983 ($ mil.)	Total Imports, c.i.f. 1983 ($ mil.)	U.S. Bilateral Economic Aid[f] FY 1983 ($ mil.)
1.8	59	97	53	11	17	37,727	49,786	781.2
2.5	37	205	20	5	5	391	798	0.0
3.1	48	135	26	2	2	724	2,308	172.3
2.3	44	149	5	n.a.	n.a.	2	2	0.9
2.4	54	98	66	3	6	455	682	18.8
1.3	67	71	69	17	28	22,133	21,313	0.0
2.0	52	121	36	7	6	9,705	16,887	209.5
1.9	43	201	48	n.a.	n.a.	42[i]	103[i]	2.1
2.4	43	126	44	n.a.	n.a.	26	96	0.0
2.5	45	148	19	2	1	61	248	18.5
2.8	50	123	24	5	15	3,075	5,324	278.7
1.4	69	43	86	8	3	1,054	1,787	80.4
2.4	66	99	78	6	17	58	238	0.0
2.2	57	79	68	13	19	33,121	37,536	272.2
2.1	53	92	62	10	15	21,146	16,423	111.4
3.0	48	120	82	n.a.	n.a.	14	64	0.0
2.8	64	54	80	60	108	460[p]	120[p]	0.0
2.5	63	53	75	11	13	4,932	7,863	102.8
2.0	63	53	86	23	26	6,164	10,311	28.8
2.7	43	160	21	19	72	53	1,844	29.2
2.9	45	143	40	18	65	352	911	0.0
2.8	63	61	64	110	136	94,421	102,043	73.1
3.2	58	105	50	183	126	19,476	18,227	0.0
3.4	57	76	26	89	206	8,881	11,712	0.0
3.7	62	67	70	69	144	627	3,645	20.1
2.4	64	34	95	39	73	1,900[r]	2,100[r]	0.0
1.6	66	33	93	56	91	23,825	25,634	0.0
2.2	66	40	68	n.a.	101	767	3,659	52.2
1.8	n.a.	18	79	n.a.	n.a.	762	722	0.0
2.4	65	30	60	102	97	14,135	13,368	0.8
3.8	65	60	58	73	256	1,875	4,180	0.0
1.7	72	9	90	77	149	22,173[t]	18,796[t]	0.0
1.0	75	17	91	526	301	290,853	251,452	800.1
2.6	67	52	79	249	454	3,038	3,464	0.0
2.6	66	13	64	341	714	3,367	724	0.0
1.1	75	10	90	n.a.	n.a.	21,953	24,011	0.0
1.7	73	15	88	467	1,470	5,068	9,337	785.0
0.7	77	7	99	524	85	147,000	126,520	0.0
3.2	71	33	60	707	693	10,782	8,081	0.0
3.1	49	125	20	125	1,012	3,604	2,771	15.1
2.2	58	52	21	1,156	2,540	3,605	1,456	0.0
3.0	55	111	25	680	1,862	52,253	39,127	0.0
1.2	72	11	83	133	245	21,832	28,158	0.0
2.3	63	52	56	400	1,734	18,351	7,803	0.0

	Popu-lation mid-1984 _(mil.)_	Physical Quality of Life Index (PQLI)[a] 1981	Per Capita GNP 1982 _($)_	Per Capita GNP (Real) Growth Rate 1960-1982 _(%)_	Share of Labor Force in Industry 1980 _(%)_
LATIN AMERICA (36)					
Low-Income (1)	**5.5**	**43**	**300**	**0.6**	**7.2**
Haiti	5.5	43	300	0.6	7.2
Lower Middle-Income (11)	**29.0**	**75**	**689**	**1.1**	**21.8**
Bolivia	6.0	53	570	1.7	24.2
Cuba	9.9	95	700[h]	n.a.	n.a.
Dominica	0.1	87	710	−0.8	n.a.
El Salvador	4.8	69	700	0.9	22.4
Grenada	0.1	92	760	1.6	n.a.
Guyana	0.8	88	670	1.7	45.0
Honduras	4.2	63	660	1.0	14.6
Nicaragua	2.9	71	920	0.2	19.9[i]
St. Kitts-Nevis	0.04	84	750	1.1	n.a.
St. Lucia	0.1	86	720	3.4	n.a.
St. Vincent	0.1	83	620	0.6	n.a.
Upper Middle-Income (18)	**338.5**	**77**	**2,070**	**3.6**	**23.8**
Antigua & Barbuda	0.1	84	1,740	−0.2	n.a.
Argentina	29.1	89	2,520	1.6	28.0
Barbados	0.3	93	3,670[v]	4.5	25.3
Belize	0.2	89	1,080	3.4	16.5
Brazil	134.4	74	2,240	4.8	24.4
Chile	11.9	85	2,210	0.6	19.4
Colombia	28.2	77	1,460	3.1	21.2
Costa Rica	2.5	91	1,430	2.8	23.0
Dominican Republic	6.3	70	1,330	3.2	18.0
†Ecuador	9.1	73	1,350	4.8	17.1
Guatemala	8.0	60	1,130	2.4	20.5
Jamaica	2.4	91	1,330	0.7	25.2
Mexico	77.8	80	2,270	3.7	25.8
Panama	2.1	88	2,120	3.4	18.1
Paraguay	3.6	80	1,610	3.7	20.4
Peru	19.2	69	1,310	1.0	18.2
Suriname	0.4	78	3,030[w]	n.a.	32.0
Uruguay	3.0	90	2,650	1.7	32.4
High-Income (6)	**20.8**	**84**	**4,311**	**1.9**	**27.5**
Bahamas	0.2	89	3,830	−0.4	n.a.
Guadeloupe	0.3	86	4,200[m]	n.a.	n.a.
Martinique	0.3	89	4,680[m]	n.a.	n.a.
Netherlands Antilles	0.2	83	5,150[m]	n.a.	n.a.
Trinidad & Tobago	1.2	91	6,840	3.1	39.0
†Venezuela	18.6	83	4,140	1.9	26.8

Population Growth Rate[b] (%)	Life Expectancy at Birth[c] (years)	Infant Mortality per 1,000 Live Births[d]	Literacy[e] (%)	Per Capita Public Education Spending 1980 ($)	Per Capita Military Spending 1980 ($)	Total Exports, f.o.b. 1983 ($ mil.)	Total Imports, c.i.f. 1983 ($ mil.)	U.S. Bilateral Economic Aid[f] FY 1983 ($ mil.)
2.2	54	112	23	4	4	412	620	46.2
2.2	54	112	23	4	4	412	620	46.2
2.3	63	68	77	76	51	5,316	6,320	414.7
2.8	51	129	63	38	19	766	424	63.0
1.0	74	17	95	162	114	983	1,638	0.0
1.7	65	13	94	n.a.	n.a.	1,006	1,411	n.a.
2.6	63	75	62	29	11	1,010	1,041	245.6
1.7	70	15	98	n.a.	n.a.	21	42	n.a.
2.0	70	43	92	59	24	292	188	0.1
3.4	59	86	60	20	12	736	691	106.0
3.6	57	88	90	26	28	391	698	0.0
1.5	64	46	98	n.a.	n.a.	31[u]	47[u]	n.a.
2.6	70	23	82	n.a.	n.a.	42[i]	117[i]	n.a.
1.9	65	60	96	n.a.	n.a.	38	23	n.a.
2.3	65	63	80	69	22	70,477	51,652	575.3
1.0	66	31	88	n.a.	n.a.	34[g]	139[g]	n.a.
1.5	71	44	93	157	58	7,910	4,660	0.0
0.9	71	26	99	233	36	328	554	0.0
2.4	70	27	91	n.a.	n.a.	73	93	17.8
2.3	64	75	76	63	13	21,898	16,844	0.4
1.8	68	42	89	113	132	3,835	2,754	2.8
2.1	63	56	81	24	12	3,101	4,888	3.9
2.7	73	27	90	117	0	1,072	986	214.1
2.6	62	66	67	24	19	1,006	1,411	63.1
3.6	62	80	81	49	26	2,550	1,650	26.6
3.5	59	66	46	21	14	1,220	1,054	29.7
2.0	71	16	90	76	9	725	1,404	103.5
2.6	66	54	83	78	11	21,168	8,219	8.2
2.1	71	21	85	87	9	480	2,868	7.4
2.7	65	46	84	18	21	252	478	3.2
2.5	58	85	80	19	26	3,288	2,642	93.5
2.0	69	35	65	n.a.	n.a.	368	384	0.1
0.9	71	39	94	78	90	1,169	624	1.0
2.7	68	40	83	187	44	24,431	21,134	0.1
2.0	69	22	93	n.a.	n.a.	1,962	3,062	0.0
1.3	70	26	83	n.a.	n.a.	79	556	0.0
1.1	70	16	88	n.a.	n.a.	173	645	0.0
2.1	62	25	93	n.a.	n.a.	3,693	8,253	0.0
1.9	72	31	95	170	14	2,344	2,503	0.0
2.8	68	41	82	188	46	16,180	6,115	0.1

	Popu-lation mid-1984 *(mil.)*	Physical Quality of Life Index (PQLI)[a] 1981	Per Capita GNP 1982 *($)*	Per Capita GNP (Real) Growth Rate 1960-1982 *(%)*	Share of Labor Force in Industry 1980 *(%)*
OCEANIA (10)					
Lower Middle-Income (5)	**4.1**	**50**	**806**	**2.0**	**7.7**
Papua New Guinea	3.4	45	820	2.1	7.7
Solomon Islands	0.3	70	660	1.3	n.a.
Tonga	0.1	78	520[g]	n.a.	n.a.
Vanuatu	0.1	n.a.	800[h]	n.a.	n.a.
Western Samoa	0.2	84	940[h]	n.a.	n.a.
Upper Middle-Income (1)	**0.7**	**86**	**1,950**	**3.2**	**22.4**
Fiji	0.7	86	1,950	3.2	22.4
High-Income (4)	**19.0**	**97**	**10,549**	**2.2**	**33.2**
• Australia	15.5	97	11,140	2.4	32.8
French Polynesia	0.2	83	7,980[m]	n.a.	n.a.
New Caledonia	0.1	84	8,230[h]	n.a.	n.a.
• New Zealand	3.2	96	7,920	1.5	35.0
EUROPE (30)					
Lower Middle-Income (1)	**2.9**	**82**	**820**	**n.a.**	**25.3**
Albania	2.9	82	820[g]	n.a.	25.3
Upper Middle-Income (3)	**83.3**	**75**	**1,896**	**4.0**	**21.6**
Portugal	10.1	86	2,450	4.8	35.1
Turkey	50.2	67	1,370	3.4	12.8
Yugoslavia	23.0	87	2,800	4.9	35.0
High-Income (26)	**729.7**	**95**	**7,991**	**3.3**	**42.9**
• Austria	7.6	96	9,880	3.9	36.7
• Belgium	9.9	96	10,760	3.6	41.1
• Bulgaria	9.0	93	4,210[aa]	n.a.	38.8
Cyprus[x]	0.7	91	3,840	5.9	26.7
• Czechoslovakia	15.5	94	9,550[aa]	n.a.	48.4
• Denmark	5.1	98	12,470	2.5	35.4
• Finland	4.9	98	10,870	3.6	34.5
• France	54.8	98	11,680	3.7	38.9
• Germany, Democratic Republic	16.7	95	10,510[aa]	n.a.	50.2
• Germany, Federal Republic	61.4	96	12,460	3.1	46.4
• Greece	10.0	91	4,290	5.2	28.0
• Hungary	10.7	93	6,460[aa]	6.3	42.6
• Iceland	0.2	100	12,150	3.2	42.1
• Ireland	3.6	95	5,150	2.9	37.3
• Italy	57.0	96	6,840	3.4	45.3
• Luxembourg	0.4	96	14,340	4.0	41.4

Population Growth Rate[b] (%)	Life Expectancy at Birth[c] (years)	Infant Mortality per 1,000 Live Births[d]	Literacy[e] (%)	Per Capita Public Education Spending 1980 ($)	Per Capita Military Spending 1980 ($)	Total Exports, f.o.b. 1983 ($ mil.)	Total Imports, c.i.f. 1983 ($ mil.)	U.S. Bilateral Economic Aid[f] FY 1983 ($ mil.)
2.9	**53**	**96**	**39**	**38**	**13**	**917**	**1,165**	**1.6**
2.9	51	102	32	38	13	822	978	0.6
3.6	65	78	60	n.a.	n.a.	51	60	0.0
2.0	58	60	100	n.a.	n.a.	11[y]	34[y]	0.0
2.5	n.a.	101	15	n.a.	n.a.	16	46	0.0
3.0	63	40	98	n.a.	n.a.	17	47	1.0
2.3	**72**	**35**	**79**	**91**	**16**	**240**	**484**	**0.0**
2.3	72	35	79	91	16	240	484	0.0
0.8	**74**	**11**	**99**	**565**	**231**	**26,137**	**25,060**	**0.0**
0.8	74	10	99	597	249	20,651	19,420	0.0
2.6	62	41	98	n.a.	n.a.	n.a.	n.a.	0.0
1.9	64	27	91	n.a.	n.a.	191	269	0.0
0.8	74	12	99	409	142	5,295	5,371	0.0
2.1	**70**	**47**	**75**	**n.a.**	**71**	**275**	**224**	**0.0**
2.1	70	47	75	n.a.	71	275[i]	224[i]	0.0
1.5	**66**	**83**	**75**	**66**	**75**	**21,594**	**29,370**	**306.0**
0.6	72	26	78	91	87	4,548	7,999	20.0
2.1	62	119	69	35	55	5,452	9,278	286.0
0.7	71	31	85	124	113	11,594	12,093	0.0
0.5	**73**	**19**	**99**	**357**	**368**	**780,263**	**806,382**	**65.0**
0.0	73	13	99	561	118	15,429	19,409	0.0
0.1	73	12	99	732	402	51,515[z]	52,927[z]	0.0
0.3	73	19	93	176	133	520	1,497	0.0
1.4	73	19	89	122	49	503	1,219	15.0
0.3	72	17	99	182	180	4,692	3,781	0.0
−0.1	75	8	99	868	314	16,004	16,241	0.0
0.5	75	7	100	585	170	12,534	12,814	0.0
0.5	76	10	99	599	492	94,945	105,415	0.0
0.0	73	12	99	304	360	24,200[i]	22,400[i]	0.0
−0.2	73	11	99	616	434	169,436	152,938	0.0
0.5	74	14	84	101	236	4,209	8,875	0.0
−0.2	71	21	99	201	103	8,702	8,508	0.0
0.9	77	7	99	500	0	740	818	0.0
1.1	73	11	98	359	87	8,592	9,164	0.0
0.1	74	14	98	321	171	73,729	80,358	13.2
0.0	73	11	100	920	143	—[z]	—[z]	0.0

	Popu-lation mid-1984	Physical Quality of Life Index (PQLI)[a] 1981	Per Capita GNP 1982	Per Capita GNP (Real) Growth Rate 1960-1982	Share of Labor Force in Industry 1980
	(mil.)		($)	(%)	(%)
Malta	0.4	88	3,800	8.0	41.3
• Netherlands	14.4	98	10,930	2.9	44.8
• Norway	4.1	99	14,280	3.4	36.6
• Poland	36.9	94	5,160[aa]	n.a.	39.3
Romania	22.7	92	4,660[aa]	n.a.	35.5
• Spain	38.4	94	5,430	4.0	40.3
• Sweden	8.3	99	14,040	2.4	34.2
• Switzerland	6.5	98	17,010	1.9	45.9
• U.S.S.R.	274.0	94	6,350[aa]	n.a.	44.7
• United Kingdom	56.5	96	9,660	2.0	42.1
NORTH AMERICA (2)					
High-Income (2)	**261.4**	**97**	**12,983**	**2.3**	**31.7**
• Canada	25.1	97	11,320	3.1	28.9
• United States	236.3	97	13,160	2.2	32.0

˙Considered by the United Nations to be one of 36 "Least Developed Countries."
†Member of the Organization of Petroleum Exporting Countries.
•Considered by ODC to be a developed country because of its per capita GNP of $3,700 or more and PQLI of 90 or above.

[a]The Physical Quality of Life Index (PQLI) is a composite index based on life expectancy at age one, infant mortality, and literacy (see Statistical Note at the beginning of these Annexes for information on the method of computation). In general, the PQLI numbers presented here measure the physical quality of life as of 1981. The PQLI numbers were prepared for the ODC by Michael Scott and M. D. Morris of the Center for Comparative Study of Development, Brown University. A working paper which discusses some of the data problems involved is available from the CCSD, Box 1916, Brown University, Providence, RI 02912.
[b]Population growth rates apply to the early 1980s and are from the Population Reference Bureau, "1984 World Population Data Sheet," supplemented with unpublished data from the U.S. Bureau of the Census.
[c]Life expectancy at birth data are drawn primarily from the World Bank, *World Tables*, Third Edition, Volume II, supplemented by data from the "1984 World Population Data Sheet," United Nations, *U.N. Demographic Yearbook* (1982), World Bank, *World Development Report* (1984), and unpublished data from the U.S. Bureau of the Census.
[d]Infant mortality data are drawn primarily from World Bank, *World Tables* (Third Edition), supplemented by data from UNESCO *Population and Vital Statistics* (April 1984), "1984 World Population Data Sheet," and unpublished data from the U.S. Bureau of the Census.
[e]Literacy data are drawn primarily from the World Bank, *World Tables* (Third Edition), supplemented by data from UNESCO, *Statistical Yearbook* (1983), unpublished data from the U.S. Bureau of the Census, and CIA, *World Factbook 1984*.
[f]U.S. bilateral economic aid includes development assistance, economic support funds (security support assistance), and P.L. 480 food aid. Aid not specifically going to an individual country (e.g. regional and interregional activities) is not included in regional subtotals or world total.
[g]Figure for 1981 from CIA, *World Factbook 1984*.
[h]Figure for DAC from *Development Co-operation, 1984 Review*.
[i]Figure for 1982 from CIA, *World Factbook 1984*.
[j]Figure for 1977.
[k]Figure for 1981 from *1983 World Bank Atlas*.
[l]Figure for 1981.

Popu-lation Growth Rate[b] (%)	Life Expec-tancy at Birth[c] (years)	Infant Mortality per 1,000 Live Births[d]	Liter-acy[e] (%)	Per Capita Public Education Spending 1980 ($)	Per Capita Military Spending 1980 ($)	Total Exports, f.o.b. 1983 ($ mil.)	Total Imports, c.i.f. 1983 ($ mil.)	U.S. Bi-lateral Economic Aid[f] FY 1983 ($ mil.)
0.6	71	14	83	99	16	326	733	0.0
0.4	76	8	99	947	373	65,428	62,554	0.0
0.2	76	7	99	1,197	409	17,977	13,481	0.0
1.0	73	20	99	135	121	47,928	4,351	24.8
0.5	71	29	98	117	61	9,328	6,918	0.0
0.6	74	9	92	117	107	19,734	29,193	12.0
0.0	77	7	100	1,350	459	27,410	26,114	0.0
0.3	76	8	99	831	331	25,587	29,190	0.0
1.0	72	28	100	231	490	33,065	35,451	0.0
0.1	74	11	99	494	478	91,639	100,032	0.0
0.7	**75**	**11**	**99**	**591**	**590**	**277,280**	**333,135**	**0.0**
0.8	75	10	99	784	195	76,745	63,255	0.0
0.7	75	11	99	571	632	200,535	269,880	—

[m]Figure from Population Reference Bureau, "1984 World Population Data Sheet."
[n]Figure for 1980 calculated from CIA, *Handbook of Economic Statistics* (1983).
[o]Figure for 1979.
[p]Figure for 1981 from *The World Almanac and Book of Facts 1984* (New York: Newspaper Enterprise Association, Inc.)
[q]Figure for 1980 from DAC, *Development Co-operation, 1982 Review.*
[r]Figure for 1980 from *World Almanac and Book of Facts 1984.*
[s]Figure for 1981 from DAC, *Development Co-operation, 1983 Review.*
[t]Figure for 1982 from Republic of China, *Statistical Yearbook of the Republic of China 1983.*
[u]Figure from CIA, *World Factbook 1984.*
[v]Figure calculated from CIA, *Handbook of Economic Statistics 1983.*
[w]Figure for 1981 calculated from CIA, *Handbook of Economic Statistics 1983.*
[x]Despite their attainment of a GNP per capita of $3,700 or above and a PQLI of 90 or above, Cyprus, Romania, and Trinidad and Tobago continue to be considered advanced developing countries by the ODC.
[y]Figure for 1980 from UNCTAD, *Handbook of International Trade Development Statistics* (Supplement, 1981).
[z]All external trade of the Belgium-Luxembourg Customs Union is listed under Belgium.
[aa]From CIA, *Handbook of Economic Statistics 1983.*

Note: All regional and income group averages are weighted by population; a country is excluded if data are not available for the particular indicator in question. Low-income countries have per capita GNPs under $420. Lower middle-income countries have per capita GNPs in the range $420-1,069. Upper middle-income countries have per capita GNPs in the range $1,070-3,699. High-income countries have per capita GNPs of $3,700 or above.

Sources: Unless otherwise noted, population and population growth data are from the "*1984 Population Data Sheet.*" Per capita GNP and growth rates are from World Bank, *World Development Report 1984.* Share of labor force in industry, life expectancy, infant mortality, and literacy are from World Bank, *World Tables,* (Third Edition). Per capita public education and military spending data are from Ruth Leger Sivard, *World Military and Social Expenditures* (1983). Export and import data are from IMF, *Direction of Trade Statistics Yearbook* (1984). U.S. bilateral economic aid figures are from U.S. AID, *U.S. Overseas Loans and Grants and Assistance for International Organizations.*

E-2. PQLI Map of the World

Notes: Each country's PQLI (Physical Quality of Life Index) is based on an average of life expectancy at age one, infant mortality, and literacy.

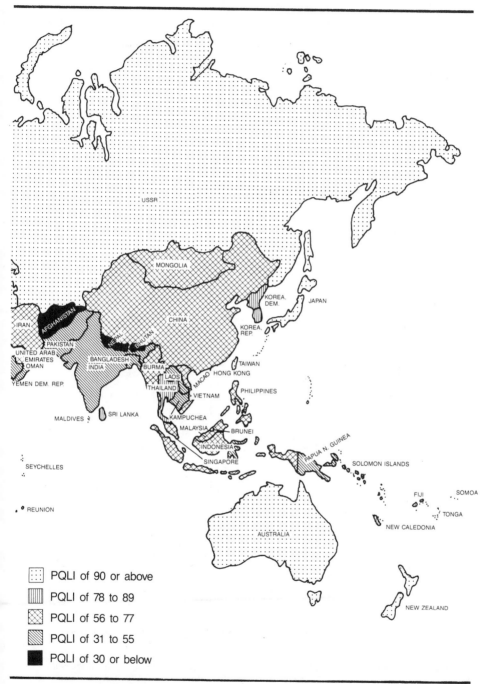

PQLI of 90 or above

PQLI of 78 to 89

PQLI of 56 to 77

PQLI of 31 to 55

PQLI of 30 or below

Countries left blank are those for which a PQLI rating is not available.
Source: Annex E, Table E-1.

E-3. Two Measures of the Gap Between Developing and Developed Countries

Whether measured by income or by physical quality of life, the absolute gap between rich and poor countries is large and growing.

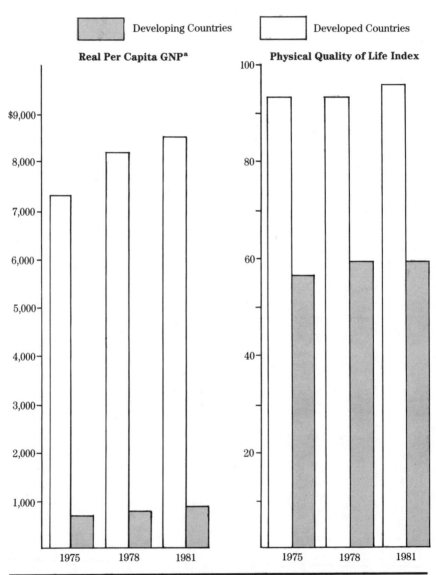

[a]In constant 1980 dollars; value expressed in 1980 prices and converted to dollars at 1980 exchange rates.

Sources: Real per capita GNP figures are from Ruth Leger Sivard, *World Military and Social Expenditures, 1983;* PQLI figures are calculated by the Overseas Development Council.

E-4. Average Annual Real Growth of Selected Indicators, by Region, 1970-1983

	All Developing Countries (%)	Latin America and Caribbean	Sub-Saharan Africa[a]	North Africa and Middle East (percentages)	South Asia	East Asia[b] and Pacific	Industrial Countries (%)
GNP:							
1970-1980	5.8	5.9	3.8	8.8	3.5	6.6	3.3
1981	2.2	-0.8	1.3	3.1	5.9	5.2	1.3
1982	1.3	-1.4	-1.0	1.2	2.8	5.5	-0.6
1983[c]	0.8	-3.8	-2.3	-6.0	6.5	7.1	2.3
GNP Per Capita:							
1970-1980	3.6	3.3	-1.0	5.7	1.0	4.8	2.5
1981	0.2	-3.0	-1.9	0.1	3.6	3.6	0.7
1982	-0.8	-3.6	-4.1	-1.7	0.5	3.7	-1.4
1983[c]	-1.3	-6.0	-5.4	-8.6	4.1	5.4	1.7
Manufacturing Production:							
1970-1980	7.7	6.3	4.0	7.5	3.8	11.1	3.0
1981	0.2	-9.4	6.3	5.7	8.2	5.8	0.3
1982	4.5	4.6	-3.7	2.7	5.6	5.9	-3.5
1983[c]	n.a.	n.a.	n.a.	-0.2	n.a.	n.a.	3.4
Agricultural Production:							
1970-1980	2.8	3.4	1.3	2.9	2.3	3.5	1.7
1981	4.1	5.4	4.4	-9.3	5.1	5.7	3.5
1982	3.1	1.7	1.7	2.6	-1.5	5.9	1.1
1983[c]	2.4	2.1	1.6	0.3	8.2	1.4	-6.7
Gross Investment:							
1970-1980	8.8	7.0	6.0	19.3	5.0	8.7	2.1
1981	3.3	-1.4	8.4	17.7	2.0	1.0	0.7
1982	-2.9	-19.1	-13.2	3.8	0.7	5.1	5.9
1983[c]	n.a.	-14.1	n.a.	-2.9	7.4	5.1	2.0

a Includes South Africa.
b Includes China.
c Preliminary.
Source: World Bank, *Annual Report 1984*, Table 1.

E-5. Relative Shares of Selected Resources and Expenditures of Developing and Developed Countries (percentages)

The developing countries have more than three-quarters of the world's population, but much smaller shares of the world's teachers, physicians, and annual income.

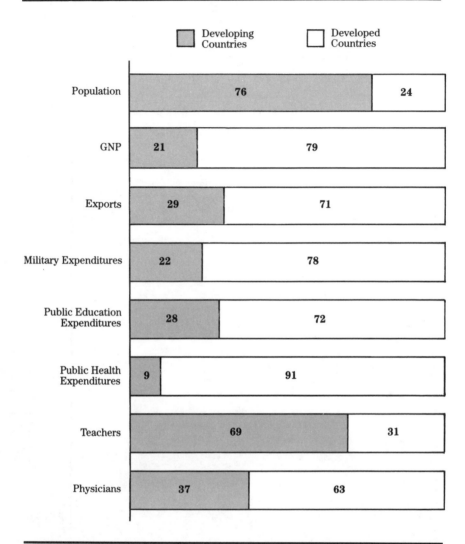

Note: World population, 4.7 billion in mid-1984; world GNP, $13.4 trillion in 1982; world exports, $1.8 trillion in 1983; world military expenditures, $543 billion in 1980; world public education expenditures, $579 billion in 1980; world public health expenditures, $444 billion in 1980; teachers worldwide, 32.1 million in 1980; physicians worldwide, 3.9 million in 1980.

Sources: Population, GNP, and export figures are based on Table E-2. Military expenditures, public education expenditures, public health expenditures, teachers, and physicians figures are based on Ruth Leger Sivard, *World Military and Social Expenditures, 1983.*

231

E-6. Real Global Gross Domestic Product (in real 1980 $ billions)

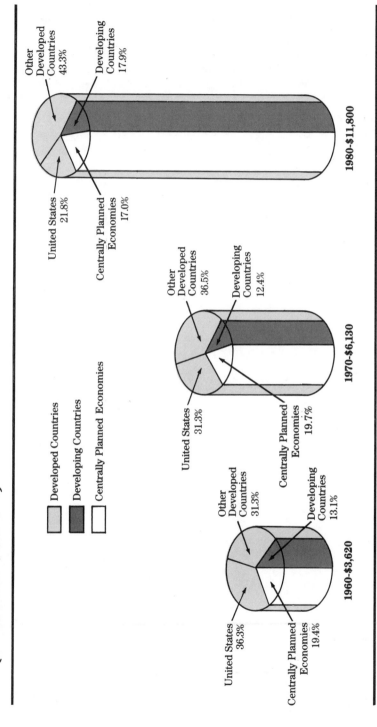

Developed Countries

Developing Countries

Centrally Planned Economies

1960-$3,620

United States 36.3%

Other Developed Countries 31.3%

Developing Countries 13.1%

Centrally Planned Economies 19.4%

1970-$6,130

United States 31.3%

Other Developed Countries 36.5%

Developing Countries 12.4%

Centrally Planned Economies 19.7%

1980-$11,800

United States 21.8%

Other Developed Countries 43.3%

Developing Countries 17.9%

Centrally Planned Economies 17.0%

Source: UNCTAD, *Handbook of International Trade and Development Statistics, 1983*, Table 63.

E-7. Labor Force Growth Rates and Projections (average annual rates)

Now that East Asia no longer has the fastest-growing population, it is in Latin America, Africa, and South Asia that the labor force is growing fastest. These are also the regions where the prospects for creating enough new jobs are bleakest.

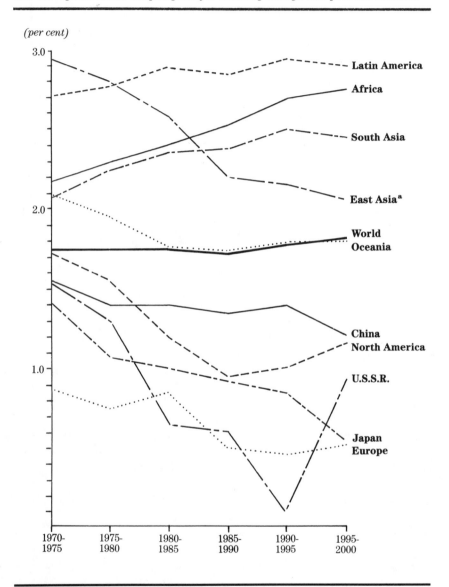

(per cent)

---

[a]Excludes China and Japan.

Source: International Labour Office, *Labour Force Estimates and Projections, 1950-2000* (Geneva: 1977).

E-8. Average Daily Caloric Intake Per Person, as a Percentage of Requirement

Not only is there a gap between developed and developing countries in caloric intake, but there is considerable variance among developing countries. By the end of the 1970s, the least developed countries were worse off than at the beginning. Although both Africa and the Far East showed improvement in the late 1970s, their averages still remained below the minimum daily requirement.

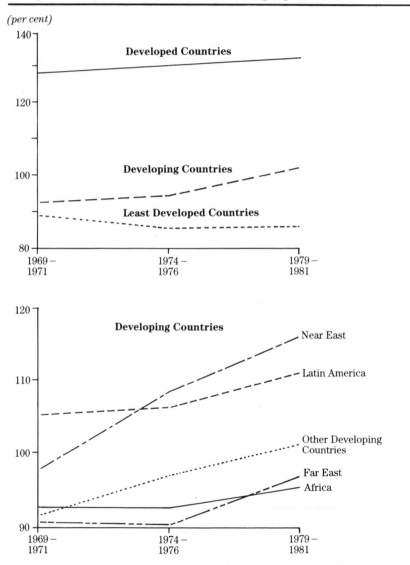

Source: Food and Agriculture Organization,"Current World Food Situation"(April 1984),p. 3.

About the Overseas Development Council and the Contributors

The Overseas Development Council is an independent, nonprofit organization established in 1969 to increase American understanding of the economic and social problems confronting the developing countries and to promote awareness of the importance of these countries to the United States in an increasingly interdependent international system.

In pursuit of these goals, ODC functions as a center for policy analysis, a forum for the exchange of ideas, and a resource for public education. Current projects fall within four broad areas of policy concern: trade and industrial policy, international financial issues, development strategies and development cooperation, and political and strategic aspects of U.S. economic relations with the Third World.

ODC's program is funded by foundations, corporations, and private individuals; its policies are determined by a governing Board and Council. In the selection and coverage of issues addressed by the current ODC program, including the U.S.-Third World Policy Perspectives series, the ODC staff and Board also benefit from the advice of members of the ODC Program Advisory Committee.

John W. Sewell is president of the Overseas Development Council.

The Editors

John W. Sewell has been president of the Overseas Development Council since January 1980. From 1977 to 1979, he was the Council's executive vice president, directing ODC's programs of research and public education. Prior to joining the Council in 1971, Mr. Sewell directed the communications program of The Brookings Institution. He also served in the Foreign Service of the United States and in the Research Bureau of the Department of State.

A contributor to several of ODC's past *Agenda* assessments of U.S. policies and performance in U.S.-Third World relations, he was also recently a co-author of *Rich Country Interests and Third World Development,* and of *The Ties That Bind: U.S. Interests in Third World Development.* Mr. Sewell is a frequent lecturer, commentator, and author on U.S. relations with the developing countries.

Richard E. Feinberg has been vice president of the Overseas Development Council since 1983 and is co-editor of the ODC's U.S.-Third World Policy Perspectives series. After coming to the Council in 1981 as a visiting fellow, he became an ODC senior fellow and director of the foreign policy program. From 1977 to 1979, Feinberg was Latin American specialist on the policy planning staff of the U.S. Department of State, prior to which he served as an international economist in the U.S. Treasury Department and with the House Banking Committee. He is currently also adjunct professor of international finance at the Georgetown University School of Foreign Service. Feinberg is the author of numerous books as well as journal and newspaper articles on U.S. foreign policy, Latin American politics, and international economics. His most recent book is *The Intemperate Zone: The Third World Challenge to U.S. Foreign Policy* (1983).

Valeriana Kallab is vice president and director of publications of the Overseas Development Council and co-editor of the ODC's U.S.-Third World Policy Perspectives series. Before joining ODC in 1972 to head its publications program, she was a research editor and writer on international economic issues with the Carnegie Endowment for International Peace in New York. She was co-editor (with John P. Lewis) of *U.S. Foreign Policy and the Third World: Agenda 1983* and (with Guy F. Erb) of *Beyond Dependency: The Third World Speaks Out* (1975). She is a member of the U.S. National Commission for UNESCO.

Contributing Authors

Paul R. Krugman has been professor of management and economics at the Massachusetts Institute of Technology since 1979. From 1982 to 1983, while on leave from MIT, he served as the senior staff member for international economics at the Council of Economic Advisers. His research interests include both international finance and longer-term issues of international trade. His most recent publication (with Elhanan Helpman) is *Market Structure and Foreign Trade: Increasing Returns, Imperfect Competition, and the International Economy.*

Stephen L. Lande is an international trade expert and a professional negotiator. As vice president of Manchester Associates, Ltd. (Washington, D.C.), an international business consulting firm, Mr. Lande is an advisor to several U.S. and foreign corporations. He has also been a consultant to the Organization of American States, the U.S. Agency for International Development, the National Investment Council of Panama, and the government of Mexico. From 1973 to 1982, Mr. Lande served in the Office of the U.S. Trade Representative as both an Assistant U.S. Trade Representative and Chief Negotiator, and established the bilateral relations section of the agency. Mr. Lande was also in charge of the implementation and administration of the U.S. Generalized System of Preferences and responsible in USTR for developing the U.S. government's Caribbean Basin Initiative.

Craig VanGrasstek is research director of Manchester Associates, Ltd., and a specialist in Latin American economic and political affairs. He is also a freelance journalist and consultant whose other assignments have included consultant to the Carnegie Endowment for International Peace, Bogota (Colombia) correspondent for the *Journal of Commerce,* and research assistant in the Latin American Program of the Woodrow Wilson International Center for Scholars (Smithsonian Institution). Mr. VanGrasstek recently completed a year as a Fulbright Fellow at the University of the Andes in Bogota.

Christine E. Contee is a fellow of the Overseas Development Council, as well as the Council's public affairs officer. She recently received an M.S. from Georgetown University, and has contributed to ODC's Policy Focus series of briefing papers.

Anthony Lake is Five College Professor of International Relations at Mount Holyoke College. He was the director of policy planning in the State Department during the Carter Administration. Mr. Lake previously served as a Foreign Service Officer in Vietnam and then in the State Department and on the National Security Council Staff in Washington; as director of the International Voluntary Services; and on the President-elect's transition team in 1976. He is the author of *The Tar Baby Option: American Policy Towards Southern Rhodesia;* contributing editor of *The Legacy of Vietnam;* and co-author of the recently published *Our Own Worst Enemy: The Unmaking of American Foreign Policy.*

Stuart K. Tucker is a fellow at the Overseas Development Council. Prior to joining ODC, he was a research consultant for the Inter-American Development Bank, the Urban Institute, and the Roosevelt Center for American Policy Studies. He has written on U.S. international trade policy, the U.S. costs of the Third World recession, and the U.S. Generalized System of Preferences (GSP). At the Council, Mr. Tucker is working in the areas of international trade policy and Central American development.

Overseas Development Council

Board of Directors*

Chairman: Robert S. McNamara
Vice Chairmen: Thornton F. Bradshaw
J. Wayne Fredericks

Marjorie C. Benton
William H. Bolin
Thomas L. Farmer**
Roger Fisher
Orville L. Freeman
John J. Gilligan
Edward K. Hamilton
Frederick Heldring
Susan Herter
Ruth J. Hinerfeld
Joan Holmes
Robert D. Hormats
Jerome Jacobson

William J. Lawless
C. Payne Lucas
Paul F. McCleary
Lawrence C. McQuade
Alfred F. Miossi
Merlin Nelson
Joseph S. Nye
John Petty
Jane Cahill Pfeiffer
John W. Sewell**
Daniel F. Sharp
Barry Zorthian

Council

Robert O. Anderson
Robert E. Asher
William Attwood
Marguerite Ross Barnett
Douglas J. Bennet
Edward G. Biester, Jr.
Jonathan B. Bingham
Eugene R. Black
Robert R. Bowie
Harrison Brown
Lester R. Brown
Ronald B. Brown
John C. Bullitt
Goler T. Butcher
Frank C. Carlucci
Lisle C. Carter, Jr.
Kathryn D. Christopherson
George J. Clark
Harlan Cleveland
Frank M. Coffin
John C. Culver
Ralph P. Davidson
Richard H. Demuth

William T. Dentzer, Jr.
John Diebold
Albert Fishlow
Luther H. Foster
Arvonne Fraser
Stephen J. Friedman
Richard N. Gardner
Peter Goldmark
Katharine Graham
James P. Grant
Arnold C. Harberger
Theodore M. Hesburgh, C.S.C.
Jerome Jacobson
Philip Johnston
Peter T. Jones
Vernon E. Jordan
Nicholas deB. Katzenbach
Philip H. Klutznick
J. Burke Knapp
Peter F. Krogh
Geraldine Kunstadter
Walter J. Levy
George N. Lindsay

Board Members are also members of the Council.
**Ex Officio.*

238

ODC Program Advisory Committee

Overseas Development Council
1717 Massachusetts Ave., N.W.
Washington, D.C. 20036
Tel. (202) 234-8701

A New Series from the Overseas Development Council

℗ U.S.-THIRD WORLD
POLICY PERSPECTIVES

Titles already available or scheduled for joint
publication by Transaction Books and the Overseas
Development Council in 1985:

ADJUSTMENT CRISIS IN THE THIRD WORLD
Richard E. Feinberg and Valeriana Kallab, editors

Just how the debt and adjustment crisis of Third World countries is handled, by
them and by international agencies and banks, can make a big difference in the
pace and quality of *global* recovery. Stagnating international trade, sharp swings
in the prices of key commodities, worsened terms of trade, high interest rates,
and reduced access to commercial bank credits have slowed and even reversed
growth in many Third World countries. Countries must bring expenditures into
line with shrinking resources in the short run, but they also need to alter prices
and take other, longer-range steps to expand the resource base in the future—to
stimulate investment, production, and employment. Already low living standards make this an especially formidable "adjustment" agenda in most Third
World nations.

Contents:

Richard E. Feinberg—The Adjustment Imperative and U.S. Policy
Albert Fishlow—The Debt Crisis: Round Two Ahead?
Tony Killick, Graham Bird, Jennifer Sharpley, and Mary Sutton—
    The IMF: Case for a Change in Emphasis
Stanley Please—The World Bank: Lending for Structural Adjustment
Joan M. Nelson—The Politics of Stabilization
Colin I. Bradford, Jr.—The NICs: Confronting U.S. "Autonomy"
Riordan Roett—Brazil's Debt Crisis
Lance Taylor—Mexico's Adjustment in the 1980s: Look Back
    Before Leaping Ahead
DeLisle Worrell—Central America and the Caribbean: Adjustment
    in Small, Open Economies

200 pp.   ISBN: 0-87855-988-4 (paper) **$12.95**
No. 1, May 1984   ISBN: 0-88738-040-9 (cloth) **$19.95**

UNCERTAIN FUTURE: COMMERCIAL BANKS IN THE THIRD WORLD

Richard E. Feinberg and Valeriana Kallab, editors

The future of international commercial lending to the Third World has become very uncertain just when the stakes are greatest for the banks, the developing countries, and the international financial system. New approaches are needed that take into account the interests of both banks and developing-country borrowers, and that promise to ease the present unstable mix of misperceptions, obligations, needs, and expectations. Having played an essentially creative role in the recent past—how will the banks respond in the period ahead, when financing will be even more urgently needed?

Contents:

Richard E. Feinberg—Overview: Restoring Confidence in International
  Credit Markets
Lawrence J. Brainard—More Lending to the Third World?
  A Banker's View
Karin Lissakers—Bank Regulation and International Debt
Christine A. Bogdanowicz-Bindert and Paul M. Sacks—
  The Role of Information: Closing the Barn Door?
George J. Clark—Foreign Banks in the Domestic Markets
  of Developing Countries
Catherine Gwin—The IMF and the World Bank: Measures to
  Improve the System
Benjamin J. Cohen—High Finance, High Politics

144 pp.   ISBN: 0-87855-989-2 (paper) **$12.95**
No. 2, September 1984   ISBN: 0-88738-041-7 (cloth) **$19.95**

U.S. TRADE POLICY AND DEVELOPING COUNTRIES

Ernest H. Preeg and contributors

North-South trade relations are deeply troubled. U.S. exports to developing countries declined by $18.2 billion for 1980-83, at the cost of some 1.1 million jobs in the U.S. export sector. Many developing countries face financial crises that can only be resolved over the longer run through resumed expansion of trade. In this volume, distinguished practitioners and academics identify specific policy objectives for the United States on issues that will be prominent in the proposed new round of GATT negotiations: adjustment of U.S. firms and workers to imports from developing countries, including sensitive sectors such as textiles and steel; transition or "graduation" of the newly industrialized countries of East Asia and Latin America to a more reciprocal basis of access to markets; special benefits for the poorest or least developed countries; and preferential trading arrangements.

Ernest H. Preeg, a career foreign service officer and currently visiting fellow at the Overseas Development Council, has had long experience in trade policy and North-South economic relations. He was a member of the U.S. delegation to the GATT Kennedy Round of negotiations and later wrote a history and analysis of those negotiations, *Traders and Diplomats* (The Brookings Institution, 1969). Prior to serving as American ambassador to Haiti (1981-82), he was deputy chief of Mission in Lima, Peru (1977-80), and deputy secretary of state for International Finance and Development (1976-77).

Contents:

224 pp.
No. 4, April 1985

ISBN: 0-87855-987-6 (paper) **$12.95**
ISBN: 0-88378-043-3 (cloth) **$19.95**

DEVELOPMENT STRATEGIES: A NEW SYNTHESIS

John P. Lewis and contributors

Contrary to the widespread popular view that few development efforts have worked, many Third World national development ventures in fact have been comparatively successful when measured against historical precedents. But growth rates have slowed, and the international economic environment is now much less favorable to growth and development progress than in the 1960s and even the 1970s. What has been learned from past development promotion experiences? And what approaches hold promise for the harsher economic circumstances of the 1980s and 1990s?

In this volume, prominent analysts of the development process—including experts (some from the Third World) with experience in both policy design and policy implementation—consider how to promote development effectively in the future. New syntheses of policy are proposed that seek to reconcile the goals of growth, equity, and adjustment; to strike fresh balances between agricultural and industrial promotion and between capital and other inputs; to reassess the strength and breadth of the case for outward-oriented strategies; and to reflect the interplay of democracy and development.

John P. Lewis is professor of economics and international affairs at Princeton University's Woodrow Wilson School of Public and International Affairs. He is simultaneously senior advisor to the Overseas Development Council and chairman of its Program Advisory Committee. From 1979 to 1981, Mr. Lewis was Chairman of the OECD's Development Assistance Committee. He has served as a member of the U.N. Committee for Development Planning, of which he was also rapporteur from 1972 to 1978. For many years, he has alternated between academia and government posts (as Member of the Council of Economic Advisors, 1963-64, and Director of the U.S. AID Mission to India. 1964-69), with collateral periods of association with The Brookings Institution and The Ford Foundation. His recent writings have focused on South Asian development and North-South economic relations.

Contributors: Irma Adelman, Jagdish N. Bhagwati, Alex Duncan, Atul Kohli, John P. Lewis, John Mellor, Leopoldo Solis and Aurelio Montemayor.

224 pp.
No. 5, September 1985

ISBN: 0-87855-991-4 (paper) **$12.95**
ISBN: 0-88738-044-1 (cloth) **$19.95**